Belief Matters

Belief Matters

Pete Briscoe
and Todd Hillard

MONARCH
BOOKS

Oxford, UK & Grand Rapids, Michigan, USA

Published in association with the literary agency of Alive Communications, Inc.,
7680 Goddard Street, Suite 200, Colorado Springs, CO 80920 USA,
www.alivecommunications.com

First published in the UK in 2008 by Monarch Books,
(a publishing imprint of Lion Hudson plc),
Wilkinson House, Jordan Hill Road, Oxford OX2 8DR
Tel: +44 (0) 1865 302750   Fax: +44 (0) 1865 302757
Email: co-ed@lionhudson.com
www.lionhudson.com

ISBN: 978-1-85424-880-0 (UK)

Distributed by:
UK: Marston Book Services Ltd, PO Box 269, Abingdon, Oxon OX14 4YN;

Scripture (unless otherwise noted) is taken from
The Holy Bible: New International Version, electronic edition,
Grand Rapids: Zondervan, © 1996, 1984

The pronunciation keys for the 'definable' words come from
The American Heritage® Dictionary of the English Language, Fourth Edition,
© 2006 by Houghton Mifflin Company.

This book has been printed on paper and board independently certified as having
come from sustainable forests.

British Library Cataloguing Data
A catalogue record for this book is available from the British Library

Printed and bound in Malta by Gutenberg Press.

Contents

Acknowledgments   7

  1. Belief Matters   9
  2. Saying 'I Believe'   21
  3. The Supreme Being   33
  4. Superior Strength   47
  5. Sovereign Shaping   61
  6. The Son   75
  7. The Supernatural Conception   89
  8. The Sacrifice   101
  9. The Sensational Sunday   117
10. The Seat   133
11. The Sure Return   147
12. The Sanctifying Spirit   163
13. The Saints   179
14. Second Chances   195
15. Starting Over   211
16. The Sustained Life   225
17. Saying 'Amen!'   241

Plotting the Truth   249
Notes   253

Rarely does a son have parents he can...
Love
Be proud of
Share life with
Rely upon
Learn from
Model after
and Laugh with.

But this son does.

To Jill and Stuart Briscoe, my cherished parents,
friends and mentors who taught me the truths found
within these pages as we woke up, ate food, walked
along and experienced life together.

I love you.

Acknowledgments

This book has been a joy to write – not only because of the subject matter but because relationships intertwined in these pages.

- My agent Beth Jusino, my assistant Becky Blanchard and my elders and fellow pastors at Bent Tree, all in their unique ways contributed to this work.
- My wife Libby and kids Cameron, Annika and Liam sacrificed time with me so I might invest it in these words. Thank you, dear family.
- Todd Hillard made this book happen with his calm demeanour and his excellent persistence... and in the process, his heart melded with mine.

To each and to all I owe great gratitude. Our joy will be in this book being read, digested and used to ground earnest disciples in their walk with Jesus Christ.

And allow me to thank my best friend. Jesus, this work was not only written for you, it was written by you as you invested in me and enabled me. I'm yours; this book is too.

Pete Briscoe
March 2008

The Apostles' Creed

I believe in God the Father Almighty, maker of heaven and earth; and in Jesus Christ his only Son our Lord; who was conceived by the Holy Ghost, born of the Virgin Mary, suffered under Pontius Pilate, was crucified, dead and buried. He descended into hell; the third day he rose again from the dead. He ascended into heaven, and sits on the right hand of God the Father Almighty. From thence he shall come to judge the quick and the dead. I believe in the Holy Ghost, the holy catholic church, the communion of saints, the forgiveness of sins, the resurrection of the body, and the life everlasting. Amen.

CHAPTER 1

Belief Matters

Belief matters.

It is quite impossible to over-emphasize that fact.

Belief matters.

Belief determines our perceptions of reality.

Belief shapes every thought, decision and action.

Belief defines the parameters of what is possible.

Belief emerges from the soul – from that inner core of our being that defines who we are and what we do.

Belief even alters the contours of eternity.

Belief is also really amazing. I mean, think about it for a minute. God has built into your soul the capacity to ponder ideas and concepts – and I'm not just talking about simple things that you can see or touch. You have the ability to contemplate things like love, truth, injustice, success... the most phenomenal issues of our existence – purpose, meaning, direction and vision for life. We have the capacity to believe all these things.

❧ DEFINITION

---

believe (bĭ-lēv´) 1. To accept as true or real. 2. To have faith, confidence, or trust.

Everybody believes. *Everybody.* Even those who say they believe in 'nothing' still believe that that 'nothing' exists. Every human has a grid of thought, a matrix of memories and a pool of ponderings that make up their system of belief.

Yes, everybody believes, but belief only has a *positive* effect when what you believe is actually *true* and *real.* In the end it really doesn't matter how much you believe. (Remember, according to Matthew 17:20, faith as tiny as a mustard seed can move mountains.) What matters is *what* you believe. You can believe with all your heart that the brakes on your car will work, or that a chair will hold you up, or that a fat guy in a red suit will squeeze himself down your chimney, but if that's not an objective fact, what you ultimately experience is going to be very different from what you believe.

That's where *truth* comes in. We may believe in God, but do we know what is true about him? If we have distorted beliefs about him, our experience of him will be crippled.

✏️ Definition

truth (trōōth), *n.* 1. Something that conforms to reality, actuality. 2. Sincerity; integrity. 3. That which is considered to have the ultimate meaning and value of existence.

Some people believe that there is no such thing as truth. But even that gets a little bit complicated, because if you ask them, 'Is it true that there is no such thing as *truth*?' they will answer 'Yes!' without seeing the contradiction. I know that's odd, but do you see why this is important? *People believe that it is true that there is no such thing as truth.*

✏️ Contemplation

I know that after I leave, savage wolves will come in among you and will not spare the flock. Even from your own number men will arise and distort the truth in order to draw away disciples after them.   ACTS 20:29–30

Again, the facts are this: Everybody believes, and whether we like it or not, truth exists. Now here's the key point. This is where the power comes in. It sounds so simple that you might overlook its magnitude.

When what we believe is truth, then we have 'true belief'. True belief is *having confidence in what is right and aligning ourselves with it.*

Think about that for a moment. When that fact is understood on a heart level, a new zeal becomes ignited in the soul; a sense of urgent importance begins to fuel new priorities; a burning desire emerges from within. True belief can take your life to a totally different level. This isn't just philosophy, or theology, or psychology. *Belief and truth are reality.* When our beliefs are aligned with truth, our lives become aligned with what is real – and that is really powerful.

That means that your energy and your decisions are consistent with the spiritual and physical laws that govern our existence. A harmony emerges – our choices begin to coincide with the way things are supposed to be. Why? Because *belief matters and what you believe matters.*

? QUESTION

Do you think most people think about the connection between 'truth' and 'belief' and the decisions they make? Why or why not?

Unleashing truth in a sceptical world

'Heaven Is a Place on Earth' – that's the belief that Lisa Miller investigated for the 28 January 2008 issue of *Newsweek*. She was referring to the growing influence of Scientology and its deceased founder, L. Ron Hubbard. In the process, she addressed the idea that Suri (the young daughter of Tom Cruise and Katie Holmes) is the reincarnation of Hubbard. She noted that Madonna, Kate Hudson and other influential stars have professed a belief that they will one day return in a new body.

But it is not just people with too much time and too much money who are falling for this nonsense. According to a Harris poll, 40 per cent of Americans aged 25 to 29 believe they will return in a different body after they die. If the woman in the cubicle next to you or a guy lacing up his shoes in the locker room were to tell you that they believed in reincarnation (it seems as though there is a three-in-ten chance that it could happen), how would you respond?

That's just one of countless examples of people sincerely believing things that most Christians would regard as untrue. What can we do about it? What can *you* do about it? You have a unique sphere of influence; there is no one else in the entire world who knows all the same people you know. So if God wants to reach people in your unique sphere with truth, you might be the best candidate for a shoulder-tap from the Almighty.

Each of us must learn to stand on the bedrock of truth. When Cameron, our first son, was five or six years old, he came home one day and said, 'Daddy, do we believe in re-in-ter-car-circumcism?' (he meant reincarnation)

'Why do you ask?' I responded.

'Because there's a boy in my class who says after we die, we're going to come back as something else, like a bug or a king, depending on whether we were good in this life or not. Is that true?'

I opened my Bible and sat him on my lap. Together we read Hebrews 9:27: 'man is destined to die once, and after that to face judgment...'

That was all he needed, and off he went to play.

It is vital that we identify the essential foundation of belief on which all other convictions are built. In a world filled with lies and doubt, speaking truth is an important and natural extension of true belief... and I don't just mean speaking to other people. The person who most needs to hear truth *from* you *is* you.

After that, God may give you numerous opportunities to share what you believe with other people. But before you can *communicate* what you believe, you must be *certain* of what you believe.

That's what this book is all about. The journey in the pages ahead will weave its way through history and theology into your present world. The adventure of discovering true belief will take you to some of the farthest points on our globe and into some of the deepest corners of your soul. As the adventure continues throughout life, speaking truth will become a normal part of the ongoing discovery.

Why a Creed?

In this book, we're going to use the Apostles' Creed as an outline to investigate truth and belief. Why?

At the dawn of Christianity, as faith began to spread throughout the nations, the new 'believers' faced a challenge. Most individuals did not have access to the Old Testament books, and God's Holy Spirit was still moving in the minds of men to write the words that would eventually become our New Testament. As the ink was drying on these final parchments of written Scripture, truth was spreading along dusty roads and across dangerous seas, carried in the hearts of men and women. Thousands of believers were being baptized... and many of them knew that their proclamation of belief might require the shedding of their own blood as martyrs.

✒ QUOTATION

> *... a few hundred years ago the most cruel punishments were inflicted, not merely*
> *upon criminals dangerous to the State, but upon innocent men and women,*
> *the best and noblest people of their time, whose only offence was a refusal to*
> *renounce their faith...*   JOHN FOXE[1]

But what did they actually believe? To what had they committed their lives? New-found faith was overflowing from their hearts, and this faith needed to be put into words. They needed some sort of declaration – a unifying verbal proclamation – something that said, 'This is what I believe.' The Latin word for such a proclamation is *credo*. From this word we get the English word 'creed'. Creeds and proclamations of faith have been a part of baptism ever since Jesus commanded us to baptize the disciples of all nations 'in the name of the Father, and the Son and the Holy Spirit' (Matthew 28:19).

Over the centuries, four great creeds emerged from the early church. The Nicene Creed, the Chalcedonian Creed, the Athanasian Creed and the Apostles' Creed have been used to define and clarify what we, as believers in Christ, actually believe.

During those dynamic and dangerous early years, it was forbidden for a believer to put the Apostles' Creed into writing. Taught only to those who were willing to risk their lives by being baptized, it was stored in the heart and passed on as a statement of faith and as a profession of dedication shared by those who truly believed. In time, the Creed was integrated into worship services, became central to doctrinal statements around the world, and is now a part of seminary studies.

✍ CONTEMPLATION

> I have given them your word and the world has hated them, for they are not of the world any more than I am of the world... Sanctify them by the truth; your word is truth.
>
> JESUS' PRAYER, JOHN 17:14, 17

Today, we have the distinct advantage of having the Word of God in written form. The Bible is a living and active document that speaks the truth and verifies the truth, yet the creeds continue to be very important proclamations and declarations of faith:

- They draw the line between Christ-followers and the unbelieving world.
- They are statements of belief that communicate our faith – words that harmonize with the truth that God had placed inside each of us.
- They summarize the written Word of God.
- They resonate with the eternal truths of Scripture.
- They point us in the direction of the miraculous, the supernatural and the incredible.

For centuries, the Apostles' Creed has stood as a unifying proclamation for Christians around the globe. It condenses vast amounts of theological power into a single statement. For generations, this declaration of belief has stood the test of time and scrutiny. Thoroughly biblical, it gives a framework to protect against false teaching and sets a standard for the core teaching of all Christians. By focusing on the essentials of faith, it continually draws us back to what is clearly communicated in the Bible – and it is silent where the Bible is silent.

Used as a matrix of faith and devotion, the simple outline of the Apostles' Creed weaves a grid of truth and forms a tapestry containing all the essential beliefs of Christianity. It also gives us a dynamic source of doctrine that we can plug into when it is time to speak the light of truth into the darkness of unbelief. *Just as it was for the early church, the Creed is a tool that brings fresh vibrancy and clarity to true belief.*

Why the Apostles' Creed? Because it's a tool – a man-made tool to help us articulate, remember and apply truth. It's nothing more than that (it's not some magical mantra that unleashes some supernatural result), but it's certainly nothing *less* than that!

By the time you have finished reading this book:

- You will be able to outline the major theological aspects of your faith from memory.
- You will be able to turn to a series of key Bible passages that support your beliefs.
- You'll be able to communicate the depth and details of your faith with those who don't believe as you do.
- You'll be able to explore the wonders of the Christian faith at new levels. With both humility and confidence, you will venture into the great mysteries of belief, experiencing the reality of God and Jesus Christ in new ways.

? QUESTION

How might your life be changed by this study of the Creed? Is there anything in particular that you would like to see God strengthen in your beliefs?

Does that sound impossible? It's not. We have always had the capacity to do these things, but what we have lacked is *a plan*, some sort of guide that can get us from where we are to where we so deeply desire to be; we need a *map*.

M.A.P.S.

Just as we use road maps to navigate through new territory, we will use 'M.A.P.S.' to navigate through the Apostles' Creed. (That's a little acronym that stands for *Meditate, Apply, Plot and Speak*.) You will be amazed at how simple it is, and how short bursts of focused attention will make a huge difference in your understanding of belief, and how true belief will begin to truly change your life.

✎ *Meditate*

Meditate in your heart upon your bed, and be still.   PSALM 4:4 (NASB)

Belief is different from knowledge (a mental awareness of information). The Bible makes it clear that knowledge alone makes us arrogant (1 Corinthians 8:1). Information that is in the head but is not in the heart only leads to problems. On the other hand, King David said, 'Thy word have I treasured in my heart, so that I might not sin against Thee' (Psalm 119:11). It's going to be easy to memorize the majority of the information that I will present in this book. But truth cannot rest in the mind only; it must get to the heart.

We must go beyond a superficial recognition of fact. We must be willing to go deep, deep into the truth of these realities and deep into our own souls to contemplate their implications in our lives.

In the pages ahead we are going to be treading on holy ground. We're going to be discussing thoughts more powerful and more important than any other topic we could possibly talk about.

The key to the Creed is not the words themselves, but rather what these words *mean* – who and what they point to. If we meditate upon the meaning of the words, the truth can finally be unleashed in humble obedience and profound life-change.

❧ QUOTATION

> ... the Creed asks, 'What meaning have you found? What truth do you claim? For what purpose are you living?' Life itself raises these questions. How can anyone help asking 'what' and 'why' when surrounded by an infinite sky?   RON JAMES[2]

❧ *Apply*

> Incline your ear and hear the words of the wise; and apply your mind to my knowledge.   PROVERBS 22:17

One day I asked my dad what the key was to great preaching. He said, 'It's like everything else in life, Pete: it's more simple than we think. Every good sermon has a *What?* section where you explain the text and its meaning. This must be followed by a *Now what?* portion where you connect truth to everyday life and point to specific changes in what people think, feel and do. The problem with a lot of preachers, though, is that they never get to the *Now what?*, so that people leave thinking "So what?"'

The Apostles' Creed is great stuff – full of good *What?* As we work our way through and meditate on the biblical truths it contains, we will naturally be led to a point of decision where we must face *Now what?* The words of the Creed are not an end in themselves. The Creed points to truth. The truth is intended to change our lives. Life-change comes from clearly understanding what we have heard and then allowing God to make these truths a reality. As we choose to act in a way that is consistent with belief, as Christ enables us, we bring glory to him and him alone.

At the end of each chapter there will be a place for reflection on this level. Not only will you meditate on what the belief *means*, but you'll have a chance to listen to God – to listen to what he wants to *do* through you because of your belief. There are no canned answers at this point. During the application section you'll go one-on-one with your Creator, listening carefully from his Word and from the stirrings of his Spirit in your spirit, telling you *now what* it is that should happen... and even more importantly, he will show you *how* you are to do it.

Be prepared for the unexpected; God's ways are higher than our ways; through his revealed truth you may very well discover an *entirely* different approach to life...

℞ *Plot the passages*

> *All Scripture is inspired by God, and profitable for teaching, for reproof, for correction, for training in righteousness, so that the man of God might be adequate, equipped for every good work.*   2 TIMOTHY 3:16 (NASB)

At the end of each chapter, using only a pen and a highlighter, you will transform your Bible into a complete theological textbook (and that's a good thing!). In the past you've probably felt intimidated by the immensity and complexity of the Bible and overwhelmed by the prospect of studying theology.

No more! In the back of this book, you'll find two special copies of the Apostles' Creed. The Creed has been broken down into phrases. Each phrase covers a specific topic and each topic is linked to a key verse. You will link this verse to several other supporting verses, plotting a course through the Bible. As you plot each phrase of the Creed, you will create a network of passages throughout the Bible forming an extensive web of truth. By the time you are done, you'll have a complete map at your fingertips – a cross-referenced guide that you can use for the rest of your life to reference the truths that are illuminated in the Apostles' Creed.

Confusing? It won't be after you try this once in the next chapter. It's a little hard to explain – a little like standing at the bottom of the mountain trying to describe to a student how to snow-ski. Don't worry, when we get to the top you'll figure it out as we move along!

Go ahead and tear out the first copy of 'Plotting the Truth' right now and insert it in the front of your Bible. Leave the second copy in this book for future reference. (It might be a good idea to actually copy this page on to a blank page in either the front or the back of your Bible.)

Then be ready with a highlighter and a pen for the next chapter!

❧ *Speak*

> *But we speak God's wisdom in a mystery, the hidden wisdom which God*
> *predestined before the ages to our glory.*   1 CORINTHIANS 2:7

Speak truth?! I can feel some of you going tense right now. Visions are running through your head of street preachers raining words of damnation down on rush-hour commuters. You see yourself whapping your neighbour over the head with a Bible as you gag her with a tract...

Erase that! Take a breath.

Speaking truth is God's business – he only desires to speak through you, and he can do that any way he chooses. You will find that you can trust him to use you in a way that is consistent with the gifts and strengths he has given you.

In *Love Your God With All Your Mind*, J.P. Moreland tells the story of a dinner party where the hostess was more than happy to chat, but her husband remained silent throughout the entire meal. When the topic of boats came up, however, the comatose husband sprang to life. He owned two boats! Everyone else had an opportunity to finish their meals as he talked at great length.

The moral of the story: *It is amazing how much easier it is to talk about topics when you have depth of understanding; it breeds confidence and brings clarity, and God will use that to make you a more effective mouthpiece for him.*

Who do we speak truth to? First (before we speak *out* to others), we need to allow God to speak *to* us personally. Affirming truth to ourselves on an ongoing basis leads to freedom – the kind of freedom that comes when our lives are aligned with the way God designed us to live. In good times and bad, we must be able to say, 'This is true; this I believe.'

Second, we need to speak truth to others. These are uncertain times in our world... and people know it. A very high percentage of people in our culture still believe in God and some still believe that the Bible is God's Word. They are looking for answers to the perplexing problems and questions that we face in our modern world. The Apostles' Creed is a very helpful outline that we can use to give biblically sound answers to the questions they're asking.

Finally, the truths contained in the Apostles' Creed can turbo-boost our worship experience. When we allow the truth in our heart to reverberate back to the Lord, it can ignite praise and worship in many different forms. Our prayers, our service, our songs... every breath is an opportunity to speak back to him our awe for who he is. When we worship in spirit and truth as we are commanded (John 4:24), we make a connection between who we are and who God is, allowing us to experience infinite truths in our small finite minds.

By using the Creed as a tool, you will be able to speak truth from your lips – but should these words make the jump from your lips to your brain, and then from your brain to your soul, your life will be absolutely transformed – transformed when you say, *I believe*...

... And in a very special way, when we say the Creed as an extension of our inner conviction – as a proclamation of our devotion and intentions – the words mix with the echoes of our spiritual heritage. When we say them, understanding what they mean and believing it from the heart, we join the standing ranks of the multitudes of Christian brothers and sisters who have gone before us... many of whom paid for their faith with their lives.

Why the Creed? Because *belief matters... and what you believe matters.*

The Apostles' Creed is a remarkable tool for discovering belief, solidifying belief and articulating belief. It takes thirty seconds to recite the Creed. It takes a lifetime to ponder it. It will take an eternity to experience it.

Welcome to the journey!

I believe in God the Father Almighty, maker of heaven and earth; and in Jesus Christ his only Son our Lord; who was conceived by the Holy Ghost, born of the Virgin Mary, suffered under Pontius Pilate, was crucified, dead and buried. He descended into hell; the third day he rose again from the dead. He ascended into heaven, and sits on the right hand of God the Father Almighty. From thence he shall come to judge the quick and the dead. I believe in the Holy Ghost, the holy catholic church, the communion of saints, the forgiveness of sins, the resurrection of the body, and the life everlasting. Amen.

CHAPTER 2

Saying 'I Believe'

❧ DEFINITION

belief (bi-lef'), *n.* The mental act, condition, or habit of placing trust or confidence in a person or thing.

I do believe. Help my unbelief!   A FATHER SPEAKING TO JESUS CHRIST

We skipped Sunday School.

We weren't the first to do it, but it was a glorious feeling nevertheless. Marc, Mike and I shuffled toward the small lake at the east end of the church property. The lake was frozen over... or so we believed. In a display of boyish confidence and courage, Mike waltzed forward onto the ice without a second thought and began sliding about without a care. I hesitated, hearing in the back of my mind a little voice (probably my mother's) saying, 'No, Peter. No!' But in the front of my mind I was hearing a bigger little voice (undoubtedly mine) saying, 'Yes, Peter. Yes! Don't be a wimp. Be a man – go for it!' Somewhere in my mind a decision was being made. Was this safe? Was it worth the risk? Did I *believe* the ice would hold me? I made the decision. Both Marc and I eased onto the ice.

Bad choice.

What was strong enough to support one boy was completely inadequate to hold three. In an instant we were swallowed by the icy teeth of the dark waters, devouring us whole in spite of our breathless thrashing and frantic lunges for the safety of the shore and for air. The fight for life continued... until we realized that the water was only about three feet deep (still deep enough if you're only five feet tall, but hardly life-threatening). Our feet settled into the murky slop on the pond's bed, leaving us muddy, soaked to the bone and with plenty of explaining to do.

I had believed; I had made a conscious choice to place my faith in the strength of the ice. But in spite of my sincerity, what I believed was false.

In reality, we were fortunate that day. Every autumn the Wisconsin newspapers are filled with four-sentence articles about the pick-up trucks carrying groups of ice-fishermen that break through the thin ice and disappear in the dark. And every year boys venture onto thin ice over waters deeper than three feet. The drivers of the trucks and the boys in search of adventure believe the ice will hold. But it doesn't. (And the parents of many of those boys experience the fact that belief really matters – that belief is often a matter of life and death.)

Wiser ice-fishermen, on the other hand, also believe that the ice will hold. But they have something that the boys do not: wisdom and information. They wait until they know with certainty that the ice will sustain them. Many drive their trucks out to little ice villages where people fish in huts discreetly crammed with easy chairs, satellite TVs, refrigerators, stoves and enough beer to sustain a football team for a lifetime. Road signs and stop signs regulate the traffic flow down the ice-streets...

They too believe that the ice can hold them. And it does.

Yes, belief matters, but...

The accepted wisdom of our day says, 'It doesn't matter what you believe as long as you believe it sincerely.' That is a lie. We would never accept that type of rea- soning when it comes to non-spiritual things, and there is absolutely no reason why we should accept that idea when it comes to issues of faith. It *does* matter what you believe, because if what you believe in is false, you can be as sincere as you want, but you're really just sincerely wrong.

People in cults believe with sincerity. But is what they believe in worthy of their trust? The ice looks as if it will sustain them; it looks safe. But is it? The icy waters of false faith are, unfortunately, a harsh and bitter eternal reality for far too many people.

Belief matters every second of every day. It matters in the moment-by- moment thoughts that flow through your mind hour after hour. Belief matters in those obvious moments when important issues of life hang in the balance:

- A flood of negative circumstances rushes through your life. The existence of a good God begins to seem very questionable. What kind of a framework do you use to combat growing doubt?
- You hear a knock on your door. Two nicely dressed men want to teach you about truth... about salvation. Apparently using Scripture as their guide, they begin to teach you – but the things they are teaching don't seem com- pletely accurate. Can you figure out what is wrong? Can you defend your family and lovingly communicate why they are in error?
- A co-worker stops by your desk and notices that you have a Bible verse on your calendar. She asks you, 'Tell me everything that you know about Jesus.' Where do you start?
- You reach mid-life. Nothing you have been working for seems to be worth the sacrifices you make. There are choices ahead – choices that will

determine the course of the rest of your life. On what basis will you make those choices? What do you use to evaluate your options?

- After years of faithful prayer and worship, the 'God experience' is drying up. Your words and your songs seem to be going nowhere. Where do you go to start to bring authentic praise and worship back into your faith?

- Perhaps you are standing on the edge of a great compromise. Conflicting thoughts and desires are pulling back and forth. The tension is great. Where do you go to begin to resolve the inner conflict?

In those times – when belief seems to matter the most – where can we turn to determine right from wrong? Where do we go to test our thoughts and our ideas to determine whether they are worthy of our belief?

To the Bible, that's where.

I know that this isn't a given in our society any more. The Bible is approached with scepticism at first, rather than acceptance. Understandably, many give it a questioning look, since they have been told that it is filled with fables and inaccuracies. Others have felt the bitter sting of Scripture being misused to justify racism, abuse, manipulation and condemnation. Approaching the Bible with scepticism is understandable and even *acceptable*. Questioning the authority of the Bible is fine *as long as you're willing to investigate it honestly and factually.*

Many a sceptic who began their investigation of the Bible with a cynical disbelief walked away with a dynamic and devoted level of belief in that book. If you have questions about the Bible's accuracy and authenticity, start digging and keep searching until you have solid answers to your doubts. Books like *More than a Carpenter* by Josh McDowell are a great place to start. At the end of honest investigation, you will find a document that is alive and used by God to speak into our hearts today. The Scriptures open windows of illumination that are ignited by God's Spirit to show us things that we could never discover or verify on our own.

✍ CONTEMPLATION

For the word of God is living and active. Sharper than any double-edged sword, it penetrates even to dividing soul and spirit, joints and marrow; it judges the thoughts and attitudes of the heart.   HEBREWS 4:12

The Bible tells us when we are on thin ice, headed for the dark and murky depths. Equally important, it points to a life of freedom and adventure. It tells us where, when and how we are to skate about freely with confident abandon.

❦ QUOTATION

A lie, believed as truth, will affect your choices as if it is true, even though it's a lie.'
                                                            BILL EWING, *REST ASSURED*[3]

Not only is the Bible the place we go to *test* our belief; the Bible tells us about the *importance* of belief. Hundreds of times in the Old and New Testaments, the issue of belief is addressed. Here are just a few:

All things are possible to him who believes.   MARK 9:23

Then they asked him, 'What must we do to do the works God requires?'
    Jesus answered, 'The work of God is this: to believe in the one he has sent.'
                                                            JOHN 6:28–29

Believe in the Lord Jesus Christ, and you will be saved.   ACTS 16:31

Abraham believed God, and it was credited to him as righteousness.   ROMANS 4:3

Belief is also the key that opens the door to the most amazing possibility: a relationship with God based on grace and love (rather than fear and performance). God is asking us to step onto the ice – the type of ice that he has confirmed as safe and good in his Word.

I stepped onto the ice spiritually when I was four years old. We were living in England at Cedar Home, our small house on the grounds of Capernwray Bible School. While Dad was teaching, I was spending enormous amounts of time combing the verdant hills with my friend, throwing chestnuts at unsuspecting sheep. (If you hit a sheep on the head with a nut, it was worth more points than a shot that harmlessly bounced off its fluffy coat.)

One day my mum whisked me into the car for a fairly long drive to the grocery store. We had time to talk – which was good, since some of the essential truths my parents had been teaching me were starting to raise questions in my developing mind. *Why did Jesus have to die on the cross? How does his death make any difference for me? Why does Dad say, 'This is going to hurt me more than you' before he spanks me? How do I ask Jesus, a grown man, into my heart?* (I couldn't figure out how he could really fit very well.)

As the English countryside whipped past my window, my mum slowly and carefully walked me through the eternal truths of the gospel. Somewhere inside me something clicked. It was all coming together and it all made sense.

In the store between the fruits and the vegetables, I grabbed my mother's hand and said, 'Mum, let's do this!'

'What?' she asked.

'Let's get Jesus in my heart, right now.'

As my mother guided me, I inched onto the ice, nervous and unsure... The ice held and it holds me still. God is ice like nothing else. Never thawing; never giving way; always firm beneath my feet, though I often slip and slide.

My questions continue, of course. I often ask 'Why?' and sometimes hear no answer. There are times when I fear that everything at my feet is cracking and giving way... but it never does. When I am faithless, he remains faithful. When I am weak, he is strong. When I look back on that day in England, I know I believed. Today in Dallas, I still believe. Belief matters to me.

💱 QUOTATION

Faith and doubt are by no means mutually exclusive; doubt is rather the shadow which everywhere follows faith and trust.   WOLFHART PANNENBERG[4]

The essence of belief

Some beliefs matter more than others, of course. It's not a big deal if you believe it's going to be sunny today and it turns out to be cloudy. On the other hand, if you don't believe that you have cancer but you actually do, the consequences can be much more severe. While many of our beliefs will have greater or lesser earthly consequences, none of them matter more than our beliefs about and in God. Throughout Scripture, belief about God is directly tied to the most valued aspects of our existence – to things like joy, peace and purpose...

? QUESTION

Think about your friends and co-workers for a moment. Do you think they consciously *consider beliefs about God when facing major life decisions? Why or why not?*

For example, take a look at the life of Abraham and Sarah. When we pick up their story in the Bible, we find them way beyond a mid-life crisis. Nice couple, but they're coming up on their hundredth birthdays and they haven't had any children yet. (A major downer, particularly in their culture, where status was directly linked to offspring.) They're getting a little bit discouraged about the possibilities. But God comes to them and makes a promise – a promise so unbelievable that it shook their belief to the core:

> *Abram fell face down, and God said to him, 'As for me, this is my covenant with you: You will be the father of many nations. No longer will you be called Abram; your name will be Abraham, for I have made you a father of many nations. I will make you very fruitful; I will make nations of you, and kings will come from you.'*
>
> GENESIS 17:3–6

That's a lot to dump on a man who is ninety-nine years old. In Romans 4 Paul expands on Abraham's response to this promise. Listen to his words carefully, for Paul not only describes Abraham's belief, but he reveals the essence of belief.

Belief is confidence in a powerful person

> *He [Abraham] is our father in the sight of God, in whom he believed – the God who gives life to the dead and calls things that are not as though they were.*
>
> ROMANS 4:17

Abraham and Sarah didn't have a lot of confidence, but their confidence was in the right place. That's the most important aspect of belief; that we believe in God. Our strength comes not from ourselves, but from God. It's when we place our trust in him to do what he promises to do through us that we find true freedom and peace. That's why it's so critical that we understand (as best we can with our limited abilities) who God is and who he has revealed himself to be. Because it's not our belief that matters; it's our belief *in him* that makes all the difference.

Belief is comfort in the midst of pain

> *Against all hope, Abraham in hope believed and so became the father of many nations...*
>
> ROMANS 4:18

Abraham had hoped before, only to have his dreams crushed again and again. Life is difficult and life is painful. Contrary to popular belief, God never promised that life would be pain-free. He does, however, promise to be present in the midst of the pain – and thus he gives us the comfort of hope beyond hope.

I don't know what issues you are facing today. I don't know where you've been or what the future looks like from where you stand. But if you have opened your life to Jesus Christ, I do know that God is with you and in you right now.

When you unleash that truth in your soul, true comfort can be found in the midst of any pain you are enduring.

Belief is candid about perplexing problems

Without weakening in his faith, he faced the fact that his body was as good as dead – since he was about a hundred years old – and that Sarah's womb was also dead.   ROMANS 4:19

Belief doesn't ignore the facts; it faces the facts and then applies faith. Abraham was very objective about his problem. He assessed the situation for what it was. As we go through life, our hopes and dreams are often shattered like fine china falling against cold concrete. But what a difference it makes when we face those bitter realities head-on. Instead of disintegrating under the stress, we can apply accurate biblical truth to the situation! God's Word gives us the perspective that we need to put the facts in their place so that we can respond in faith to what God says is true.

? QUESTION

In your opinion, do you think most people are searching for truth? Do you think they are content with the superficial aspects of life, or do you think they are looking for something real and deep? Give an example to support your opinion.

Belief is consistent in its progress

Yet he did not waver through unbelief regarding the promise of God, but was strengthened in his faith...   ROMANS 4:20

Belief is something that grows. You don't get one shot that lasts your whole life. Do you know how long Sarah and Abraham waited for God to fulfil his promise? Almost thirteen years! Abe and Sarah weren't travelling to the best infertility clinics in Palestine all these years; they weren't getting their 'readings' from the lab or trying various procedures. At their age, it's doubtful they could do anything! No, they were just waiting, taking care of the flocks, keeping the tent dust free, cooking meals, cleaning dishes... and waiting. Thirteen years is a long time; plenty of time for Abraham's faith to be made stronger than it was at the time he received the promise.

That encourages me. That means that where I am today in my belief is not where I will have to be tomorrow. I have a full lifetime to be strengthened in faith and to be bolstered in my belief. So do you.

Belief culminates in praise

> *… but was strengthened in his faith, and gave glory to God.*   ROMANS 4:20

It's important to note the timing of Abraham's praise. His son was not born yet, so his praise emerges in the midst of his pain. He is still grappling with perplexing problems, but standing on the promise he received, he gives glory to God for things he cannot yet see. Abraham's heart, like our hearts, has the capacity to worship and give thanks for things we cannot see. Because the fulfilment of God's promise is certain, our praise of God need not waver (even when our circumstances don't align with our personal desires).

Belief is being convinced of promises

> *… being fully persuaded that God had power to do what he had promised.*
>   ROMANS 4:21

On some TV channels you will hear preachers claiming promises that God has never made. This is obviously dangerous, and the need to know exactly what has been promised (and what hasn't) is imperative. That being said, God has the ability and the integrity to do what he says he will do. What he says in his word is worthy of belief, and it's our job to take him at his Word. That's the foundation of faith and that faith changes everything.

Sometimes it changes what is; often it only changes our *perception* of what is. Belief is the absolute core of our existence and being. When you say, *I believe*, it changes the way that you live and it changes who you really are. That's why belief matters so much.

℘ QUOTATION

But each time we come to repeat the Creed, we must be careful not to slur over its opening words.   D. BRUCE LOCKERBIE[5]

M.A.P.S.

✍ *Meditate*

Okay, let's make this personal. Hopefully you're sitting somewhere where you can do some thinking and praying without being distracted. You're looking for a place where your mind can be quiet and ponder belief on a deeper level than maybe you're used to.

Ask God to guide your thoughts as you consider those first two simple words of the Creed:

I believe...

✍ *Apply*

Which of the six aspects of belief do you find most encouraging? Which one seems the most outrageous? Which one might apply to a situation you are facing right now?

Talk to God about that right now. Let him know that you want to be 'a doer of the word, not merely a hearer' who deludes himself/herself (James 1:22).

✍ *Plot the passages*

- Key word: *Belief*.
- Key passage: Romans 4:17–21.
- Supporting passages: Mark 9:23–24; John 6:28–29; Acts 16:31; Romans 4:2–3.

If you have a pen and highlighter with you, let's get started so you can see how this works and how easy it is:

1. Pull out the 'Plot the Truth' sheet (it's either in your Bible already or still in the back of this book). Notice that the key word for 'I believe' is *Belief*, and the key passage is Romans 4:17–21.
2. Turn to Romans 4:17–21 in your Bible and highlight it.
3. In the margin next to Romans 4:17–21 write 'Believe, Mark 9:23' (the first supporting passage on the list).
4. Turn to Mark 9:23–24 and highlight it; then write 'Believe, John 6:28–29' in the margin next to it. (See how this is going to work?!) Repeat the process until you have completed all the passages.
5. You have just begun to build a scriptural scaffolding that you can use for the rest of your life as a reference to truth and belief. Excellent work! In the future, when you find passages that speak about belief (there are tons of

them!), go to the last verse in the chain and write yourself a note to the new text. In this way you can keep the chain growing as you grow.

⁂ *Speak*

Remember that the truth is to be communicated in three different directions: (1) to yourself as a reminder of what is true; (2) to others who are ready to listen; and (3) to God in worship and praise.

Speak to self

My belief in God is:

- Confidence in a powerful person.
- Comfort in the midst of pain.
- Candid about my problems.
- Consistent in progress.
- Culminating in praise.
- Convinced of God's promises.

Speak to others

⚘ QUOTATION

Seek first to understand and then be understood.   STEVEN COVEY[6]

Since everyone believes, asking them about *what* they believe is a great conversation starter. People love to talk about what they believe (particularly if they feel they are safe and won't be judged or condemned).

Consider getting together with someone you know and simply asking them what they believe. Listen well without interrupting. You'll learn a lot! After you're fairly sure that you understand what they believe, ask God to show you how he wants to speak truth through you to them.

Now that you have read this chapter, what do you have to say to those who are skating confidently on very, very thin ice?

Speak to God

In Mark 9:24 we find one of most honest prayers in the whole Bible. A man has come to Jesus with a son who is possessed by a violent evil spirit. The man desperately asks if Jesus is able to help him. Jesus tells him, 'All things are possible to him who believes.' As we speak to God about what we have learned in this chapter, perhaps our most honest response to God is the same words that the father exclaimed to Jesus:

Lord,
I do believe. Help my unbelief.
Amen.

* * *

Meanwhile, back in Wisconsin...

Our minds raced as we pulled ourselves from the pond and slogged back towards the church building. Desperately we tried to concoct verbal manipulations that we would employ to try to avoid the imminent retribution (a situation made more stressful by the fact that I was the preacher's kid).

As our death-march back to certain punishment continued, Mike noticed that his watch had slipped off his wrist during our thrashing about in the lake. We ran back to the broken ice but the watch was nowhere to be seen... and our lips were chattering so hard that we abandoned the search in favour of the chastisement (and hot chocolate) that awaited us back in the church.

'I'm going to find that watch in the spring and I bet you $10 it will still work!' Mike declared with great confidence. I took the bet.

Four long, cold months later, the three of us found ourselves knee-deep and bare-footed, feeling around for the watch. 'I just know it will still be working!' Mike kept saying.

Against all odds, we found it, dried it off, wound it up and – you guessed it – it worked perfectly!

'How did you know?' I asked as I handed over my $10.

'Because even when it takes a licking, Timex keeps on ticking,' he replied (quoting the watch manufacturer's well-advertised creed).

Mike had heard their creed and he had *believed* it. His belief impacted his decisions and his decisions blessed his life. Through our foolishness something valuable had been lost in those cold waters. Through Mike's belief, it had been found again. Yes, we learned some important lessons from that lake.

Like the Timex motto, the Apostles' Creed will become to us a powerful reminder. We can use it as a declaration of our belief and as a tool to communicate our pledge of allegiance of faith. As it is memorized, applied, plotted through the Bible – and then spoken with the conviction of true belief – it will be used by God to grow us, change us and bless us.

The Creed begins with *'I believe...'* – and those two words mark the beginning of a remarkable quest for life-changing truth. That's why I look forward to seeing those beliefs embedded in our hearts – because belief matters and belief unleashes the power of truth through our lives... even in a sceptical world.

*I believe **in God the Father** Almighty, maker of heaven and earth; and in Jesus Christ his only Son our Lord; who was conceived by the Holy Ghost, born of the Virgin Mary, suffered under Pontius Pilate, was crucified, dead and buried. He descended into hell; the third day he rose again from the dead. He ascended into heaven, and sits on the right hand of God the Father Almighty. From thence he shall come to judge the quick and the dead. I believe in the Holy Ghost, the holy catholic church, the communion of saints, the forgiveness of sins, the resurrection of the body, and the life everlasting. Amen.*

CHAPTER 3

The Supreme Being

✒ DEFINITION

Theology (thē-ŏl´[e]-jē), *n.* The study of God and religious truth.

Biography (bī-ŏg´r[e]-fē), *n.* The story of a person's life.

Do you know why most of us miss the adventure? It's because we've never learned to plug our theology into our biography. TIM HANSEL[7]

God.

That's a very simple word: 'God'. Three letters; one syllable; very easy to say. In America, we see this word on our money; we print it on our bumper stickers and plaster it on billboards. Preachers say it with such confidence, as if they have the meaning of this word all figured out – 'God' squished into a box of fancy-sounding words and quotations by long-dead theologians. Too often we hear this word thrown around casually and carelessly, like punctuation at the beginning or the end of a sentence.

God. What does that word mean? Does belief in that little word matter? The answer is an unquestionable 'yes'. That little word means everything. It has caused wars and it has healed families. It has been the source of great comfort and great abuse. It causes some to feel peace and others to boil with anger...

Polls tells us that 90–95 per cent of Americans 'believe in God'. I'm assuming that if you're reading this book you 'believe in God' too. But do you know what you believe when you say that? What do you mean when you say 'God'?

❧ QUOTATION

The music that really turns me on is either running toward God or away from God. Both recognize the pivot, that God is at the center of the jaunt. BONO

The three big questions

The issue of 'God' cannot be avoided. Immediately, when we consider our belief in God, three vitally important questions must be addressed:

- Do you know *about* him?
- Do you *know* him?
- Do you *make him known*?

... And do you see the need for all three?

- To know God, but to not know *about* him... is that possible?
- To know about God, but to not *know* him... is that not tragic?
- To know God, but to not *make him known*... is that conceivable?

These three questions about God have been central in the history of all humanity. Consider Moses, one of the great leaders of the Old Testament:

> *Moses said to the Lord, 'You have been telling me, "Lead these people," but you have not let me know whom you will send with me... If you are pleased with me, teach me your ways so I may know you and continue to find favour with you.'*
> EXODUS 33:12–13

Teach me your ways so I may know you... It's a humble but desperate request, isn't it? We must know about him so that we can know him, so that we can then make him known. What we believe about God is the most important thing about us. It's easy to see why those who wrote the Apostles' Creed started off with 'I believe in God the Father'.

❧ QUOTATION

What comes into our minds when we think about God is the most important thing about us.
A. W. TOZER[8]

God the *Father*

We need to take a quick step backwards before we move forward, because when I say the word 'father' your mind is forming a mental picture based on how you see your own father. Sometimes this picture is a mosaic of all the fathers you see around you, but are earthly fathers a good picture of your heavenly Father? Is God like them?

It depends. For some of us, the word 'father' brings up feelings of comfort and security. For others, just hearing the sound of his footsteps in the hall outside our bedroom door causes us to try to hide from abuse or violation. You might look back at your father and say, 'If God's anything like my old man, I don't want to have anything to do with him!'

So when we talk about 'God the Father' our minds (and not our emotions) must dominate. We need to make a clear distinction between our earthly father and our heavenly Father. The Holy Spirit and the Bible (and not our feelings or earthly experiences) must shape our thinking when we try to figure out what we mean by 'God the Father'.

Throughout the Bible we find the perfect picture of a perfect Father. In Exodus 33, after Moses requests God to teach him his ways, God reveals no less than fourteen fatherly traits about himself, each of which is amplified in many other places throughout the Bible.

These traits also make a decent model for those of us who are fathers on earth, but they aren't intended to be a guilt trip to try to make us perform better. They are intended to encourage us all, as God's kids, with the wonderful news of our perfect Parent who cherishes, values and adores us.

He's around

The Lord replied, 'My Presence will go with you...'   EXODUS 33:14

When Moses asked who would go with him, God said, 'I will go with you.' We find this throughout Scripture. Wherever you go, God will be there.

My Dad travelled a lot when I was young. When we were living in England, he would sometimes be in the States for months at a time. We missed him terribly. (One of the reasons why we moved to Milwaukee in 1970 was so that my father could be more involved in our lives – so he could be 'around' more.) During the years of his absence, my Mum pointed me to the 'Fatherness of God'. She taught me that he is *always* around, no matter where I am or what I am doing. While Dad was gone, I was forced to seek God's Fatherness in my life... and his presence became a reality to me.

God is with you right now – as you read these words he is with you – intricately involved in your individual life as a very present Father. No valley is too deep, no mountain too high... You might even try to run away from God or turn your back on him, but the moment you stop, you'll realize that he is still there with you.

✍ CONTEMPLATION

The Lord your God is with you, he is mighty to save. He will take great delight in you, he will quiet you with his love, he will rejoice over you with singing.

ZEPHANIAH 3:17

He is comforting

... and I will give you rest.   EXODUS 33:14

God will give us *rest*? Some of us had fathers who pushed us and pushed us to the brink of mental and physical exhaustion. God the Father is different. Yes, he has things for you to do – and those things are very important – but Scripture makes it clear that those things are done by depending on *God's* strength working through us, rather than by us using *our* strength to try to do things for him.

✍ CONTEMPLATION

It was I [God] who taught Ephraim to walk, taking them by the arms; but they did not realize it was I who healed them. I led them with cords of human kindness, with ties of love; I lifted the yoke from their neck and bent down to feed them.

HOSEA 11:3–4

He elevates

Then Moses said to him... 'How will anyone know that you are pleased with me and with your people unless you go with us? What else will distinguish me and your people from all the other people on the face of the earth?'   EXODUS 33:16

I was chaplain to the Milwaukee Brewers baseball team a number of years ago. That was a big deal. Where I used to live, the Brewers were the gods of the bat, ball and diamond. Every devout Wisconsinite watched them on TV. Those who could afford tickets would regularly make the pilgrimage to County Stadium to worship in person. But to enter into the locker room? That was the 'holy of holies' – the inner sanctuary of the temple where no mortal fan would ever think of gaining access.

But I had a way in: Paul Molitor. Paul was the captain of the team and because I knew him, I was welcome in the lockers – I was even allowed to speak to them face to face. I shared with the whole group thoughts from the Bible, and they listened... all because of Paul. He elevated me to a different level in the eyes of these amazing athletes. They were willing to listen to me because of my relationship with him.

God the Father does the same thing for us. His presence in our lives *distinguishes* us from others. Some may not recognize God as being the source of our uniqueness, but he is. When we become aware of our position as God's children, we start to project that in our behaviour and attitude... we become elevated, changed, unique in the world... and many will be willing to listen to us as we make him known, as a natural extension of that relationship with the Father.

He provides

> *And the Lord said to Moses, 'I will do the very thing you have asked...'*
> EXODUS 33:17

God does not give us everything that we want. He gives us what we need. He is a provider.

As the God who knows everything, he knows what we need far better than we do. In short, God owns everything (Psalm 50:10–12), God is generous (Acts 14:16–17), and God is aware of our needs (Matthew 6:31–32). In confidence, therefore, we can not only ask God for what we hope he will provide, but we can be confident that *he is already providing, right now, the very things that we need.*

⠬ QUOTATION

> *If God owns everything and knows everything, if he loves us and is perfect and holy in all he does, then everything he gives and everything he withholds can rightly be recognized as a good gift from him, even if we are unable to see it as such.*
> GEORGE Q. HAUSER[9]

If this is true, shouldn't our prayers be focused on aligning our desires and will with what God clearly says that we need?

? QUESTION

> *Can you tell the difference between your desires and what a loving Father knows that you need? Do you believe that God is providing for you right now everything that you truly need, just as he will provide for you in the future? Why or why not?*

He is pleased

> *... because I am pleased with you...*   EXODUS 33:17

Maybe it was through art, maybe through fiery, angry sermons – I don't know where, for sure – but somewhere along the line many of us got the idea that God the Father is angry, and he's sitting up in heaven on a cloud... and he is keeping score... all the time. He has a list of laws and rules in one hand and a lightning-bolt in the other; he's just waiting for you to screw up. And when you do? *Kapow!* Is that accurate? No, not even close.

God is pleased with us. God told Moses that he would do these things because he was pleased with him. Now you might say, 'Yeah, that's because it's Moses. I am no Moses.' Moses is supposed to be this great godly leader, right? Well, he's supposed to be, but he's not. Do you know what happened right before this passage? Moses' followers built a huge golden idol and they were worshipping this thing instead of God. If Moses was supposed to be some great leader, shouldn't he have been more effective? But in reality, his people were a mess... just like we are, just like *you* are. But still, God finds pleasure in us, in spite of us.

He is interested

> *... and I know you by name.*   EXODUS 33:17

How important would you feel if your father had 5 billion kids' phone numbers in his mobile phone, and you were just one of them? How much attention could one man give that many children? Almost none... unless it was your *heavenly* Father. God, it turns out, has no limitations on his power, his knowledge, or his ability to be everywhere for everyone all at once.

One New Year's season I was sitting with thousands of college students at the Urbana conference at Illinois University. The arena was packed to the rafters. At one point in the programme they asked us all to pray, out loud – 20,000 students praying at the top of their lungs! I was overwhelmed not by the noise or the cumulative effect, but by the simple fact that God was capable of hearing all the prayers, deciphering the desires, formulating each request and answering each one perfectly. In my ear my prayer was the only one I could really hear; all the other prayers were in the background, but for God the Father, *every* prayer was the *only* one he could hear. No such thing as background prayers... Every moment of every day, millions of prayers are cast heavenward – each one like the only one.

God knows your name by heart, and it's always on his heart. If you have a thorn in your foot, he cares about it even though there may be floods and famine elsewhere on the planet. That means he can give you 100 per cent of his attention and not have any less for anyone else. *Your* number is '1' on God's speed dial:

> *Are not five sparrows sold for two pennies? Yet not one of them is forgotten by God. Indeed, the very hairs of your head are all numbered. Don't be afraid; you are worth more than many sparrows.*   LUKE 12:6–7

He is compassionate

After the little idol-worshipping 'incident' (in which 3,000 people died), God gave the Ten Commandments to Moses again, and then revealed even more about who he is as God the Father:

> *The Lord, the Lord, the compassionate...*   EXODUS 34:6

I love the passages that talk about God being compassionate. Verses like this show that God the Father has emotion. Again, many of us have never seen this in our earthly fathers... and the emotions we usually saw were sometimes really frightening. But when we find out that God is compassionate, we find out that he really cares and he feels that caring. From the depth of his heart, from the core of emotion, God is compassionate toward you and me.

That is a very radical thought, if you think about it... so think about it. 'Compassion' simply means 'with passion' – but step back from the simple meaning of this word and contemplate the implications of these three words: *God. Compassion. You.* Your heavenly Father is not mechanical in his love for you; *he feels it*.

I was in the Philippine Islands with a mission team during my time at college. In one village we came across a boy with leprosy. He was shunned by all – an untouchable. The gracious pastor of the tiny evangelical church in town reached out with his hands, but he was the only one who was willing to embrace the grotesque face, the stumps for hands, the disfigured legs... I could barely look at him, let alone touch him. I'll never forget the morning I came around the corner and found this little boy sitting on the lap of one of my teammates, Randy. Randy had taught him how to play 'Patty Cake'. As stumps hit palms and the distorted face burst into a twisted but pure smile, I saw a picture of the compassion of God: God with me on his lap...

✍ CONTEMPLATION

... for the Lord your God is gracious and compassionate. He will not turn his face from you if you return to him.   2 CHRONICLES 30:9

He is gracious

... and gracious God...   EXODUS 34:6

Compassionate *and gracious*. That's the God we call Father. His grace changes the rules on all things. Where we are constantly bombarded and judged in the world because of our performance, our appearance, and our possessions, God deals with us in no such way. He lavishes his best on us, even though we have done nothing in and of ourselves to deserve it. What can you say to that? How do we respond to such love?

✍ CONTEMPLATION

For it is by grace you have been saved, through faith – and this not from yourselves, it is the gift of God – not by works, so that no one can boast.

EPHESIANS 2:8–10

He is patient

... slow to anger...   EXODUS 34:6

I'm learning this one the hard way. I am coaching my son Liam's basketball team now. The little guy is just in elementary school, with years of learning ahead of him... and I am embarrassed by how often I expect him to be where I was when I played in college! I see what he is doing, expect something else, deal with him in 'coach' lingo, and see his eyes well up with tears. Oh, how I sometimes wish it was God coaching that team and not me! I am impatient with him, expecting him to be today what he will one day be.

God knows our weaknesses, he knows how we have been made, and he gives us slack when others might just cut us off. Amazingly, he sees us as we are 'in Christ', and knows full well who he is shaping us to become. He recognizes the process of development and growth and is thoroughly patient with us as we trudge along the path.

✍ CONTEMPLATION

The Lord is compassionate and gracious, slow to anger, abounding in love... As a father has compassion on his children, so the Lord has compassion on those who fear him; for he knows how we are formed, he remembers that we are dust.

PSALM 103:8, 13–14

He is loving

... abounding in love... maintaining love to thousands...   EXODUS 34:6–7

This one attribute of God is at the core of all we seek – it's the answer to all the questions we ask about knowing about him, knowing him, and making him known. Deep inside each and every one of us is the desire to be loved. And while we might find that love in limited measure in other things, the true love that we seek can only be found in him, because he *is* the love that we seek:

Dear friends, let us love one another, for love comes from God. Everyone who loves has been born of God and knows God. Whoever does not love does not know God, because God is love. This is how God showed his love among us: He sent his one and only Son into the world that we might live through him. This is love: not that we loved God, but that he loved us and sent his Son as an atoning sacrifice for our sins.   1 JOHN 4:7–10

✿ QUOTATION

It is staggering that God should love sinners; yet it is true. God loves creatures who have become unlovely and (one would have thought) unlovable... love among men is awakened by something in the beloved, but the love of God is free, spontaneous, unevoked, uncaused. God loves men because he has chosen to love them.   J. I. PACKER, *KNOWING GOD*

He is faithful

... and faithfulness...   EXODUS 34:6

Because God is God, he doesn't get side-tracked; he doesn't get distracted; he doesn't get bored. He has everything he needs right now. He has absolutely no reason to leave you, or give up on you, or go somewhere else. Do you get that? You really need to think about it, because no human being is like that.

My Dad is a faithful man. In fact, I know what I'm going to say about him at his funeral: 'He was faithful to his Saviour, to his bride, and to his calling.' We were fortunate to have that kind of human faithfulness in our family (imperfect as it was). But compared to God, Dad's faithfulness is miniscule. God never changes, never flounders, never turns his back.

When we believe that God is perfectly faithful (as he is), peace and relief descend on our fearful souls. He's not going anywhere, he'll keep his promises, and he'll follow through with his pronouncements. This makes the faith walk possible *and* logical.

✍ CONTEMPLATION

And surely I am with you always, to the very end of the age.   MATTHEW 28:20

He is forgiving

> *… and forgiving wickedness, rebellion and sin.*   EXODUS 34:7

Guilt is huge… and heavy. Like a lead anchor strapped to our feet, our sins, both big and small, from the past can submerge us in the ocean of shame. God the Father, however, forgives the one who believes in him. And he does so completely. You might need to let that soak in for a moment.

The Bible is a description of the method that God used to forgive you. The New Testament shows you the person whom he has chosen: Jesus Christ. It also shows you the method: the crucifixion and resurrection. It's all because he is a forgiving Father.

He is just

> *Yet he does not leave the guilty unpunished; he punishes the children and their children for the sin of the fathers to the third and fourth generation.*   EXODUS 34:7

The loving side of God, however, does not erase the fact that he is also fair. Everything that he does is right and good – meaning that he cannot overlook sin. We can thank him that he has forgiven our sins and paid the price for them in the person of Jesus Christ when he died on the cross, but for those who refuse such a gift as this, his punishment and his judgment will be swift and just.

It's unpopular, and it's uncomfortable, but it's true. It is good as well. Without an awareness of God's holy justice, we would have complete mayhem in our world and total subjectivity in our relationship with him.

? QUESTION

Which of these attributes of God are most attractive to you? Which ones make you uncomfortable? Are there any that you doubt?

He is praiseworthy

Moses bowed to the ground at once and worshipped.   EXODUS 34:8

It's one thing to know all of these things in our head (to know this *about* God), but what a tragedy it would be if it never went further than this. God's revelation causes a response in the heart of those who are sensitive to his leading. Moses asked God to teach him his ways. God taught him with words that were clear and powerful. When Moses received this revelation, he saw himself in proportion to the God he now knew. And how did he respond?

He bowed down. He worshipped.

And then God began to make himself known to others through Moses. God had revealed himself as Father. Moses saw himself as a child. And together they walked forward in truth to the glory of God.

❧ QUOTATION

'Knowing' in the Biblical sense is a very intimate thing. It implies to actually experience. It is not just head knowledge, cerebral assent, or muscular posing. John 8:32 says, 'You shall know the truth and the truth shall make you free.' You participate; you experience life and make it 'biographical.' So, your theology becomes your biography.   TIM HANSEL, *HOLY SWEAT*

M.A.P.S.

❧ *Meditate*

Ask God to guide your thoughts as you consider these words from the Creed:

I believe... in God the Father.

✖ *Apply*

Review the fatherly attributes of God described in this chapter.

Which attributes of God the Father are you not experiencing?

If you were to choose to believe these things, what steps of faith would naturally follow?

✖ *Plot the passages*

- Key word: *Father.*
- Key passage: Exodus 33:12–17.
- Supporting passages: Hosea 6:3; Psalm 103:8–14; Zephaniah 3:17; 2 Chronicles 30:9; 1 John 4:7–10.

✖ *Speak*

Speak to self

I believe in God, my perfect Father, because:

- He's around.
- He's comforting.
- He elevates.
- He provides.
- He's pleased.
- He's interested.
- He's compassionate.
- He's gracious.
- He's patient.
- He's loving.
- He's faithful.
- He's forgiving.
- He's just.
- He's praiseworthy.

Speak to others

Talking about earthly fathers is an easy transition into talking about God as the perfect Father. It's really natural to compare and contrast fathers and *the* Father in regular conversation.

Think about a friend you know well who doesn't believe in God the Father. What do you know about their earthly father that could be a springboard in talking about some of the fourteen attributes of God?

Who do you know who needs to hear about God the Father? Are you praying for the opportunity to tell them about him?

Speak to God

Heavenly Father,
I want to know you; really know you. I don't want to just know about you, and I don't want to know you like a casual acquaintance. You have revealed yourself in the Word. Now, please reveal yourself in my heart. Lead me toward a pure understanding of you as my perfect Father. Then let the reality of you in my life be a light of truth to those in the darkness around me.
Amen.

*   *   *

God.

That's a very simple word: 'God'. Three letters; one syllable; very easy to say.

How could such a word ever describe the Almighty Father whom we find defined in the Bible? It can't. No words can; and yet in the Bible God reveals himself to be the one whom we can not only know *about*, but the one whom we can know *personally*, and then make known to *others*.

We have barely tasted a drop of water in the ocean of God's essence in this chapter. We are standing on the shore with our toes barely wet. Are you ready to wade in deeper, or perhaps even jump head-first into our experience of knowing God?

Let us acknowledge the Lord;
let us press on to acknowledge him.
As surely as the sun rises,
he will appear;
he will come to us like the winter rains,
like the spring rains that water the earth.   HOSEA 6:3

*I believe in God the Father **Almighty**, maker of heaven and earth; and in Jesus Christ his only Son our Lord; who was conceived by the Holy Ghost, born of the Virgin Mary, suffered under Pontius Pilate, was crucified, dead and buried. He descended into hell; the third day he rose again from the dead. He ascended into heaven, and sits on the right hand of God the Father Almighty. From thence he shall come to judge the quick and the dead. I believe in the Holy Ghost, the holy catholic church, the communion of saints, the forgiveness of sins, the resurrection of the body, and the life everlasting. Amen.*

CHAPTER 4

Superior Strength

'I believe in God' is not simply one belief among many. When we say 'we believe in God,' we are saying that we have embarked upon a path in which God is the overriding concern, the ultimate power, and the only one to whom our allegiance is properly due.   DAVID S. CUNNINGHAM[10]

Calvin Miller tells the story of a little girl who asked her father what God was like. Pulling her onto his lap, he said:

Think of God this way: Suppose you took all your sand in your sandbox and scooped it into a little mountain in the yard. Then suppose you went up and down the block and got all the sand in all your friends' sandboxes and added it to that mountain.

'Then suppose you went everywhere in the world and got all the sand in all the sandboxes of the world and added it to this mountain. Then, after you got all the sand in all the sandboxes, you went to all the beaches of the world and got all the sand from all those beaches and continued to add it to your mountain of sand. Then, at last suppose you went to all the deserts of the world and got all of that sand and added it to the mountain. Finally, you would have a terribly large mountain.

'Then, let us say you licked your index finger and went up and stuck it on the side of that huge mountain. When you drew your finger back, some grains would be stuck to your finger. But let us suppose that you took your other index finger and flicked away all of the grains that had stuck to your finger, except for one grain.

'That one grain of sand would represent what we know about God, and the mountain that was left would represent what we had yet to learn about him.[11]

That's not an exaggeration; in fact, the grain is an *overstatement* of the amount we know about God compared to what there is to know. It will no doubt take an eternity to understand him! But still we press on to know him and follow him, as we are commanded.

There are two sides to God's coin. On one side is the word 'Father'. We can relate to the Father thing. Our perceptions of 'God as Father' may be warped by our perceptions of our earthly fathers, but at least we have something to compare him to (imperfect as that something might be).

We have no comparisons when we talk about God being 'Almighty'. Humans have concocted a variety of different words to try to describe this aspect of God. Some call him the 'sovereign' one. Some say that he is 'transcendent'. Words like this might help describe him, but all words, no matter how descriptive, fall short of the fact that he is truly indescribable.

❧ Definition

sovereign (sŏv'[e]r-ĭn), *n.* One that exercises supreme, permanent authority, especially in a nation or other governmental unit, as a king, queen, or other noble person who serves as chief of state; a ruler or monarch.

transcendent (trăn-sĕn'd[e]nt), *adj.* 1. Surpassing others; pre-eminent or supreme. 2. Lying beyond the ordinary range of perception. 3. Being beyond the limits of experience and hence unknowable. 4. Being above and independent of the material universe.

Meanwhile, back in the Middle East...

When we last left Moses, he had asked God to describe himself so that he would know who it was that was 'going with him' as they made the trek to the Promised Land. God had revealed at least fourteen attributes about his character. But then Moses pushed a little bit further:

> *Then Moses said, 'Now show me your glory.'*   EXODUS 33:18

God says 'no' to this request – and for good reason. Moses is asking if he can step beyond the boundaries of human understanding and know God in ways that are truly unknowable. God holds back. He knows that if his glory were fully exposed it would blow Moses' mind into a million pieces; his soul would not be able to absorb it; his body would not be able to tolerate it... To see God in all his glory would kill him.

When the Apostles' Creed describes God 'Almighty', that's what it is talking about. We're standing on holy ground, on the edge of the infinite, at the pinnacle of something that is not just wonderful and awesome, but even dangerous.

So, while we might be able to see God as a 'Father', we must also in humility and wisdom recognize that God is 'farther'. There are critical aspects of God that we have no ability to understand or embrace, and thankfully God shows great restraint. He reveals himself only up to the level that we can handle. What's on the other side? Power, wisdom and awesomeness echo from God's being farther, much farther, than our ability to understand or experience.

Yes, we can know about God. We can even know him in a personal way. But in other ways he is completely unknowable... *infinitely beyond* our comprehension. As Chip Ingram says, 'We can know him truly, we cannot know him exhaustively.'[12]

There are some really impressive theological terms that describe God's attributes and abilities. Several of them began with the prefix 'omni-', which means 'all' or 'total':

- Omni*present* – God is everywhere (Psalm 139:7–12).
- Omni*potent* – God has all power (Jeremiah 32:17, 27).
- Omni*scient* – God is all scientific... No, that's not it – at least, not how the word 'science' is used today. The root of the word 'science' is actually 'knowledge', so this simply means that God knows everything (1 John 3:20).

In Luke 1:37 the angel Gabriel proclaimed, 'Nothing is impossible with God.' You've probably heard something like this before – but have you ever really thought about it? *Anything* that he chooses to do that is in accordance with his character, he *can* do.

God also knows everything. The problem, of course, is that we can't grasp the expanse of his might or wisdom. He's just in a totally different league than we are! He is Father, but he is also *farther* – farther than our minds can reach.

? Question

Why might someone be uncomfortable with the truth that God the Almighty knows everything about them? What attributes of God the Father would ease their concerns?

✍ Contemplation

'For my thoughts are not your thoughts, neither are your ways my ways,' declares the Lord. 'As the heavens are higher than the earth, so are my ways higher than your ways and my thoughts than your thoughts.'   ISAIAH 55:8–9

Check out these letters written by children in Sunday school:

Dear God,
Are you really invisible or is that just a trick?
Lucy

Dear God,
Is it true my father won't get into heaven if he uses his bowling words in the house?
Anita

Dear God,
I went to this wedding and they kissed right in church. Is that okay?
Neil

Dear God,
Maybe Cain and Abel would not kill each other so much if they had their own rooms. It works with my brother.
Larry

Dear God,
I think the stapler is one of your greatest inventions.
Ruth

Dear God,
I bet it is very hard for You to love all of everybody in the whole world. There are only four people in our family and I can never do it.
Nan

I love kids. I love the simplicity of their faith and the innocence in their belief. Their assumptions about God crack me up… but sometimes I honestly wonder if our perceptions of God as adults are really any better. Compared to what there is to know about God, we know about 0.000000036 per cent more than the children who wrote the letters above… Maybe we have a single grain of sand more than they do, but that's about it.

When Moses asked to see his glory, it was like asking God to pour the oceans through a thimble. The thimble couldn't possibly handle it. We couldn't possibly handle it.

No, God won't reveal himself *fully*, but with what he has revealed *partially*, we can respond in several ways:

- We are to *respect* him greatly.
- We are to *reverence* him continually.
- We are to *replace* him with nothing.

❧ QUOTATION

Our real idea of God may lie buried underneath the rubbish of conventional religious notions and may require an intelligent and vigorous search before it is finally unearthed and exposed for what it is. Only after an ordeal of painful self-probing are we likely to discover what we actually believe about God.   A. W. TOZER[13]

Golden calves

Okay, let's back up the horses for just a minute to make sure that you know what this means. When we start talking about God being Almighty, it's not time to mess around; this is serious business... life-and-death serious.

Before this whole conversation took place between God and Moses, Moses had just been up on Mount Sinai where he had an intense glimpse of the glory of God. Now he was descending the mountain with supernaturally carved tablets containing the law of the holy and powerful God.

What does he find? While he was gone the Israelites made a large golden calf... and they were dancing for it, worshipping it as if their lives depended upon it.

> He said to Aaron, 'What did these people do to you, that you led them into such great sin?'
>
> 'Do not be angry, my Lord,' Aaron answered. 'You know how prone these people are to evil. They said to me, "Make us gods who will go before us..." So I told them, "Whoever has any gold jewellery, take it off." Then they gave me the gold, and I threw it into the fire, and out came this calf!'   EXODUS 32:21–22

Make us gods who will go before us. That is the essence of *idolatry*. Idolatry takes place *anytime* we allow *anything* to take the place of God as the central life-giving almighty force in our life.

In the Western world, golden calves are pretty much out of vogue, but in their place we have managed to create a huge list of other things that become our substitute for God... And honestly, just like the Israelites, we dance and worship these things as if our lives depend upon them:

- Girlfriends, boyfriends
- Careers
- Money
- Reputation
- Cars, houses, clothes
- Knowledge
- Comfort
- Security
- Kids and kids' sports

The list goes on and on.

✍ CONTEMPLATION

Formerly, when you did not know God, you were slaves to those who by nature are not gods. But now that you know God – or rather are known by God – how is it that you are turning back to those weak and miserable principles? Do you wish to be enslaved by them all over again?   GALATIONS 4:8–9

? QUESTION

In your neighbourhood, what are some of the things that people use to take the place of God in their lives?

We often make a distinction between people who believe in God and those who do not. If someone knows about God, we think that that is better than them not knowing about God. But that is not the distinction the Bible makes. The Bible says that people either believe in the true God or they believe in idols.

Those idols can be metal or they can be mental, but there is a constant temptation to put trust in idols rather than in God. Things that we can touch and see and feel continually lure our passion and faith away from the true Almighty God:

Is there any God besides me? No, there is no other Rock; I know not one. All who make idols are nothing, and the things they treasure are worthless. Those who would speak up for them are blind; they are ignorant, to their own shame. Who shapes a god and casts an idol, which can profit him nothing?   ISAIAH 44:8–10

The problem with idols is that God and God *only* is Almighty. There is not a single idol on the face of the earth that we can fully depend on to meet our needs. They simply aren't *able* to do so... and so they eventually leave our hearts empty, our expectations broken and our dreams shattered. Even the idols that appear to be able to sustain us will ultimately crumble at the moment of death, for they are completely unable to help us beyond the grave.

The only One able

God (merciful as he is) was unwilling to blow Moses out of the water by showing him his glory. But even so, God was willing to show him the *effects* of his glory. He allowed Moses to see his back, to see the results of his abilities.

God does that same thing today. Because he's almighty, there are certain things that he and only he is able to do. We may not be able to understand how or why he does these things – for his ways and his motives are far beyond our own – but as a consequence of the things that we cannot see, there are certain things that we can see that reveal God's glory to us.

God is able to save us

> *Therefore he is able to save completely those who come to God through him, because he always lives to intercede for them.*   HEBREWS 7:25

At the core of the gospel is the truth that God is able to find someone who has been lost. He can find them and he can save them. He can do this physically, emotionally and spiritually. Though we have rebelled and gone our own way, God is able to reverse the consequences of our arrogant, ignorant choices. He is able to save us from the wrath and judgment that we are due because he paid the penalty for those sins himself when he came to earth as a man and died on the cross in our place.

❧ QUOTATION

> *If you have not chosen God, it will make no difference in the end what you have chosen. For you have missed the purpose for which you were formed, and you will have forsaken the only thing that satisfies.*   WILLIAM LAW[14]

He is able to empower us

> *And God is able to make all grace abound to you, so that in all things at all times, having all that you need, you will abound in every good work.*   2 CORINTHIANS 9:8

Because of God's grace, we are able to do things that we would be unable to do on our own. How does that work? I have no idea! I don't know how it is that he energizes our thoughts or the molecules in our flesh to allow us to accomplish things and choose things that we couldn't without his strength. But we know that he does. His Word promises that, and from time to time when we obey him and allow him to work through us, we also experience it.

He is able to uphold us

> *No temptation has seized you except what is common to man. And God is faithful; he will not let you be tempted beyond what you can bear. But when you are tempted, he will also provide a way out so that you can stand up under it.*
>
> 1 CORINTHIANS 10:13

We are constantly bombarded with temptation in this world. God says that he will give us a way out when we need it. It's not a matter of whether *he* will, it's only a matter of whether *we* will take the way of escape. How does he do this? How does he manipulate circumstances so that we always have the option of whether or not we are going to give in to temptation? I really don't know how he does that. But he's almighty; he can do whatever he wants and I'm thankful that he at least gives me the option to do what's right in times of temptation.

When I was playing basketball in college we had the opportunity to take a trip to Europe to play some international teams. Our travels took us to Amsterdam. I was completely ignorant about the reputation of the city and apparently my coach was too, because he gave us a night off to 'enjoy the great city of Amsterdam'.

Walking the dark streets with some of my teammates, we happened across the red light district – a clean, legal, organized and repulsive venue for selecting and soliciting prostitutes. I glanced into a large window-pane and was mortified to see an almost naked young woman enticing me towards her. I was terrified. My eyes reflexively glanced down at the cobblestone street and stayed there. I had memorized 1 Corinthians 10:13 as a child, and the Holy Spirit instantly brought that verse to mind. Out loud, for the benefit of my equally terrified teammates, I started to quote the verse. 'Eyes down boys!' I shouted. 'Remember, no temptation has seized us except that which is common to man... Keep walking, follow me... God is faithful, he won't let this go too far, and he will provide a way out for us. Look for it, guys; where is it?' I looked up and saw a cross-street leading to a quiet residential street. Recognizing it as our 'way out', we sprinted for the safety.

I get shivers down my spine thinking about how I could have messed up my life that night. A pocket of extra money, a beautiful woman, every natural instinct ready to pull me down... I could have made a decision of lifelong regret. But God upheld us and showed us the way out of the cesspool to safety.

He is able to work in us

> *Now to him who is able to do immeasurably more than all we ask or imagine, according to his power that is at work within us, to him be glory in the church and in Christ Jesus throughout all generations, for ever and ever! Amen.*
> EPHESIANS 3:20–21

This is definitely one of the great mysteries of the faith – and yet one of the most practical and profound. For some reason, in some way, God works through the person who knows him and trusts him to bring honour and glory to himself. Get it? I don't. How does he do that in all believers all of the time? I have no idea. But I'm really glad that he does. Without God living through us, it wouldn't be just difficult to live the Christian life. Without God's working through us, it would be *impossible* to live. But because he does, he is able to do *immeasurably* more than we can even dream, more than we can imagine. This is no exaggeration! We cannot measure the ways that he is able to work in us. Only the Almighty could do such things.

? QUESTION

> **What does it mean to believe in a God who is unbelievable? What is it like to know a God who is unknowable?**

He is able to transform us

> *But our citizenship is in heaven. And we eagerly await a Saviour from there, the Lord Jesus Christ, who, by the power that enables him to bring everything under his control, will transform our lowly bodies so that they will be like his glorious body.*
> PHILIPPIANS 3:20–21

God is in the business of remodelling. Big time. He is able to transform our spirits, our minds, and one day he will even transform our bodies. Sometimes the remodelling is painful and ugly as he comes in and tears out the walls, the furnishings, the old appliances that he knows must go if we are to reflect Jesus Christ outward through authentic lives. Somehow, he can take our broken lives, distorted beliefs and decaying bodies and transform them into something glorious, reflecting his glory.

✎ QUOTATION

The atheist finds himself enslaved by the need to prove himself an unbeliever. In denying the existence of God he finds nothing greater than himself and other selves in the universe. His greatest creed centers in 'I believe in myself.'

D. BRUCE LOCKERBIE

He is able to purify us

To him who is able to keep you from falling and to present you before his glorious presence without fault and with great joy...   JUDE 24

When Christ comes into our lives, he usually comes giving us a heightened awareness of sin. This can weigh heavily on our minds, but thankfully the purpose of this awareness is to teach us one of the great realities of Christian spirituality: We are unable to purify ourselves from the stain of our sin.

Maybe you've been on the receiving end of sin. Even if it wasn't your 'fault', the sins against you can leave you under a heavy weight of shame and filth. You wish you could wash yourself both from the outside and from the inside from what has happened to you... but you can't. You're not able to.

But God is able. God is able to purify you both from the sins you have committed and from those that have been committed against you.

God the Father, God the Father Almighty... When we say we believe in this God, we may not be able to see all of his glory, but he allows us to see the *effects* of his almightiness. He is able to do far above and beyond anything that we can imagine or think. We might try to describe that with all sorts of theological words or with earthly analogies. But in the end all we can do is stand with our hearts and hands raised toward heaven in worship...

M.A.P.S.

✎ *Meditate*

Ask God to guide your thoughts as you consider these words from the Creed:

I believe in God the Father Almighty.

✼ *Apply*

We have a tendency to try to figure God out. When we can't figure him out, we tend to take things into our own hands and fix them according to our own limited knowledge and abilities.

Where are you trusting in your own abilities?

If you truly believed that God is almighty, how might that change some of your daily decisions?

What is one thing that you would like to see happen in light of your belief in God the Almighty?

✼ *Plot the passages*

- Key word: *Almighty*.
- Key passage: Luke 1:37.
- Supporting passages: Isaiah 55:8–9; 44:8–10; Hebrews 7:25; 2 Corinthians 9:8; Ephesians 3:20–21; Jude 24–25.

✼ *Speak*

Speak to self

I believe that God is able to:

- Save me.
- Empower me.
- Uphold me.
- Work through me.
- Transform me.
- Purify me.

Speak to others

One of the best ways to *tell* people about what you believe about God is to *ask* them what they believe about God. Some people are used to being preached at, and none of them like that very much. But everyone loves to be listened to.

Review the attributes and abilities of God described in this chapter. Make a list of questions that would help someone tell you what they really believe about God.

Ask that God would give you a chance to sit down with someone who is ready to talk. Simply ask people *what* they believe about God and *why* they believe that. But don't respond or argue with them, just listen!

When you are through with all your questions, after they are convinced that you care about what they believe, they will ask you what you believe. Guaranteed.

Speak to God

My Almighty Father God,

My desire is to respect you greatly, to show reverence to you continually, and to replace you with nothing.

You are able to do many things that are impossible and you are the only one with the ability to make this desire a reality in my soul. I sincerely and humbly ask that you would do so.

Amen.

*   *   *

Cynthia lay on my office floor in the foetal position, crying, for four hours.

One of the most gifted worship leaders I had ever seen, she was a mainstay on our platform, leading our congregation in worship practically every week. But her world was now crashing down around her. Her marriage, her family, her friendships, her ministry... everything, as she once knew it, was stripped from her in a moment's time as she spoke her sin out loud. Her life had been forever altered in exchange for a temporary pleasure.

I had confronted her with facts that exposed her secret shame. Cynthia had been having an affair.

For two weeks, her life hung in the balance as she retreated into a cloud of inconsolable grief and despair. She was full of sorrow, yet still unrepentant. No one knew what decision Cynthia would eventually make. But God was already proving himself able – able to work a miracle in the heart of her husband. In the midst of his devastation and brokenness, Roland found freedom in the choice of forgiveness, then made the decision to seek reconciliation if Cynthia would choose to stay.

As the supernatural power of Christ moved in her life, Cynthia came to the end of herself, turned away from her sin and toward her God of grace, and emerged from her 'death bed' exhausted, but ready to receive love and help from the body of Christ.

In the months that followed God displayed his almighty ability in unimaginable ways. He worked through a group of faithful, merciful, Holy Spirit-led women, who surrounded Cynthia with loving support and accountability. I watched in wonder as the Almighty empowered, upheld, transformed and purified this broken couple, reshaping them into healthy, surrendered and thoroughly authentic people – with nothing to hide and everything to gain from their Father Almighty.

Almost two years to the day of my confrontation, Cynthia stood on the platform of our church sanctuary again, the first time since her sin had surfaced. She confessed it all, describing how unsuspecting she had been in the journey that had led to her sin, and how in hindsight now, she could clearly see that she 'settled' in her marriage, believing that 'this is as good as it's going to get', instead of longing for the *fantastic* marriage God had intended for them. She explained that she had fallen for the enemy's lie, believing that her unmet needs could be taken care of in the arms of another man, rather than in the goodness and provision of her heavenly Father. She spoke of what happened when the lie was revealed for what it was... the despair, the depression, the brokenness... and finally the discovery and acceptance of the love and grace of God.

Humbly she asked for forgiveness from the congregation she had betrayed, and God's grace and mercy emerged from their hearts. And then, taking the microphone for the first time in nearly two years, she sang 'Amazing Grace, how sweet the sound...' as if singing it for the first time, every note and every lyric of grace delivered with fresh meaning, by a life that had been transformed by an able God who is both almighty and the perfect Father.

> *We must try to speak of His love. All Christians have tried, but none have done it very well. I can no more do justice to that awesome and wonder filled theme than a child can grasp a star. Still... as I stretch my heart toward the high, shining love of God, someone who has not before known about it may be encouraged to look up and have hope.*
> A. W. TOZER, *KNOWLEDGE OF THE HOLY*

*I believe in God the Father Almighty, **maker of heaven and earth**; and in Jesus Christ his only Son our Lord; who was conceived by the Holy Ghost, born of the Virgin Mary, suffered under Pontius Pilate, was crucified, dead and buried. He descended into hell; the third day he rose again from the dead. He ascended into heaven, and sits on the right hand of God the Father Almighty. From thence he shall come to judge the quick and the dead. I believe in the Holy Ghost, the holy catholic church, the communion of saints, the forgiveness of sins, the resurrection of the body, and the life everlasting. Amen.*

CHAPTER 5

Sovereign Shaping

In the beginning, God created the heavens and the earth.   GENESIS 1:1

... the truth is personal. God is not merely the Creator in abstraction, in theory, or as a postulate. God is my *Creator, who has placed me here for a reason.'*

RON JAMES[15]

What if...

What if there really is a God who is both our Father and yet a little bit farther – an intimate one, an ultimate one, an almighty one?

What if this God is 'creator of heaven and earth'? Could those five words – *creator of heaven and earth* – communicate truth with huge personal implications?

Because, what if this God not only created heaven and earth, but the most valuable of all the things he made was... *you*?

Not long ago, a big Fortune 500 tech company ran an ad campaign based on those two words: 'What if...?' The thirty-second commercials showed individual engineers and executives doing something normal. A guy would be in the shower, or a woman would be driving her car... and all of a sudden, as if the clouds parted and a brilliant sunbeam broke through, 'Boom!' – a concept or an idea would descend. The person would then grab the phone and call a co-worker and ask the question, 'What if...?'

What were they selling? I don't even remember! But what they were really marketing was the life-changing implications of ideas, illumination, inspiration, and most of all, *possibilities*.

'What if...?'

What if God really is maker of heaven and earth? What if God not only *made* you, but *is making* you... still transforming you, shaping you and moulding you with purpose and vision?

What if all of his other attributes as an almighty Father of love and power and creativity were to be focused in on your soul like a laser beam?

And what if you really believe that? What would be the possibilities?

In the beginning

'In the beginning God created the heavens and the earth.' That's Genesis 1:1, the first line of the Bible. Does it sound simplistic? Maybe; but just because it's simple doesn't mean that it isn't one of the most profound, reality-shaking truths that we will ever embrace. Let's consider some of the implications of this simple belief.

God created out of nowhere

Get this: God is 'pre-existent'. Time as we know it is a by-product of his creation of the heavens and the earth. Before he created matter and distance, there was no such thing as 'time', yet God existed before these things existed. That's pretty simple but a little bit mind-boggling too. He *created* time and space and matter, *but that means that he must exist in some realm beyond the time, space and matter...* and quite frankly, I don't think any of us have the capacity to imagine what that really means. In the beginning, God created, yes – but that means that he existed before the beginning. Wow.

He created out of nothing

Theologians have a favourite term, *ex-nihilo*; it simply means 'out of nothing' in Latin.

When God started creating, he didn't have any materials to work with. He started with zippo, zilch, nada. It was *ex-nihilo* all the way. So how did he do it? By his words. The Hebrew word for 'speak' in Genesis 1 is *a'mar*. In Hebrew script, it looks like this: אָמַר.

God said. He made the call and it was so. He could just say 'stars', and entire galaxies began swirling. He could just say 'mountains', and there they were – the Himalayas. He *is* God the Father Almighty, and this display of his creative power alone leads us to fall on our faces in terrified and humble worship.

? QUESTION

Do you really believe that God has this kind of creative ability and power? Why do you think many people deny or disbelieve that he does?

The facts are simply this: At one point in the history of the universe, there was no universe. Every rule of common sense and every law of physics points to the fact that things don't just suddenly appear – nor do they organize themselves without outside help. First there was nothing; then there was something.

There is great debate about what happened after that first 'something' was created. Men and women who sincerely believe the Bible are debating the details about how, how long, and in what order God created.

✍ CONTEMPLATION

> By faith we understand that the universe was formed at God's command, so that what is seen was not made out of what was visible.   HEBREWS 11:3

At this point, it's important to understand a basic hermeneutical concept: *authorial intent.* What was the author trying to communicate in this passage of Scripture? *That God the Father Almighty is the maker of heaven and earth.* That's all he said in this particular passage. That's all God apparently wanted us to focus on.

✎ DEFINITION

> **hermeneutics** (hûr'm[e]-nōō'tĭks) *n.* 1. Bible interpretation. 2. A fancy word some people say to sound smart when they could have just said 'Bible interpretation'. (I don't know the etymology of the word, but I'm guessing the first guy that used it was named Herman – only joking!)

The debate will continue, but remember: No one has ever offered a factual explanation for how 'something' came out of 'nothing'. 'Someone' (God) outside of that 'something' must have caused it.

Setting the stage

From the Genesis 1 account, it would appear that God created the heavens and the earth in three different phases.

Stage 1: Formlessness

> *Now the earth was formless and empty, darkness was over the surface of the deep, and the Spirit of God was hovering over the waters.*   GENESIS 1:2

First, there was nothing. The first 'something' that God created appears to have been a wet, undefined, shapeless blob of matter.

Stage 2: Form

Whatever this formless blob was (and I doubt that we have the ability to under-stand what it might have been), God started to separate things, sort things and create order out of the chaos.

> *And God said, 'Let there be light,' and there was light. God saw that the light was good, and he separated the light from the darkness... And God said, 'Let there be an expanse between the waters to separate water from water...' And God said, 'Let the water under the sky be gathered to one place, and let dry ground appear...' And God said, 'Let there be lights in the expanse of the sky to separate the day from the night, and let them serve as signs to mark seasons and days and years...'*   GENESIS 1:3–4, 6, 9, 14

Stage 3: Fullness

Finally, when the stage was set, God created life itself – things to fill the heavens and the earth.

> *Then God said, 'Let the land produce vegetation...' And God said, 'Let the water teem with living creatures, and let birds fly above the earth across the expanse of the sky.' And God said, 'Let the land produce living creatures according to their kinds: livestock, creatures that move along the ground, and wild animals, each according to its kind.' And it was so.*   GENESIS 1:11, 20, 24

If you say that you believe these things – that God created the heavens and the earth as Genesis 1 lays it out – sooner or later your beliefs are going to have a head-on collision with the theory of evolution. My Dad once wrote:

> *Today the believer who stands up and says, 'I believe in God the Father Almighty, maker of heaven and earth' had better recognize that a lot of people are going to regard that statement with the utmost skepticism, if not total derision. And as a result of that, they're going to have to go back to their drawing board and find out if they really do believe in a maker of all things. Why? Because our world deserves to have people who believe what they believe and know why they believe it and can articulate it.*[16]

We won't take the time to go into the evolution/creation debate here. But let me say firmly that the theory of evolution is in serious trouble. This theory might have made some sense back in the 1800s when Charles Darwin was doing his writing, but we know so much more now than he did. He knew very, very little about the complexity of the cell; he knew nothing about the phenomenal amount of information in the DNA code (DNA hadn't even been discovered back then). He had no concept of biochemistry and the intricate universe of organization and activity that sustains life. He wasn't even aware of the massive gaps between species in the fossil record.

We know about those things now. While textbooks and professors still teach this theory as fact, they do so out of either a misguided interpretation of the facts or a personal bias against God. Let me say this very directly: If you have nagging doubts about the theory of evolution, get the facts and get them now. If you are willing to do a little reading, there is no reason to stumble over Darwin's *theory* when the *facts* that support God's creation are so strong.

At the dinner table recently I asked my teenage son what he was studying in science. 'The Big Bang theory,' was his response. 'It's so stupid!'

'Really?!' I replied. 'Why do you say that?'

'Because God made it – that's why...'

I thought for a moment before I spoke, realizing that what I was about to say might rock his world... 'Could it be that God used a Big Bang to create the universe? Someone would have had to cause that first "pop".'

He looked puzzled; I could see the gears cranking...

As believers we need to think clearly and wisely, not swallowing theories as fact *nor dismissing fact as fiction*. Belief matters, and if we aren't thinking well, we will lose credibility and our voice.

When we look at the complexity of creation, the fingerprints of God are everywhere. You can even see his created order in the symmetry of mathematics:

$1 \times 8 + 1 = 9$
$12 \times 8 + 2 = 98$
$123 \times 8 + 3 = 987$
$1234 \times 8 + 4 = 9876$
$12345 \times 8 + 5 = 98765$
$123456 \times 8 + 6 = 987654$
$1234567 \times 8 + 7 = 9876543$
$12345678 \times 8 + 8 = 98765432$
$123456789 \times 8 + 9 = 987654321$

$1 \times 9 + 2 = 11$
$12 \times 9 + 3 = 111$
$123 \times 9 + 4 = 1111$
$1234 \times 9 + 5 = 11111$
$12345 \times 9 + 6 = 111111$
$123456 \times 9 + 7 = 1111111$

1234567 x 9 + 8 = 11111111
12345678 x 9 + 9 = 111111111
123456789 x 9 + 10 = 1111111111

9 x 9 + 7 = 88
98 x 9 + 6 = 888
987 x 9 + 5 = 8888
9876 x 9 + 4 = 88888
98765 x 9 + 3 = 888888
987654 x 9 + 2 = 8888888
9876543 x 9 + 1 = 88888888
98765432 x 9 + 0 = 888888888

Brilliant, isn't it? And look at this symmetry:

1 x 1 = 1
11 x 11 = 121
111 x 111 = 12321
1111 x 1111 = 1234321
11111 x 11111 = 123454321
111111 x 111111 = 12345654321
1111111 x 1111111 = 1234567654321
11111111 x 11111111 = 123456787654321
111111111 x 111111111=12345678987654321

What if...

What if God really is the Creator of heaven and earth? It's worth stopping for a while – maybe a good long while – to stare at the stars, ponder the beauty of wildlife, peer into a microscope at the phenomenal complexity of life... just the slightest bit of meditation can launch our thoughts and our belief into new possibilities.

But *what if* God wasn't finished yet?

Saving the best for last

It is safe to say that each individual in the sea of humanity is on a quest for meaning, purpose and direction in life. Whether we do it through war or through peace, through materialism or through self-sacrifice, each of us is trying to find our place in the heavens and the earth.

? QUESTION

Do you think it's possible for a person to find meaning in life if they don't believe in God? Why or why not?

Is it possible to grasp these things if we don't know from where we have come? I don't think so. In order for us to move into the future with an awareness of our destiny and with a sense of fulfilment, we must know the truth about our past... and we must *believe* it.

✍ CONTEMPLATION

From birth I was cast upon you; from my mother's womb you have been my God.

PSALM 22:10

From birth I have relied on you; you brought me forth from my mother's womb. I will ever praise you.

PSALM 71:6

For you created my inmost being; you knit me together in my mother's womb.

PSALM 139:13

Genesis 1 reveals at least three important principles about our humanity:

God created humans in his own image

Then God said, 'Let us make man in our image, in our likeness, and let them rule over the fish of the sea and the birds of the air, over the livestock, over all the earth, and over all the creatures that move along the ground.' So God created man in his own image, in the image of God he created him; male and female he created them. GENESIS 1:26–27

There are certain characteristics about God (some of which we studied in the last chapter) that are reflected in the way that he has created us. There are certain aspects of our humanity that are unique to us, that set us apart from all other animals. Exactly what these are and how he gave them to us is not clear from this passage. But there is one thing I can say for sure: in the last century there has been a lot of talk about the equality of women. But the 'equality' of women is not a new concept. Men and women have been equal since Genesis 1. 'Man' is defined as 'male and female' and both genders are created in the image of God.

From the very beginning God proclaimed men and women to be the pinnacle of his creative genius, for God breathed into the souls of both men and women a special ability – an ability to love, an ability to choose, an ability to think beyond the heavens and the earth and ask, 'What if...?'

He commissioned them

God blessed them and said to them, 'Be fruitful and increase in number; fill the earth and subdue it. Rule over the fish of the sea and the birds of the air and over every living creature that moves on the ground.' Then God said, 'I give you every seed-bearing plant on the face of the whole earth and every tree that has fruit with seed in it. They will be yours for food. And to all the beasts of the earth and all the birds of the air and all the creatures that move on the ground – everything that has the breath of life in it – I give every green plant for food.' And it was so.

GENESIS 1:28–29

It was the world's first job description. God blessed them and told them to multiply – which implies, well, sex. On that first night in the garden you can hear the first romantic discussion taking place. You can see the first expectant look on Adam's face, but Eve is probably having the first headache, so Adam looks at her and says, 'Listen, honey – you heard what God said...'

What did God say? He said, 'Go make some babies and make the most of what I have given you on this earth. Rule over it and eat from it...'

❧ Quotation

To confess God as our Almighty Father and Creator, as we have seen, means that we must have an enduring sense of belonging in a purposeful world and that we accept the limits and the challenge of our stewardship over it. JOHN R. MAY[17]

It had been quite a week, and when God was done he took Sunday off – but not before he stood back and looked at his work and all that had been created out of nothing:

God saw all that he had made, and it was very good. And there was evening, and there was morning – the sixth day. GENESIS 1:31

It was very good... but it didn't last. The pinnacle of God's creation was headed for 'the fall'. Through a mixture of temptation and lies, our ancestors made a conscious decision to believe a lie (that they could become like God too). Every generation since has been born into a river of deceit that flows from this most basic lie: we should be our own god, creating our own destiny and purpose, living independent of the One who truly made us.

Now we are left only with shattered reflections and twisted images of the perfection of God's original creation. The heart of men and women is continually drawn back to 'nature' and ways of life that seem far removed from the fingerprints of humanity, but even the wilderness is just a twisted and distorted remnant of God's perfection.

Into such a world we have been born. With a slap on the butt after the pain of delivery, we enter alone into a world of uncertainty and difficulties.

An eternally extreme makeover

God made you. There is no getting around that fact, nor can you dodge the responsibility that comes with it. Your ancestors blew it; you blow it. 'Life sucks and then you die.' End of story.

Or is it?

What if God not only *made* you, but is still *making* you?

What are the possibilities if God is not finished yet? Is it possible that the Creator is still in the business of moulding and shaping our lives? The Bible says it's not only possible, it's reality.

He is re-creating

> *Therefore, if anyone is in Christ, the new creation has come: The old has gone, the new is here!*   2 CORINTHIANS 5:17

Make sure you get this right: God really isn't in the business of taking old stuff and giving it a facelift or a new paint job. God works from the inside out. He takes the old stuff and he *obliterates* it and *replaces* it with something new. (That's what the Apostle John called being 'born again' – John 3:3.) God doesn't just go for the remodel job; he tears down and rebuilds.

I recently watched a TV show called *Extreme Makeover Home Edition*. I'm embarrassed to admit it, but it made me cry. A family had lost their home to a flood. The *Makeover* team showed up and sent the family on a nice beach holiday while the crew completely gutted the place and rebuilt it from the inside out... in just one week!

When the family returned they didn't find a few updates or additions; they found a miniature-version Disney World! Fantasy rooms for each family member, a quiet nook for Mum and Dad, a back garden complete with climbing-wall and zip-line! (Does anyone else wonder how these poor families pay the taxes on these incredible houses? Sorry, I digress.)

The point I'm trying to make is that the house gets a complete transformation from the inside out, and this type of transformation is possible for us too. When it comes to the spiritual things in our life, God has gutted us out and made us a brand-new creation. *Extreme Makeover LIFE Edition!*

He is reconciling

> *All this is from God, who reconciled us to himself through Christ and gave us the ministry of reconciliation: that God was reconciling the world to himself in Christ, not counting people's sins against them.*   2 CORINTHIANS 5:18–19

In 1846, the poet Elizabeth Barrett Browning married her husband Robert against her parents' wishes. They disowned her completely, yet Elizabeth wrote a letter to them every week, begging for reconciliation. She never heard from them until one day, when she received a package from her mother. Inside were all the letters Elizabeth had written; and every letter was unopened. She took some of those letters and published them, and now they are among the gems of English literature.

What if...? What if her mother had opened those letters and heard the truthful yearnings in Elizabeth's heart?

The Bible, from cover to cover, is a package of love letters from God to you. From beginning to end, you read the yearnings of God's heart, begging for reconciliation. Even though we are the ones who turned out backs on him, he continues to reach out with a message that shouts, 'Life can be different!' His love as a Father reaches across our rebellion; in his open hand he offers reconciliation to all who will take it.

✍ QUOTATION

To rely on the 'Creator of heaven and earth' is to rely on the one who will 'do a new thing' (Isaiah 43:18–19). Our attention is focused not backward on some earlier age of perfection, but forward to the reconciliation of all things through that love made manifest in the cross and resurrection of Jesus Christ.

THEODORE W. JENNINGS[18]

He is re-commissioning

And he has committed to us the message of reconciliation. We are therefore Christ's ambassadors, as though God were making his appeal through us. We implore you on Christ's behalf: Be reconciled to God.   2 CORINTHIANS 5:19–20

In the Garden of Eden everything existed in harmony and unity. We live in a world of conflict now – a world where lies have deadly consequences and where the truth desperately needs to be proclaimed.

In this broken world, God is commissioning us again. He calls us to be a part of a rescue mission that broadcasts the good news about God's continued creative works to those around us – to those who desperately need his healing touch.

We don't just get to make babies and watch our pets. We are called to be 'ambassadors' of Christ' (2 Corinthians 5:20), proclaiming through our words and displaying through our actions the re-creation that we have experienced and continue to experience through a relationship with Jesus Christ.

That's the new commission.

What if...?

What if you believed it?

M.A.P.S.

❧ Meditate

Ask God to guide your thoughts as you ponder these words from the Apostles' Creed:

I believe in God, the maker of heaven and earth.

❧ Apply

Review the main points of this chapter, then consider carefully this quote from Ron James:

God is my Creator, who has placed me here for a reason – to be open to God's will, to place myself and all my powers at God's disposal, to join in the redemptive purpose for all creation. This Creator is the God I confess in the Creed when I say, 'I believe in God the Father Almighty, maker of heaven and earth.'[19]

Sincerely ask God to show you what he wants to do through you because of your belief in his creative and re-creative power.

✖ *Plot the passages*

- Key word: *Creator*.
- Key passage: Genesis 1:1–31.
- Supporting passages: Hebrews 11:3; Psalm 139:13–14; 2 Corinthians 5:17–20; Ephesians 2:10.

✖ *Speak*

Speak to self

I believe in God, the Maker of heaven and earth, and I believe that:

- God created out of nowhere.
- God created out of nothing.
- God created humans in his own image.
- God is re-creating me in the image of Jesus.
- God is reconciling me with himself.
- God is re-commissioning me to be an ambassador of true belief.

Speak to others

Creation vs. evolution is a hot topic. Sometimes this is due to a misinterpretation of the facts or a lack of facts altogether. If this topic of conversation comes up frequently for you (or if you have your own questions about evolution), you'll want to study the issue so that you can give solid responses to others and yourself.

Many times, however, evolutionists have formed their beliefs not because of science, but because of painful life experiences. Once again, listen carefully to the people. Ask them lots of questions about what they believe. Understand the roots of their beliefs before you plant new seeds of truth.

Who do you know who is interested in issues of creation? Who do you know who needs to hear about the re-creative transformation that God is willing to give?

Speak to God

My God and my Creator,

I worship you today for who you are as my Maker and my Re-creator! The Bible says that the stars and the sky declare your glory – and I believe that. Everywhere I look, I see the results of your creative powers. I can do nothing except praise you and bow before you in light of all that you have made.

And Lord, thank you for re-creating me. I thank you that I'm not the person I was before you came into my life. Thank you for reconciling me to yourself. I can think of no greater gift and I know that it was purchased at great cost.

Thank you, again.

Amen.

*   *   *

Experiencing God's continued creative powers begins with the words, *'I believe... I believe in the maker of heaven and earth.'*

What if...?

What if there really is a God who is both our Father and yet a little bit farther – an intimate one, an ultimate one, an almighty one?

What if...?

What if this God is 'creator of heaven and earth'? Could those five words – *creator of heaven and earth* – communicate truth with huge personal implications?

Because, what if this God not only created heaven and earth, but the most valuable of all the things he made was... *you*?

2 Corinthians 5:17 says, 'Therefore, if anyone is in Christ new things have come. The old has gone; the new is here!' What if you *really* believed that God has done what he says he has?

God, who is rich in mercy, made us alive with Christ even when we were dead in transgressions – it is by grace you have been saved. And God raised us up with Christ and seated us with him in the heavenly realms in Christ Jesus... and this not from yourselves, it is the gift of God – not by works, so that no one can boast. For we are God's handiwork, created in Christ Jesus to do good works, which God prepared in advance for us to do.   EPHESIANS 2:4–6, 8–10

I believe in God the Father Almighty, maker of heaven and earth; and **in Jesus Christ his only Son our Lord**; *who was conceived by the Holy Ghost, born of the Virgin Mary, suffered under Pontius Pilate, was crucified, dead and buried. He descended into hell; the third day he rose again from the dead. He ascended into heaven, and sits on the right hand of God the Father Almighty. From thence he shall come to judge the quick and the dead. I believe in the Holy Ghost, the holy catholic church, the communion of saints, the forgiveness of sins, the resurrection of the body, and the life everlasting. Amen.*

CHAPTER 6

The Son

Christianity does not begin with a theory, no matter how finely spun. Christianity does not begin with an abstraction, no matter how poetic. Christianity begins with a person, an actual, factual, historical, tangible, human, believable person, Jesus of Nazareth, whom we confess to be the Christ. RON JAMES[20]

I think the most important thing that happens within Christian spirituality is when a person falls in love with Jesus. DON MILLER[21]

The man sits down and asks her for a drink.

She is used to this, of course – men approaching her, asking for something, taking what they desire and then leaving her alone... empty... again.

But there is something different about this man. Definitely not a local. Perhaps a traveller who has found himself on the wrong side of the tracks? Strange. Inappropriate. Uncomfortable. A man of his high class stooping to proposition one as low as her.

'Why you askin' me for a drink, Mister?'

She anticipates another classic pick-up line... but his words don't follow the path that she is used to. The conversation diverts...

'If you really knew who I was, you'd be the one asking me for a drink,' he responds coolly.

'I'll take whatever you're servin',' she says with a smile.

'Then go get your husband and come back.'

'Ain't got no old man,' she says, confused again by the direction of his words.

'I know that. You've had five of them and the one you're with now doesn't wear your ring.'

'Mister, are you some sort of prophet?' she asks the stranger, hoping to draw his attention away from her flushed cheeks, away from the painful reality of what he knows about those who have shared her bed. 'My people have been worshipping up in these parts for a long time...'

'Yes, but you worship what you do not know,' he says. 'But the time is coming – in fact now is – when those who worship will worship from the spirit with truth.'

'Don't know much about that,' she says. 'But I do know that the special man is coming; a talker, a holy man, a Lord... and I'm trusting that he'll explain it to us all.'

Then Jesus declared, 'I who speak to you am he.'

Belief matters. It really does – but not because there is value in belief alone. Value must be found in that in which we believe. Belief in a trustworthy person or thing launches us across an important threshold, into new territory of faith and action.

We are not unlike the Samaritan woman who met Jesus at the well in the narrative above (see John 4). For no human can meet him and remain unchanged *if* we believe in him as he is.

But exactly who did she meet? Who is this messiah-man? The Apostles' Creed distinguishes him from all other men with this phrase:

Jesus Christ his only Son our Lord.

From this brief phrase we can pick out four things that place this person infinitely above and beyond anyone else we can imagine or think about – things that make him (and him only) worthy of our belief and trust:

- He is a Man.
- He is Monogeneous.
- He is Messiah.
- He is Master.

Man

In the movie *Jesus Christ Superstar* Mary Magdalene sings, *I Don't Know How to Love Him*. She is no stranger to men, of course, but as she finds herself in a new kind of love, she wrestles with the fact that he's just another man like all the rest.

Jesus Christ was 'just a man' in the sense that he was fully human. His humanity was obvious both in his words and in the way he lived his life. One day when he got in trouble with the authorities, he responded this way to the Jews:

'If you were Abraham's children,' said Jesus, 'then you would do the things Abraham did. As it is, you are determined to kill me, a man who has told you the truth that I heard from God. Abraham did not do such things.'   JOHN 8:39–40

A lot is happening in this passage, so much that you might overlook a subtle but important point: Right there in the middle of verse 40, Jesus says that he is 'a man'. 'Jesus' was a common name for men in Palestine; it still is in Latin American countries. Several other things clearly confirm his humanness:

He was physical

> *So he came to a town in Samaria called Sychar... Jacob's well was there, and Jesus, tired as he was from the journey, sat down by the well... When a Samaritan woman came to draw water, Jesus said to her, 'Will you give me a drink?' (His disciples had gone into the town to buy food.)*   JOHN 4:5–8

This much is pretty clear: The man Jesus had a body with limitations like ours. He got tired; he got thirsty. A few verses later we read, 'Meanwhile his disciples urged him, "Rabbi, eat something"' (John 4:31), so he obviously had a need for food as well.

He was emotional

Like most men, Jesus had a handful of friends. One of those was a man named Lazarus. But Lazarus got sick and his sister sent word to Jesus, saying, 'Lord, the one you love is sick' (John 11:3). Jesus *loved* his friend... and he also knew death's unavoidable complement: grief. When Lazarus died, Jesus responded with great emotion:

> *... he was deeply moved in spirit and troubled.*
> *'Where have you laid him?' he asked.*
> *'Come and see, Lord,' they replied.*
> *Jesus wept.*
> *Then the Jews said, 'See how he loved him!'*   JOHN 11:33–36

'Jesus *wept*...' (John 11:35). That's the shortest verse in the Bible. (If you want to start a Scripture memory programme, I recommend this as your first verse. Pretty hard to mess it up!) But just because it's short doesn't mean it's insignificant. The word 'wept' is the same word used to describe a horse that is deeply snorting through its nostrils – we are talking about deep, soul-shaking sobs of emotional pain.

On the flip-side, Jesus also experienced joy. 'I have told you this so that my joy might be in you, and so that your joy may be complete' (John 15:11). I believe that Jesus was a man full of laughter and happiness. Like any man, he was physical and he experienced the full rainbow of human emotion.

? QUESTION

Do you think most people are comfortable believing in an emotional Jesus? Why or why not?

Monogeneous

✒ Definition

Monogeneous (m[e]-nŏj´[e]-n[e]s), *adj.* One of a kind. *Mono* means 'one'. *Genas* means 'kind' or 'nature'. It is the word from which we get 'genes', 'gender' and 'genetic'.

Monogeneous simply means that Jesus is 'one of a kind'. What kind of a kind? *God's* kind. That's what the Creed means when it states 'his only Son'. There is a powerful and unique oneness between Jesus and the Father that shows up in four ways:

1. His relationship with the Father

> *For God so loved the world that he gave his only begotten Son.*   JOHN 3:16

To say that God gave his only begotten Son is to make a radical claim: *this* Son came from *that* Father. There is a direct, unseverable, Father–Son relationship between God the Father and God the Son.

✒ Contemplation

No man has seen God at any time; the only begotten God, who is in the bosom of the Father, He has explained Him.   JOHN 1:18 (NASB)

✒ Quotation

When the Creed called God maker of heaven and earth, it parted company with Hinduism and Eastern faiths in general. Now by calling Jesus Christ God's only Son, it parts company with Judaism and Islam and stands quite alone.

J. I. PACKER[22]

2. His pre-existence with the Father

> *In the beginning was the Word, and the Word was with God, and the Word was God. He was with God in the beginning. Through him all things were made; without him nothing was made that has been made.*   JOHN 1:1–3

The Greek word for 'word' is *logos*. Douglas J. Soccio writes:

> *The Greek word logos is rich and complex, meaning all of the following: 'intelligence', 'speech', 'discourse', 'thought', 'reason', 'word', 'meaning',... the logos was the rule according to which all things are accomplished and the law which is found in all things.*[23]

Basically, God had a perfect idea (an idea that was separate from anything material), and out of that idea he created everything, including the heavens and the earth. The Son was (and is) a partner in creation with the Father. So all the characteristics of God as the 'maker of heaven and earth' describe Jesus too!

In order for him to be there 'in the beginning' of creation, he had to exist *before* the beginning. This is clearly one of the attributes that prove that Jesus is one of a kind with God.

✑ CONTEMPLATION

He is the image of the invisible God, the firstborn over all creation. For by him all things were created: things in heaven and on earth, visible and invisible, whether thrones or powers or rulers or authorities; all things were created by him and for him. He is before all things, and in him all things hold together. COLOSSIANS 1:15–17

3. His unity with the Father

Throughout the New Testament (and particularly in the books written by John) we see a special personal connection between Jesus and the Father. This was a unique one-of-a-kind relationship – interestingly, it's the kind of relationship that Jesus prayed we would have with him and the Father through the Spirit:

> *Before long, the world will not see me any more, but you will see me. Because I live, you also will live. On that day you will realize that I am in my Father, and you are in me, and I am in you.*   JOHN 14:19–20

Clearly there was a very special connection between the Son and the Father – a unity that we can be a part of even while we are on earth.

4. His association with the Father

Jesus claimed not only to be unified with or close to the Father; he claimed *oneness* with the Father, *making himself God's equal*:

[Jesus said...] 'I and the Father are one.'

Again the Jews picked up stones to stone him, but Jesus said to them, 'I have shown you many good works from the Father. For which of these do you stone me?'

'We are not stoning you for any good work,' they replied, 'but for blasphemy, because you, a mere man, claim to be God.'   JOHN 10:30–33

Wow. Picture that. The religious elite are staring Jesus down. His own people have picked up stones and are ready to pulverize his body. He has a clear opportunity to deny his claim to be God, but he doesn't! The claim stands: *Jesus claimed to be God.*

The Jews wanted to kill him for his claim to be God. The Greeks, on the other hand, couldn't accept that he was a real man! In the Greek culture, gods were a dime a dozen. You could find a temple to a different god on every street corner – but the claim that God had taken on human form? That was unthinkable for the Greek. (If Jesus was intending to win friends and influence people, he sure could have chosen a better marketing strategy!)

As Christians, we are stuck somewhere in between the Jew and the Greek. When we say that we understand the 'deity' of Jesus Christ or the 'incarnation' of Christ, we must confess that we believe him to be fully human and yet fully God – both in one package – something that is beyond our comprehension. Clearly, this is the work of God the Almighty. The concept of Jesus the 'God/man' should leave us wondering as much as it does understanding.

✂ QUOTATION

The Word became flesh, and then through the theologians, it became words again.   KARL BARTH[24]

We will never be able to grasp this in its entirety. But at the same time, it's amazing to see that this 'dual nature' of Jesus enables him and qualifies him to do things that are impossible for anyone else.

? QUESTION

Why is it that you can talk casually about almost any historical figure, but when the conversation turns to Jesus, many people get tense?

Messiah

Back to the woman at the well. When talking to Jesus, she verbalized a widely held expectation:

> The woman said, 'I know that Messiah (called Christ) is coming. When he comes, he will explain everything to us.'
> Then Jesus declared, 'I who speak to you am he.'   JOHN 4:25–26

The word 'Christ' is the Greek rendering of the Hebrew word for 'messiah'. They mean the same thing, just in different languages. 'Messiah' means 'anointed one'. Calling Jesus the 'Christ' identifies him as a very special ambassador with a particular *mission*. Only three different groups of people were 'anointed' in the Old Testament, and all three of these 'offices' converge in a stunning way in Jesus Christ.

Prophet

The prophets of the Old Testament were anointed with oil for a special ministry. Their job was to bring God's message to man. Most of the time these messages were, let's say, less than positive. They were often warnings of impending doom and destruction. Prophets weren't exactly the most popular guys on the speaking circuit. I'm guessing that's why they usually prefaced their messages with the words, 'Thus saith the Lord', which in effect means, 'Hey, don't blame me! I'm just the messenger here, okay?!'

We don't like bad news, but at the same time humans have a deeply felt need for knowledge. Throughout history our ancestors turned to mediums and/or fortune-tellers. (Nowadays we call them New Age channellers.) 'Just for fun' we read horoscopes and break open our fortune cookies – but aren't we always hoping that someone can tell us what's going to happen over the next horizon?

Jesus said you don't need them. As *the Christ*, the anointed one, he is the one who 'will explain everything to us'. He is our prophet, the one who communicates God's message to each of us. He is bringing God to us.

Priest

Once a year a special Jewish priest was allowed to enter the 'Most Holy Place' – an inner sanctuary of the temple where God resided in a special way. The priest would make the annual sacrifice as an important payment for the sins of the nation. Only the priest was allowed to go in there. He was the one man who represented all the people – he was bringing the people to God.

Jesus does the same thing. As the anointed one, he fulfils this priestly role for us. Read the book of Hebrews. This amazing New Testament book clearly identifies Jesus as the Christ, the perfect anointed priest who not only *makes* the sacrifice, but who *is* the sacrifice. The Christ is the perfect Lamb of God that takes away the sins of the world.

✍ CONTEMPLATION

Therefore, brothers, since we have confidence to enter the Most Holy Place by the blood of Jesus, by a new and living way opened for us through the curtain, that is, his body, and since we have a great priest over the house of God, let us draw near to God with a sincere heart in full assurance of faith, having our hearts sprinkled to cleanse us from a guilty conscience...   HEBREWS 10:19–22

What is the result? We don't need priests any more. Jesus the Christ finished the job – and continues in this role even today. He is still the perfect anointed one who brings us to God:

For Christ died for sins once for all, the righteous for the unrighteous, to bring you to God.   1 PETER 3:18

King

Meanwhile Jesus stood before the governor, and the governor asked him, 'Are you the king of the Jews?'
    'Yes, it is as you say,' Jesus replied.   MATTHEW 27:11

The third person who was anointed in the Old Testament was the King. Kings in ancient Israel were appointed by God to positions of unquestioned rule and authority. When King David was anointed with oil (1 Samuel 16:13), 'the Spirit of the Lord came upon David in power.'

As Christ the Messiah, God has anointed Jesus as the 'King of kings and Lord of lords' (Revelation 17:14; 19:16). He has a kingdom; he has power; he is the final authority and what he says goes. But presently we are in a brief period of history where Christ doesn't force his authority on anyone. Instead, he invites all to enter his kingdom as willing children, who are then free to enjoy his guidance, provision, protection and discipline.

Jesus was totally serious about fulfilling this role; ultimately he died for it. 'Above his head they placed the written charge against him: THIS IS JESUS, THE KING OF THE JEWS' (Matthew 27:37).

Master

You know the message God sent to the people of Israel, announcing the good news of peace through Jesus Christ, who is Lord of all.   ACTS 10:36

C.S. Lewis is currently best known as the author of the Chronicles of Narnia. Through this now famous series of children's books, he paints a picture of Jesus Christ as Lord for everyone to see. Though this picture is laced with fantasy and imagination, it comes from solid and deep theological roots that clearly describe Jesus Christ as Lord of all.

And this is where things get a little bit uncomfortable, because everything that we have learned about Jesus the Christ so far brings us to an unavoidable decision: will we or will we not bend the knee before him as our personal Master?

✆ QUOTATION

Any man who is merely a man and said the sort of things Jesus said would not be a great moral teacher. He would either be a lunatic on a level with the man who says he is a poached egg, or else he would be the devil of hell. You must make your choice. You can shut him up for a fool, you can spit on him and kill him as a demon, or you can fall at his feet and call him Lord and God. But let us not come with any patronizing nonsense about his being a great human teacher. He has not left that open to us, he did not intend to.   C.S. LEWIS[25]

The Apostle Paul made this very clear when he wrote to the church at Philippi:

Therefore God exalted him to the highest place and gave him the name that is above every name, that at the name of Jesus every knee should bow, in heaven and on earth and under the earth, and every tongue confess that Jesus Christ is Lord, to the glory of God the Father.   PHILIPPIANS 2:9–11

God is God. Jesus is God. The knee will bow one way or the other.

? QUESTION

What tendencies do you find in yourself that might make you resistant to bowing before Christ as your Prophet, Priest and King? Where does that hesitancy come from?

But there is yet more to Jesus' ministry. He was also the *ultimate servant*.

Flash back to Jesus' last night. The stage has been set; the prophecies are unfolding before their eyes. The sun will rise over betrayal, arrests, beatings, denials... and a waiting cross. Tonight the Christ and his disciples have just shared the Passover meal with each other – the meal that has for centuries symbolized the coming sacrificial Saviour. *This bread is my body, soon to be broken for you. This wine is my blood, flowing for your sins...*

... And then, when the meal is complete, he does a most remarkable thing. The Prophet, the Priest, the King rises from the table and lays his garments aside. He picks up a towel, pours water into the basin and begins to wash the feet of his disciples (John 13:1–5).

What does it mean that Jesus is Lord? What kind of a Lord is he? The answers lie in the dirty, dung-ridden feet of his followers becoming clean in the loving hands of the Master. This is the picture of the one who is fully man and fully God: *Jesus Christ, God's only Son, our Lord.* A *servant* master.

We are to bend the knee before the God who kneels before us as a servant of those he loves.

This is the man who asked the woman for water.

This is the God who pointed the way to an entirely different kind of living.

This is Jesus.

M.A.P.S.

❧ *Meditate*

Like the Samaritan woman at the well, like the disciple whose feet had just been washed, each of us as individuals must decide what we believe about Jesus.

Ask God to guide your thoughts as you consider these words from the Creed:

'I believe... in Jesus Christ his only Son our Lord.'

✣ *Apply*

- Review the main points of this chapter.
- Ask the Lord to guide you into specific points of action.
- Let him search your heart and show you if there's any hurtful way in you.
- Ponder whether or not you truly believe who he has revealed himself to be, or whether this is just mental information that has not been followed up with a heartfelt abandon.

Ask yourself: How would my life change if I continually placed myself in the hands of Jesus Christ as my Lord, allowing him to work through me in any way that he chose?

The Son of God modelled the future for us by washing the feet of those whom he came to serve. Ask God to reveal to you whose feet need washing today. Are you willing to bend the knee to allow Christ to serve them through you?

⚜ *Plot the passages*

I'd like to encourage you to keep highlighting and plotting these passages in your own Bible. Having these verses at your fingertips is great for sharing with others as well as reminding yourself that belief matters. Keep it up!

- Key word: *Son*.
- Key passage: John 1:1–14.
- Supporting passages: John 11:35, 10:30–33; Acts 10:36; Philippians 2:9–11; John 13:1–5.

⚜ *Speak*

Speak to self

I believe in Jesus Christ, God's only Son, my Lord. I believe that:

- He is a Man who is both physical and emotional.
- He is Monogeneous, one of a kind with God.
- He is Messiah, the anointed Prophet, Priest and King.
- He is Master, the servant Lord who calls us to follow.

Speak to others

C.S. Lewis said that Jesus was either 'Lord, liar or lunatic'. That's a great place to start meaningful conversations. Either Jesus was God, as he claimed (Lord), or he knew he wasn't God but claimed to be so (liar), or he thought he was God but wasn't (lunatic). Show people the claims that Christ made, and then ask them which category they think he fits into.

Speak to God

(Find a place alone where you can kneel.)

> *Dear God,*
> *I choose today to bend my knee before you in worship and praise. I believe that you came to earth as a man. I have faith that your Son Jesus is my living*

Prophet, Priest and King. Keep me humble, teachable – always aware of the eternal wonder of what you have done and who you are. Lord, I seek to praise you beyond my human capacity to understand you.

And now, I lay myself in your hands, ready to be used as a tool in any way you desire. You are my King – yet you are a servant King. If I'm going to live the type of life that you lived, I must depend fully on you to live that life through me. I simply cannot do that in my own strength, but through you I believe that this type of life is possible.

You are the Christ; you are the Lord; with great anticipation and submission, I kneel before you now.

I pray this in the name of Jesus Christ, God's only Son, my Lord!

Amen.

*   *   *

The Towel

Still wet, grimy from eleven pairs of feet, a towel hangs in a corner alongside a wash basin. As usual.

Tonight, though, is different. The towel was not hung there by the servant girl, but by the one they call Master, Teacher. The Master doing a servant's work for his fellow followers? That's all wrong. Somehow, though, he makes it right.

For a few moments eleven pairs of eyes fix thoughtfully on the towel and the basin. But tonight of all nights there are more pressing matters.

Wait! Is he saying wash one another's feet? What if this little band takes him seriously? What if they actually imitate their self-appointed foot washer? Tomorrow, of course, morning-after realism will unmask the thought for the nonsense it is.

But tonight, in the glow of the moment, imagination rules. Could a servant's towel be the rumpled banner of a new way? Not likely, people being what they are. But maybe. Just maybe.   DOUG MCGLASHAN, *WORLD VISION MAGAZINE*

*I believe in God the Father Almighty, maker of heaven and earth; and in Jesus Christ his only Son our Lord; **who was conceived by the Holy Ghost, born of the Virgin Mary**, suffered under Pontius Pilate, was crucified, dead and buried. He descended into hell; the third day he rose again from the dead. He ascended into heaven, and sits on the right hand of God the Father Almighty. From thence he shall come to judge the quick and the dead. I believe in the Holy Ghost, the holy catholic church, the communion of saints, the forgiveness of sins, the resurrection of the body, and the life everlasting. Amen.*

CHAPTER 7

The Supernatural Conception

As a Christian I believe that we live in parallel worlds. One world consists of hills and lakes and barns and politicians and shepherds watching their flock by night. The other consists of angels and sinister forces...   PHILIP YANCEY

For nothing is impossible with God.   LUKE 1:37

Evenrude wasn't purring when we entered the apartment. That was weird. He got his name because he hums like a motorboat all the time, except, that is, when he's in trouble. It was Christmas time and we had left him alone while we took a holiday trip. I didn't like the sheepish look on his whiskered face...

In the living-room we discovered the reason for our guilt-ridden greeting: The Christmas tree was upended, ornaments scattered and broken, lights strewn about... and the lovely black syrupy 'water' from the base? It had soaked into the Persian rug my mum had lent us... and saturated the blueprints from the new home we were building... and it had all coagulated into this blob of paper and wool and tree-needles.

As we cleaned up the mess, in my head I entertained images of TV commercials where Christmas is always warm, cosy, perfect and clean.

But Christmas isn't always like that, is it? It never really was. Just ask Mary, the mother of Jesus. On that special night in Bethlehem, contrary to popular opinion, there was no snow falling. Jesus probably wasn't even born in December at all. And the star that we hang above the stable? It was at least a couple years before the Magi followed that heavenly light to where Jesus was already living as a child.

A holy night for sure, yet one without fanfare. A few bewildered shepherds and a young Jewish couple who crassly had been ushered into a barn to deliver their baby. Nothing had changed in the world. But everything had changed in the world.

The baby's entrance into this world appeared plain and unremarkable – yet, as we shall see, the culmination of this particular pregnancy sent shockwaves through the heavens, just as the conception of this child had sent bewilderment and disillusionment into the lives of the parents. The events that led up to the pregnancy were anything but 'normal' and 'natural'.

In order to discover the mystery and miracle of the birth of Jesus, we need to back-track to nine months before that night when the Maker, the Messiah and the Master slipped almost unnoticed into an earthly existence.

Four passages speak of Christ's miraculous conception by a woman who had known no man. How did this happen? What is the significance of his birth by a virgin? What is happening in the unseen realm when this baby breathes its first gasps of earthly oxygen? What does it mean when we say: *'I believe in Jesus Christ, who was conceived by the Holy Ghost, born of the Virgin Mary'*?

Genesis 3:14 – protoevangelium

✎ DEFINITION

protoevangelium (prō′t[e]-ē′vān-jĕl′ĭ-[e]m), *n.*, from *proto* meaning 'first' and *evangel* meaning 'gospel'. The first hint of the gospel of Jesus Christ anywhere in the Bible.

The first passage that hints of something unusual to come shows up right after 'the fall'. God had completed creation and it was very good. But it was not to last. Tempted by Satan himself, Adam and Eve turn their backs on the promises of God in hope that they might become 'like God' themselves. After banishing Adam and Eve from Eden and the tree of life, God turns his attention toward the liar.

Satan has taken a cheap shot at humanity (and we fell for it), but God is right back in the devil's face with a warning:

> *The Lord God said to the serpent, 'Because you have done this, cursed are you more than all cattle, and more than every beast of the field; on your belly you will go, and dust you will eat all the days of your life; and I will put enmity between you and the woman, and between your seed and her seed; he shall bruise you on the head, and you shall bruise him on the heel.'*   GENESIS 3:14–15 (NASB)

This is a battle cry, for sure. It's a call to the fight. But in this passage we see our first hint of the 'good news' of the gospel: *the offspring of a woman will be the ultimate demise of the evil one.*

Note carefully the use of the words 'her seed'. Very unusual. When we talk about making babies, we don't talk about a woman having 'seed'; we talk about a man having seed and the woman receiving that seed. This is the *only* place in the Bible and *all* ancient literature where we are told that a woman has seed.

Something is going to be different about the conception of this child. Is it possible that the seed will *not* come from a human male?

? QUESTION

In your opinion, is a single passage like this sufficient to support a doctrine like the virgin birth of Christ? Why or why not?

Isaiah 7:14 – prophecy

The people of Judah were under attack – big time. Two nations attacking from two different directions. It was so bad that 'the hearts of Ahaz and his people were shaken, as the trees of the forest are shaken by the wind' (Isaiah 7:2). That's when the prophet Isaiah shows up with an encouraging word:

> *Then Isaiah said, 'Hear now, you house of David!... Therefore the Lord himself will give you a sign: The virgin will be with child and will give birth to a son, and will call him Immanuel.*
> ISAIAH 7:13–14

Prophecy is tricky stuff. Most of the time we aren't sure what it says until after the event takes place. Like the insinuations about a virgin birth in Genesis 3, we have to be very careful before we draw clear conclusions based solely on a prophetic message. Is this a prophecy saying Jesus will be born to a woman who has not had sex?

The word for 'virgin' in this passage is the Hebrew word *alma*. It is usually translated 'young woman'. It is sometimes translated 'virgin'. In the PBV translation of the Bible (that's the Pete Briscoe Version), I translate it 'womgin' – a combination of 'woman' and 'virgin'. (For some reason no one reads this version of the Bible – not even my mother.) So, before we jump to any hard-and-fast conclusions, we must yield to the flashing yellow light of caution: This word *alma* can be taken both ways, so it's *possible* that this child has no earthly father.

Matthew 1:18–22 – pronouncement

> *This is how the birth of Jesus Christ came about: His mother Mary was pledged to be married to Joseph, but before they came together, she was found to be with*

child through the Holy Spirit. Because Joseph her husband was a righteous man and did not want to expose her to public disgrace, he had in mind to divorce her quietly.   MATTHEW 1:18–22

Now, we finally get into the details. In the New Testament the things that may have been alluded to in the past become present reality. But what a reality! Look again at Matthew 1. That's a tough way to start a marriage! The guy decides to divorce the gal *before* the wedding even takes place? Not good.

When a couple ask me to 'do their wedding', my response is always... 'No'. They usually look shocked and slightly heartbroken until I explain, 'I will find it a great privilege, however, to be used by God to start a Christian marriage.' They giggle that cute little engaged-couple giggle and then we get to work. At the end of our first session I always take a deep breath and ask the question, 'Are you two sleeping together?' (From the Bible and from experience I know that sex before marriage is out of bounds and damaging to the future of the relationship. If I am going to shepherd a couple well, I need to know...)

I have had some fascinating answers over the years, but my favourite one was when she said, 'Yes' and he said 'No' *simultaneously*. Then they looked at each other with that not-quite-so-cute little engaged-couple look – like the look you get from a cat who has just destroyed the house with a Christmas tree.

According to this passage, Mary was *pledged* (or betrothed) to Joseph. We don't do this any more. Betrothal is somewhere in between an engagement and marriage – an extremely firm commitment, just without the ceremony and sex.

So think about this from Joseph's perspective. You're committed and you are saving yourself for her... and all of a sudden *she* shows up pregnant?

Joseph immediately shows some real character here. It looks like Mary has failed, but he does what he can to shelter her from shame and public disgrace; he plans to divorce her privately. (This move would save Mary's life too. The punishment for an illegitimate birth was death.)

But after he had considered this, an angel of the Lord appeared to him in a dream and said, 'Joseph son of David, do not be afraid to take Mary home as your wife, because what is conceived in her is from the Holy Spirit. She will give birth to a son, and you are to give him the name Jesus, because he will save his people from their sins.' All this took place to fulfil what the Lord had said through the prophet: 'The virgin will be with child and will give birth to a son, and they will call him Immanuel' – which means, 'God with us.'   MATTHEW 1:20–23

In this passage Matthew uses the Greek word *parthenos* for 'virgin', which almost always refers to a woman who has not had sex. (Note also that Matthew quotes the Isaiah passage. It was his understanding that Isaiah was pointing to a true virgin who would give birth to a child.) This is the first really clear indication of what is taking place: *The Holy Spirit has caused this pregnancy. This is the Son of God, God with us...* (Big sigh of relief. It looks like Mary is off the hook.)

How did Joseph deal with it? Initially, he was understandably *miffed*. He must have been shocked and *mystified* by this revelation from God. But he was very probably *mindful* too – Joseph, a devout Jew, would have recognized the angel's message as a quote from Isaiah 7. He may have even tied it back into Genesis 3. He may have thought, *Now I get it! We always talked about the deal with the woman's seed. That makes sense if a virgin is to have a child... She doesn't need me to have this child...*

But it didn't end there. Joseph was also *motivated*. When he woke up, he did what the angel of the Lord had commanded him. He took Mary home as his wife. He didn't have sex with her until she gave birth to her son, and he gave him the name Jesus.

Well done, young man.

? QUESTION

Can you remember an instance when, like Joseph, you were miffed, mystified, and then mindful? Were you motivated to act accordingly? Why or why not? What was the result?

Mary's version of the story follows a similar path – but instead of a dream, she gets a visit by the angel Gabriel:

> *The angel went to her and said, 'Greetings, you who are highly favoured! The Lord is with you... You will be with child and give birth to a son, and you are to give him the name Jesus. He will be great and will be called the Son of the Most High...'*
> LUKE 1:28, 31–32

I'm guessing that Mary is a little bit *miffed* at this point as well. Luke says she was 'greatly troubled' (verse 29), which is probably an understatement. This angel says she's going to be pregnant out of wedlock – by no fault of her own – and she should consider herself 'highly favoured'!

> *'How will this be,' Mary asked the angel, 'since I am a virgin?'*
> *   The angel answered, 'The Holy Spirit will come upon you, and the power of the Most High will overshadow you... For nothing is impossible with God.'*
> LUKE 1:34–35, 37

That's a lot to dump on a teenage girl. Mary has the biological sense to know that this is physically impossible. She also has the guts to question an angel. No doubt Mary was also *mystified* by this revelation from God. But the angel reminds her of something – something she is *mindful* of: 'Nothing is impossible with God' (verse 37). Is Mary *motivated* to obey?

> *'I am the Lord's servant,'* Mary answered. *'May it be to me as you have said.'*
>
> LUKE 1:38

Well done, young woman.

The moral of his-story

Those are the facts surrounding the birth of Jesus Christ – the history behind 'his-story'. Why is this in the Apostles' Creed? Why is this hinted at in Genesis 3 and alluded to in Isaiah 7? Why do Matthew and Luke take two long sections of the Gospels to explain to us that it was a virgin who gave birth? *Why is this so important?* Three reasons:

1. It solidifies the claim that Jesus Christ is the Son of God

Gabriel made it clear to Mary that this son of hers would be no regular guy:

> *He will be great and will be called the Son of the Most High. The Lord God will give him the throne of his father David, and he will reign over the house of Jacob forever; his kingdom will never end... So the holy one to be born will be called the Son of God.*   LUKE 1:32–33, 35

This clinches the point made in the last chapter: Jesus Christ is fully man and fully God. His relationship with the Father is unparalleled. Now we see that there is even a spiritual/biological connection between the Father and the Son. He was conceived by the Holy Ghost: *fully God*. He was born to a virgin woman: *fully man*. The Son of God in every possible way.

In his book *Knowing God*, J. I. Packer says that seekers many times find difficulties in the wrong places. They struggle with the atonement, the resurrection or the Gospel miracles. But he argues:

> *[The real difficultly] lies not in the Good Friday message of atonement, nor in the Easter message of resurrection, but in the Christmas message of Incarnation... This is two mysteries for the price of one... the plurality of personas within the*

unity of God and the union of Godhead and manhood in the person of Jesus...
Once the incarnation is grasped as a reality, these other difficulties dissolve.[26]

If Jesus really is the Son of God, it makes perfect sense that he would perform miracles; if he is the author of life, it makes sense that he would rise from the dead too. If the immortal one dies, it is easy to see how that death would have an impact on all of humanity. Why does it matter that Jesus was conceived of the Holy Spirit and born to the Virgin Mary? Because the incarnation makes the rest of the New Testament make sense.

A miracle? Absolutely! What is impossible by natural law, God did. He supernaturally intervened and moved molecules and electrons according to his spiritual desires... Because *nothing* is impossible for Almighty God.

✿ QUOTATION

The incarnation is in itself an unfathomable mystery, but it makes sense of everything else that the New Testament contains.   J. I. PACKER

2. It reveals the big picture

Back in Genesis 3, after Satan had tripped up Adam and Eve, God was right there in the evil one's face. God said, 'I will put enmity between you and the woman, and between your seed and her seed; he shall bruise you on the head.' This wasn't an idle threat; it wasn't even a prediction. *It was a promise.* It was a call to arms – a prophecy of Satan's defeat. Satan heard it loud and clear and the battle has been raging ever since... from Genesis to Revelation.

Don't be fooled by sweet-sounding Christmas carols. The birth of Christ was not a peaceful barnyard scene. It was a strategic and massive military move by the King of Kings. This was no 'Silent Night'. It was the Lord of Lords positioning *himself* to crush Satan...

And Satan knew it. In the book of Revelation, John gives us the rest of the story – a behind-the-scenes look at the nativity:

A great and wondrous sign appeared in heaven: a woman... She was pregnant and cried out in pain as she was about to give birth. Then another sign appeared in heaven: an enormous red dragon... The dragon stood in front of the woman who was about to give birth, so that he might devour her child the moment it was born. She gave birth to a son, a male child, who will rule all the nations with an iron sceptre. And her child was snatched up to God and to his throne...

REVELATION 12:1–5

Not exactly 'O Little Town of Bethlehem'... Probably more like *Apocalypse Now*. If the angels were doing any singing that night, they were singing battle-cries as they rose to defend the Christ-child against the attack of Satan and a multitude of demons who probably attacked with him.

✍ CONTEMPLATION

Since the children have flesh and blood, he too shared in their humanity so that by his death he might destroy him who holds the power of death – that is, the devil – and free those who all their lives were held in slavery by their fear of death.

HEBREWS 2:14–15

3. *It gives us a model for living*

The biblical account of the virgin birth of Christ is intended to bring clear glory to Jesus. He is the main player in this drama – but there are two other minor characters and we can learn a lot from them.

Mary and Joseph conducted themselves admirably throughout this whole event. As minor players in this spiritual battle, they responded in a way that certainly reflected well on their heavenly Father as well as their son (God's Son).

This young couple were cut from common stock. We have no indication from the Bible that Mary and Joseph were any different from you or me. While some claim that Mary was sinless, Scripture supports no such idea. In fact, in Luke 1:46–47, Mary praises the Lord as 'God my Saviour'. If she was sinless, she certainly wouldn't need a saviour.

Some people also pray to Mary, thinking that she is a special middle-person between us and God. But 1 Timothy 2:5 says, 'For there is one God and one mediator between God and man, the man Christ Jesus.' The only way someone can mediate between both God and man is if they *are* God and man. Mary doesn't fit that bill (but you know who does).

Others believe that Mary's mother was a virgin too (this is called the *immaculate conception*). But again, there is no indicator in Scripture that this was the case.

I'm going to say something very strong here. Please think about it carefully. Any time that the focus of our worship is taken off Jesus and placed on something else (whether it be Mary, or a Mustang convertible, or Buddha, or big bucks...), it's called *idolatry*. Those are strong words, but the Bible teaches us that our heart should be focused on Jesus Christ alone.

With that in mind, however, I'm going to suggest that Joseph and Mary make really good *role models*. Their responses to difficult and challenging situations (not to mention that they were on the front lines of a brutal spiritual war) were awesome – definitely worth emulating in the power of the Spirit.

We are on the front lines of a spiritual war as well (whether we realize it or not). We are told of this war in many places, including the end of the Christmas story according to the book of Revelation. The child was born, Satan tried to kill him at the moment of birth, but the child was spared. What happened after that?

> *Then the dragon was enraged at the woman and went off to make war against the rest of her offspring – those who obey God's commandments and hold to the testimony of Jesus.*   REVELATION 12:17

Hmmm, who is the dragon making war against *right now*? You and me, God's kids. Because of that we should plan on being:

- *Miffed.* Life is going to be filled with unexpected problems and difficulties. We should expect to feel frustrated and even angry sometimes.
- *Mystified.* When God illuminates what's really going on, and when he calls us to respond in outlandish ways (that seem to make no sense by the world's standards), we can expect to be a little bewildered – just like Mary and Joseph were.
- *Mindful.* During those times we need to remember what is true... what the Bible says is true. We must remember what we believe, because belief matters during these critical times of difficulty and decision-making.
- *Motivated.* Our belief in what is true must be followed up by decisions of submissive obedience to our Lord and a dependence upon Christ to live it out through us. Full stop.

And always remember – just as Gabriel told Mary – there is more going on than meets the eye, and the possibilities extend beyond anything we can imagine...

...because anything is possible with God... Anything.

M.A.P.S.

✐ *Meditate*

Ask God to guide your thoughts as you consider these words from the Creed:

> *I believe in Jesus Christ... who was conceived by the Holy Ghost, born of the Virgin Mary.*

✨ *Apply*

Review Joseph and Mary's journey.

Consider a challenging situation that you are facing, have faced, or might face. How does the *miffed*, *mystified*, *mindful*, *motivated* role model fit into this circumstance?

Are you basing your decisions on what you can see, or do you believe in the greater unseen battle? Are you confident that all things are possible with God?

Are you willing to obey God's specific leading?

❧ *Plot the passages*

- Key word: *Conception*.
- Key passage: Luke 1:28–38.
- Supporting passages: Genesis 3:14–15; Isaiah 7:14; Matthew 1:18–23; Revelation 12:1–5; Hebrews 2:14–15.

✴ *Speak*

Speak to self

I believe that the conception of Jesus Christ by the Holy Spirit and the virgin birth:

- Solidify the claim that Jesus Christ is the Son of God.
- Reveal the bigger picture of spiritual warfare.
- Give me a model to follow during difficult times.
- Are evidence that anything is possible for God!

Speak to others

The gospel appears in Scripture possibly as early as Genesis 3 (the *protoevangelium*). The *prophecy* about the virgin birth of Christ shows up in Isaiah 7. In the Gospels of Matthew and Luke the miraculous conception of Jesus is *proclaimed*.

But what about now? Who is spreading the good news about this gospel today?

We are. Together. As a team.

Consider this passage:

How, then, can they call on the one they have not believed in? And how can they believe in the one of whom they have not heard? And how can they hear without someone preaching to them? And how can they preach unless they are sent? As it is written, 'How beautiful are the feet of those who bring good news!'

ROMANS 10:14–15

How could your specific skills, character, personality and resources be used within God's family to spread the gospel today?

Speak to God

God of All Possibilities,

In all honesty, I'm a little bit mystified by how you revealed yourself through Mary, through Joseph, through the virgin birth of your Son. But what an incredible message of hope!

Father, use me in any way you choose to continue to proclaim this message in my world. In particular, I pray that you would show me how you desire to work through me, just as I am, as part of the worldwide team of believers who desire to speak this message to others.

Give me a conscious awareness of the spiritual battle that continues to rage around me. Give me the willingness – and then be my strength – to respond to the war and all its challenges in an honourable, appropriate way.

In the name and power of your Son Jesus Christ,

Amen.

* * *

Daddy has just tucked her in for the night. Cosy, warm and safe – yet in the darkness shadows begin to move and her imagination begins to stir...

'Daddy!' she calls across the hall. 'I'm scared!'

'Don't worry, Honey. I'm over here.'

A few minutes pass, but she senses rustling in the closet... and breath from under her bed...

'Daddy! I'm still scared!'

'Don't worry, Honey. I'm over here.'

A few more minutes pass, but the darkness is really dark... the little girl cries out again, 'That's not good enough! *I need somebody with skin on!*'

Can you relate to the little girl? I sure can. When things get tough, when I get scared – when I'm miffed, mystified, mindful and motivated... I still need somebody with skin on.

And that's what we get in Jesus Christ; that's what we proclaim when we say, '*I believe Jesus was conceived by the Holy Ghost, born of the Virgin Mary...*'

God with us. Emmanuel. God with skin.

That's the Christmas story. That's the *evangel*, the good news proclaimed from Genesis to Revelation.

*I believe in God the Father Almighty, maker of heaven and earth; and in Jesus Christ his only Son our Lord; who was conceived by the Holy Ghost, born of the Virgin Mary, **suffered under Pontius Pilate, was crucified, dead and buried**. He descended into hell; the third day he rose again from the dead. He ascended into heaven, and sits on the right hand of God the Father Almighty. From thence he shall come to judge the quick and the dead. I believe in the Holy Ghost, the holy catholic church, the communion of saints, the forgiveness of sins, the resurrection of the body, and the life everlasting. Amen.*

CHAPTER 8

The Sacrifice

... we cannot close our eyes to the reality of suffering, for it is the reality chosen by the one we name Lord and Christ. And the path he walks here is the one he bids us to follow. THEODORE W. JENNINGS, JR[27]

God weeps with us so that we may one day laugh with him. JURGEN MOLTMANN[28]

The 'foot-washing incident' was a great success.

When Jesus took out the cloth and the wash-basin and washed the feet of his followers, he showed them the new way of servant leadership. This was clear symbolism – a real attention-getter. It was a powerful conclusion to the message that he was communicating to his somewhat remedial disciples. They got it. Sermon over.

Or was it?

What if this wasn't a 'sermon illustration'? What if Christ's actions weren't symbolic; what if they were authentic, genuine – an extension of who he really was? And what if that was all just a prelude to what he really came to accomplish?

The night he washed feet, he also took the bread and the wine. He broke the bread, saying, 'This is my body'; he poured the wine, saying, 'This is my blood'. Symbolic, yes... but this was no theoretical illustration. Jesus was making a direct connection between the Passover supper and the next twenty-four hours. In the coming day *his* body would be broken; *his* blood would flow.

Blood flowed a lot in Roman times. Thousands of men were crucified as enemies of the Empire. What is the significance of *this* crucifixion? Why is *this* day spoken of more than any other day in human history? Why does *this* cross get tattooed into the arm of the biker and worn around the neck of the teenager? What does it mean to us when we say: '*I believe in Jesus Christ, who suffered under Pontius Pilate, was crucified, dead and buried...*'?

The answer can be found in the word 'atonement', a theological term which you have probably heard before.

? QUESTION

Do think Christianity has become more of a symbolic religion than a relationship-oriented faith? Why or why not?

Atonement

The film *The Passion of the Christ* stunned us all. After decades of dissecting the meaning of the cross, some of us had become desensitized to the fact that the crucifixion was a real event. As Brennan Manning wrote in *The Ragamuffin Gospel*:

> *We have so theologized the passion and death of this sacred man that we no longer see the slow unraveling of his tissue, the spread of gangrene, his raging thirst.[29]*

The blood, the sweat, the tears... It was all real that day in Jerusalem. Real whips, real nails – real suffering. How could the cross be both the highest pinnacle and the lowest valley of human history? Because it *showed* love and *was* love:

> *This is how God showed his love among us: He sent his one and only Son into the world that we might live through him. This is love: not that we loved God, but that he loved us and sent his Son as an atoning sacrifice for our sins.*   1 JOHN 4:9–10

Terms to impress your pastor and confound your friends:

❧ DEFINITION

Atonement ([e]-tōn'm[e]nt), *n.* The work Christ did in his life and death to earn our salvation.[30]

Propitiation (prō-pĭsh'ē-ā'sh[e]n), *n.* A sacrifice that bears God's wrath to the end and in doing so changes God's wrath toward us into favour.[31]

Expiation (ĕk'spē-ā'sh[e]n), *n.* What is accomplished by divinely appointed sacrifices in order to free sinners from the punishment of their sins.

Evandalism (ĭ-vān'd[e]-lĭz'[e]m), *n.* Using spraypaint to write 'John 3:16' on public structures. (I made this one up.)

Jesus was sent by God as 'an atoning sacrifice for our sins'. The word 'sin' makes people very uncomfortable. In fact, many of us have come up with our own set of 'sin-onyms' (words for 'sin' that people use so they don't have to use the word 'sin'). We might call it an 'addiction', or a 'struggle', a 'weakness'... Sometimes we just call it 'my thing'.

The Bible calls it 'sin' – an ancient archery term that means missing the bull's-eye. In spiritual terms, that means falling short of the perfect glory of God (Romans 3:23).

💬 QUOTATION

The wrath of God is his steady, unrelenting, unremitting, uncompromising antagonism toward evil in all its forms and manifestations. In short, God's anger is poles apart from ours. What provokes our anger (injured vanity) never provokes his. What provokes his anger (evil) seldom provokes ours.   JOHN STOTT

God is righteous, holy, just. He simply cannot associate with sin. God and sin are oil and water; sin separates from God, repels him, provokes anger in him... and yet, God is love (1 John 4:8).

This dichotomy is called 'the great dilemma of God'. He is a God of love and desires our intimacy and our affections. Yet he is a God of justice and must be fair in all of his dealings. He simply cannot allow evil to go unpunished. Someone had to pay the penalty... and the penalty for sin is death (Romans 6:23). The solution to the great dilemma was simple. (Costly, but simple.)

On a hill far away...

I sometimes imagine what it was like on that hill outside Jerusalem that day. Close your eyes for a moment and feel the heat of the sun; hear the shouting of the crowds; watch the blood dripping into the dirt in front of the rough beams that display the dangling body of Christ...

God himself was paying the price for my sin, for your sin – the 'atonement'. In the molecules of his flesh and in the confines of his heart he carried it all. The pain, the humiliation – even separation from the Father as he bore our sin in his body and became sin on our behalf.

✍ CONTEMPLATION

He committed no sin, and no deceit was found in his mouth. When they hurled their insults at him, he did not retaliate; when he suffered, he made no threats. Instead, he entrusted himself to him who judges justly. He himself bore our sins in his body on the tree, so that we might die to sins and live for righteousness; by his wounds you have been healed.   1 PETER 2:22–24

✿ QUOTATION

The cross is the intersecting point where God met mankind, accepted the worst abuse man could offer, and stretching out his arms in love, offered forgiveness. But the cross remains a symbol of consummate passions intertwined – love mixed with hatred, with love prevailing.   D. BRUCE LOCKERBIE[32]

As the end approached – as his final breaths were escaping his lips and the clouds of death descended – his parting message to the world was, *'Tetelesti.'* This Greek word meant 'paid in full, completely finished'. Jesus was saying that the job had been done, the debt had been paid, the task had been completed. This is the word you would use when putting your report on the boss's desk after two years of research; when finishing the final exams for your degree; when stepping across the finishing line of a marathon...

? QUESTION

What kind of characteristics and attitudes would you expect to see in someone who truly believed that all their sins were atoned for?

It was full propitiation: 'A sacrifice that bears God's wrath to the end and in doing so changes God's wrath toward us.' The problem of sin had been solved.

✿ QUOTATION

Man is alienated from God by sin, and God is alienated from man by wrath. It is by the substitutionary death of Christ that sin is overcome and wrath averted, so that God can look on man without displeasure and man can look on God without fear.   DAVID WELLS

On a hill closer to home...

I don't think we believe in the atonement. At least not completely, not in our hearts. In our heads? Maybe. Maybe we can intellectually understand some-one else making a payment for us. But when we search our souls, do we find that we really believe? Is the atonement our biography as well as our theol-ogy? I wonder...

Aren't our lives haunted by a voice that quietly screams, 'No! It can't be so!'? Isn't there a child's pride that wells up inside each of us, proclaiming, 'No! I'll do it myself!' Is not our spiritual freedom hobbled by a work ethic that demands, 'I will pay this back; I *must* pay this back!'?

We believe, but Lord, help our unbelief. Dear God, place us at the foot of the cross. Open the eyes of our hearts, Lord; we want to see Jesus – high and lifted up, pressed against coarse wood, gasping for breath in the noonday heat... We want to feel Jesus, we want to touch the drops of warm crimson dripping from his flesh... We want to hear Jesus; we want to hear him say to us in fainting breath, 'Tetelesti.'

We need to believe, Lord. We want to believe.

✍ CONTEMPLATION

When you were dead in your transgressions and the uncircumcision of your flesh, He made you alive together with Him, having forgiven us all our transgressions, having cancelled out the certificate of debt consisting of decrees against us, which was hostile to us; and He has taken it out of the way, having nailed it to the cross.

COLOSSIANS 2:13–14 (NASB)

At-one-ment

My son had just been suspended from school. Ouch!

He deserved it, no doubt. It wasn't malice – just mischief – but I was deeply disappointed. One of the reasons we have him in the public schools is so he can be light in a dark world, but now it looked as if that dark world was snuffing out his brightness.

My friend Tim was sitting in his office when I walked in and plopped down. I shared with him the headlines and the agony I was feeling... and he listened. 'What are you planning on doing?' he asked.

I told him my plans to ground my son until he graduated from college. 'Why are you smiling?' I asked.

'Because Vicky and I have learned that grounding a kid for a long time usually doesn't work. You get worn down and eventually give in and let him out early…'

For a good long time Tim's wisdom flowed. We considered options and we laughed about teenage boys. We reminded each other of the power of grace and the bigger picture of life. His comforting words got me off the ledge. By the time we bowed to pray for my son, in my heart I knew I was tremendously blessed to have such an authentic, honest, deep friendship.

I knew Tim was there for me. I knew he cared for me – and perhaps most importantly in that moment, I knew he knew what I was going through, *because he had been there as well.*

⚜ DEFINITION

---

at-one-ment (at-wŭn' m[e]nt), *n.*
1. Yet another Pete Briscoe-ism.
2. A made-up word to describe a state of unity and understanding because of a shared experience.

That afternoon I felt 'at-one' with Tim. We shared 'at-one-ment'. I believe that at-one-ment is a God-given desire, a genuine need that God programmed into our souls. It is the dream of every couple standing at the altar, the aspiration of every team that takes to the field, the hope of every woman who sits down with a cup of coffee and a friend.

To a limited extent, this oneness can be found in the company of humanity… but only to an extent. In the best situations, we get a brief taste of the acceptance and unity we crave. In the worst situations (people being what they are), our desires are turned against us, our aspirations are abused, our hopes are mocked.

? QUESTION

Where do you go to find at-one-ment? Do those sources satisfy your desire? Why or why not?

But the desire keeps us searching. Isn't there someone out there who understands, someone who can satisfy this need to belong?

Therefore, since we have a great high priest who has gone through the heavens, Jesus the Son of God, let us hold firmly to the faith we profess. For we do not have a high priest who is unable to sympathize with our weaknesses… Let us

*then approach the throne of grace with confidence, so that we may receive mercy
and find grace to help us in our time of need.*   HEBREWS 4:14–16

Jesus Christ is that someone. He offers us genuine sympathy in our struggles. He
empathizes fully with our pain. He knows what it's like because he's been there.
We can experience at-one-ment with him in the midst of all circumstances.

🎵 QUOTATION

*There can be no Christian theology which is not at every point a theology of
the cross. There can be no faith which is not a reliance upon and loyalty to the
crucified. There can be no following of Jesus which is not taking up of the same
cross.*   THEODORE W. JENNINGS, JR[33]

Jesus Christ suffered emotionally

We've already seen that Jesus Christ was a human being with emotion. He suffered from loneliness (Matthew 26:40), frustration (Mark 8:21), anger (Mark 3:5)
and feelings of abandonment (Mark 15:34). He also shared in the most painful
of all human emotions: rejection.

- He was *rejected for who he was* by the authorities who scoffed at his claim
  to be the Son of God (Matthew 26:63–66).
- He was *rejected by those who loved him* when the disciples abandoned him
  in time of need – when Peter denied him *three* times (Matthew 26:73–74).
- He was *regarded as worthless* by those in charge. At the insistence of the
  crowds, Pilate released a notorious prisoner, Barabbas. For the sake of
  political convenience he gave in to the crowd's demand that Jesus should
  be crucified (Matthew 27:15–22).

In the end, only a few women and John stayed by Jesus. When he was finally
recognized and received for who he was, it was too late.

*When the Centurion and those with him who were guarding Jesus saw the
earthquake and all that had happened, they were terrified, and exclaimed, 'Surely
he was the Son of God!'*   MATTHEW 27:54

😕 QUOTATION

Yet while none of its suffering can be exaggerated, the fact remains that the cross's greatest cause of anguish may not have been the nails impaling the hands and feet. The greater cause may have been its shame.   D. BRUCE LOCKERBIE[34]

He suffered physically

Surely he took up our infirmities and carried our sorrows, yet we considered him stricken by God, smitten by him, and afflicted. But he was pierced for our transgressions, he was crushed for our iniquities; the punishment that brought us peace was upon him, and by his wounds we are healed.   ISAIAH 53:4–5

The writers of the Gospels don't go into the gory details of the cross. They described Jesus' torture and execution in quite a matter-of-fact way. (Historians and Hollywood have willingly filled in the graphic details.) Prior to the cross, he knew the normal demands and limitations of the human body. We don't have an indication that he got sick, but he may have. We do see plenty of hunger, thirst and being physically tired. He definitely understands physical suffering.

✍ CONTEMPLATION

Christ Jesus: Who, being in very nature God, did not consider equality with God something to be grasped, but made himself nothing, taking the very nature of a servant, being made in human likeness. And being found in appearance as a man, he humbled himself and became obedient to death – even death on a cross!

PHILIPPIANS 2:6–8

He suffered spiritually

From the sixth hour until the ninth hour darkness came over all the land. About the ninth hour Jesus cried out in a loud voice, 'Eloi, Eloi, lama sabachthani?' – which means, 'My God, my God, why have you forsaken me?'   MATTHEW 27:45–46

As the sacrifice of Jesus Christ reached its climax, as the sins of the world were being paid for by his suffering and death, there was a moment where God the Father Almighty turned his back on Jesus Christ his Son. On a spiritual level,

Jesus Christ realized that his Father (with whom he had been intimately bound since eternity past) had turned away.

This suffering, the most spiritually acute of any suffering that one could imagine, was fully felt; but it did not last. When the sacrifice was complete and all that had been prophesied was fulfilled, Jesus called out with a loud voice, 'Father, into your hands I commit my spirit.' When he had said this, he breathed his last (Luke 23:46) and his inseparable union with the Father was re-established.

We suffer a cloudy spiritual existence today as well. We see God only 'dimly'. After the grave it will be 'face to face' (1 Corinthians 13:12). But since asking Christ into your life, you have the promise that Christ will never forsake you, nor will he ever reject you (1 Timothy 2:4). Spiritual dimness? Yes. Spiritual separation? Never again.

Emotional, physical and spiritual suffering... If you're like me, you perhaps dreamed of a God who always gallops into the scene on his white stallion, shoots up all the bad guys (my suffering) and then rides off into the eternal sunset with everybody in town saying, 'Wow, who was that mysterious God?' And then (in my dream) everybody is knocking down my door begging me to share the gospel with them so that they can have this God on their team too.

✍ CONTEMPLATION

I have told you these things, so that in me you may have peace. In this world you will have trouble. But take heart! I have overcome the world.   JOHN 16:33

It doesn't appear to work that way. Jesus never promised to put an end to our earthly suffering. What he promised was his presence in the midst of our suffering. Suffering was his reality; a reality that he fully experienced throughout his life – but particularly between the Last Supper and the cross. Suffering is our reality. In essence, Jesus said, 'Get used to it; but let's get through it *together*.'

✌ QUOTATION

To the abandoned child wailing in the city street, the mother weeping over her stillborn infant, the man moaning in the torture cell, the parent with no food or medicine to give a dying child, the Indian hunted down by ranchers' dogs, the one betrayed by a friend – to all the wounded and suffering, despised and dishonored, the Gospel points to Jesus and says, 'Behold your suffering, behold your God!'

THEODORE W. JENNINGS[35]

He may not rescue us the way that we wish, but in his goodness, I believe, he offers something far more valuable: *He offers himself.* I think he may even orchestrate suffering to gently pressure us to move toward himself – into at-one-ment – so that we can truly satisfy our desire in him.

Beyond the grave our at-one-ment with Jesus Christ will continue – but we will not be sharing suffering; we will join together in a grand eternal celebration that is infinitely beyond anything we can imagine or think.

> *Therefore we do not lose heart. Though outwardly we are wasting away, yet inwardly we are being renewed day by day. For our light and momentary troubles are achieving for us an eternal glory that far outweighs them all. So we fix our eyes not on what is seen, but on what is unseen. For what is seen is temporary, but what is unseen is eternal.*   2 CORINTHIANS 4:16–18

We believe, but Lord, help our unbelief. Holy Spirit, would you make this 'real' to us? As real as Jesus' pain, as real as all the suffering in us and around us... Give us an awareness of our at-one-ment in you. And thank you for making it possible on the cross.

At-one-ment in the atonement

I'm really glad that the Creed talks about God being the Almighty right up front. I, for one, need the continual reminder that he can do anything he chooses. *Anything.* Remembering this helps tremendously when I'm pondering the implications of the cross. Numerous times in Scripture it comes out that I have 'at-one-ment in the atonement'. Consider these words from Paul:

> *I have been crucified with Christ and I no longer live, but Christ lives in me. The life I live in the body, I live by faith in the Son of God, who loved me and gave himself for me. I do not set aside the grace of God, for if righteousness could be gained through the law, Christ died for nothing!*   GALATIANS 2:20–21

Passages like this perch us on the edge of the great mystery of the gospel. Paul is saying that you can have *true oneness* with Christ because *you died with him at the cross.* Quite frankly, this changes absolutely everything. Because of this:

- Christ himself has become your life – he is the one who lives in your spirit. In a profound and yet very practical way, your life has been exchanged for his.

- You can live by faith in the Jesus in you, the Jesus who died for you. Not only has the price for sin been paid, but the Spirit of Christ now lives in you... You have 'at-one-ment in the atonement'.
- You are no longer to live by 'the law' (the old rules of performance that the world and religion try to force on us). It doesn't work that way any more (if it did, then 'Christ died for nothing!').

Since you died with Christ to the basic principles of this world, why, as though you still belonged to it, do you submit to its rules: 'Do not handle! Do not taste! Do not touch!'? These are all destined to perish with use, because they are based on human commands and teachings. Such regulations indeed have an appearance of wisdom, with their self-imposed worship, their false humility and their harsh treatment of the body, but they lack any value in restraining sensual indulgence.

COLOSSIANS 2:20–23

I was sitting with my Dad on the park swings a few years ago. I was a relatively new pastor and struggling with one of the leaders in the church. I had been wounded in a recent meeting and my Dad asked for the details.

As I shared them he interrupted me, 'You don't have to take that, Pete; that is inappropriate.'

'But if I say anything, I'll probably get fired, Dad.'

'So go in tomorrow and get fired!' he responded.

A sense of rest washed over me. First, I was reminded that I didn't have to play the religious game. I only had to do what God wanted to do through me. Second, I realized that if I got booted from my first pastor's job, I didn't have to fear rejection from my Dad (I had at-one-ment with him). His opinion matters to me and that day I felt great power in his comfort.

Another snapshot of God.

Do you see him there, in your picture? He's with you on the swing, Father and child – he's listening, comforting, counselling... reminding you that the rules have changed. You don't have to put up with the pressure any more and your relationship (your at-one-ment) with him is secure, whether you fail or succeed. You have been paid for through the atonement he made on the cross. From the confidence of God's comfort emerges the courage to allow him to do bold things through you... for you know that he alone, as the Almighty, has the ability to do so!

? QUESTION

How do you picture the Father? How do you picture the crucified Christ? Is the Christ of the cross a far-off icon, or do you picture him next to you and in you now?

We believe, but Lord, help our unbelief. Dear God, open the eyes of our hearts. Lord, we want to see you in us. We want to know the truth about our crucifixion with you, about you living in us. We want to hear you, Jesus. Give us the humility to rest with you, listen to you, and allow you to give us inner comfort and courage. Then use us to your glory.

I [Jesus] am the vine; you are the branches. If a man remains in me and I in him, he will bear much fruit; apart from me you can do nothing.   JOHN 15:5

I [Paul] have learned to be content whatever the circumstances. I know what it is to be in need, and I know what it is to have plenty. I have learned the secret of being content in any and every situation, whether well fed or hungry, whether living in plenty or in want. I can do everything through him who gives me strength. Yet it was good of you to share in my troubles.   PHILIPPIANS 4:11–14

M.A.P.S.

⊱ *Meditate*

Ask God to guide your thoughts as you consider these words from the Creed:

I believe he... suffered under Pontius Pilate, was crucified, dead and buried.

⊱ *Apply*

When it comes to the *atonement* that Christ made on the cross for our sins, we tend to gravitate toward one of two lies:

1. My sin is not that serious. He didn't have to die for that!
2. My sin is too hideous. There is no way he can forgive that!

Let God search your heart and see if you believe either of these things. He will show you that *all* your sin is that serious and *all* of it is forgiven. Praise him for that!

When it comes to *at-one-ment* with Jesus, consider making it your intent to turn to Christ first, as the perfect friend who has 'been there'. This is a real choice that can be made moment by moment.

Finally, when it comes to *at-one-ment in the atonement*, I would highly recommend memorizing Galatians 2:20 and repeating it often. This is one of the powerful mysteries of the faith that is rediscovered on a continual basis. *You have been crucified with Christ. It is no longer you who live; Christ lives in you!*

❧ *Plot the passages*

- Key word: *Crucified*.
- Key passage: 1 John 4:9–10.
- Supporting passages: 1 Peter 2:22–24; Isaiah 53:4–5; Colossians 2:13–14; Galatians 2:20–21; Hebrews 4:14–16.

❧ *Speak*

Speak to self
Because I am in Christ and he is in me:

- I am not alone.
- I am understood.
- I am forgiven.
- I don't have to sacrifice myself.
- I don't have to have my needs for at-one-ment met by others.
- I don't have to purify or purge myself.

I am in Christ and he is in me... nothing happens by 'myself' any more!

Speak to others
In our society, crosses are everywhere. On buildings, on jewellery, in art... They are a great conversation-starter (and as you know, getting the conversation started always feels like the hardest part!).

So just ask! *Why do you think they put those on churches? I noticed you are wearing a cross. What does that mean to you? Do you think that is a decoration or a symbol of faith?...*

When the conversation turns back to you, you'll have a three-part outline all ready to go in your mind: (1) Atonement; (2) At-one-ment; and (3) At-one-ment in the Atonement. Nice work!

Speak to God

My Sacrificial Saviour,

I can only praise you and thank you for offering yourself as an atoning sacrifice for my sin. Thank you for paying the price. Please make this real in my heart as well as in my head.

I can only praise you and thank you for 'being there' for me in every situation. You have been here. You understand. Your presence is my great need. Thank you for filling that need perfectly.

I can only praise you and thank you as I stand back and consider the reality that I was crucified with you and you now live in me. What a miracle; what a mystery... what profound implications. I trust in you to continually reveal this truth to me as you live your life through me as you see fit.

Amen!

*   *   *

'But rules seem so much safer...'

I was wrestling with that thought as I was talking with yet another couple about my son's suspension. (I admit I was having a tough time letting go of this.) It was another at-one-ment moment with two friends who have known my son since birth, have poured their life into his, and would gladly take him off our hands if he were available (which he's not!).

'You know,' Stephanie said, 'the thing we learned over the years is that our role as parents is to teach our kids to hear the voice of the Lord and respond to him, not to try to get them to behave to certain standards. If our job is to prepare them to live in the real world in Christ, then why not teach them to do so while under our roof?'

I felt the synapses in my brain rewiring themselves... *It's not about rules. It's about Jesus.* He is the focus. That's what my son needs to learn – what I need to learn – to listen to and live in oneness with the God-man who was crucified for me, died for me and was buried for me... the one who now walks with me and lives in me.

It was another major paradigm shift in my journey:

Set your minds on things above, not on earthly things. For you died, and your life is now hidden with Christ in God. When Christ, who is your life, appears, then you also will appear with him in glory.   COLOSSIANS 3:2–4

I believe in God the Father Almighty, maker of heaven and earth; and in Jesus Christ his only Son our Lord; who was conceived by the Holy Ghost, born of the Virgin Mary, suffered under Pontius Pilate, was crucified, dead and buried. ***He descended into hell; the third day he rose again from the dead.*** *He ascended into heaven, and sits on the right hand of God the Father Almighty. From thence he shall come to judge the quick and the dead. I believe in the Holy Ghost, the holy catholic church, the communion of saints, the forgiveness of sins, the resurrection of the body, and the life everlasting. Amen.*

CHAPTER 9

The Sensational Sunday

Our Lord has written the promise of resurrection, not in books alone, but in every leaf in springtime.   MARTIN LUTHER

It's Friday, but Sunday's coming!   TONY CAMPOLO

To the crowd watching the body go limp under the Jerusalem sun, it was just another corpse... one of thousands that had been crucified under Roman rule. But more than a man died that day. With his last breath the lingering hope of the masses evaporated in the dry Jerusalem air. Jesus Christ, the self-proclaimed Son of God, was dead.

As Joseph of Arimathea prepared what was left of Jesus' tattered body for burial, as it was put in the tomb and the stone was rolled into place, the disciples huddled behind locked doors in a haze of disillusionment – in fear, I'm sure, that the soldiers would come for them next.

We can imagine the discussions, the questions, the vacuum in the room now that he was gone.

He was gone.

Now what?! In that hour of despair, could any of them have imagined what would transpire over the next three days? I don't think so. But looking back from the perspective of history, we can ask three important questions:

What happened to his soul?

What happened to his body?

Do we believe it when the Creed says: *'He descended into hell; the third day he rose again from the dead'*?

'He descended into hell'

What happened to Jesus' soul during the three days that his body lay decaying in the tomb? Let me be honest: I don't know for sure. This is the most debated phrase in the Creed. The only passage in Scripture that seems to allude to the possibility of hell comes from 1 Peter:

> *For Christ died for sins once for all, the righteous for the unrighteous, to bring*
> *you to God. He was put to death in the body but made alive by the Spirit,* through
> whom also he went and preached to the spirits in prison.
>
> 1 PETER 3:18–19 (ITALICS MINE)

This is a fascinating passage – the kind of verse that sends shivers up your spine when you meditate on what it says: *Christ died for sins, once for all...* One sacrificial act of love paying for all sins... *my* sins, *your* sins. The second half, however, is a little more obscure (okay, it's *a lot* more obscure). There are twelve words in verse 19. Five of those words have really fuzzy meanings in the original Greek. When translating them we really just have to guess between multiple possibilities. *Could* this verse mean that Jesus descended into hell? Yes, it could. But *does* it say that? Not necessarily, no.

✑ QUOTATION

This is a real problem for the expositor... This passage is open to different
interpretations, and it is not easy to explain them or to show why one view is
preferable to another. The wisest course is to admit that the details or the
passage are heavily disputed, to present one view (or at most two) and to avoid
making any applications that are dubiously debated.   HOWARD MARSHAL[36]

Calvin said Jesus descended into hell to 'culminate his humiliation'. Luther said Christ descended into hell so that he could 'display his exaltation' over Satan – a kind of in-your-face victory lap. Many think that Jesus went to Hades and preached to the people who were disobedient in Noah's day.

When the text is unclear our conclusions must be tentative – particularly when other passages don't seem to agree with our interpretation. Jesus promised the thief dying next to him that they would meet, that day, in Paradise (Luke 23:43). Moments later he committed his spirit into the hands of the Father (verse 46). The hell idea just doesn't fit very well with this, though it *could*.

So, where was the soul of Jesus during the three days his body lay in the tomb? I don't know for certain, but according to 1 Peter we do know that he was busy. He was preaching somewhere – but because this *may* have been in hell, I doubt we'll find many pastors trying to get on that circuit.

'The third day he rose again from the dead'

The personal implications of this phrase from the Creed are monumental and, thankfully, we have mounds of clear evidence to look at. We know a lot about

Jewish and Roman culture, and that adds important detail to the biblical account. Where was the *body* of Jesus?

- His body had been bandaged and packed with up to seventy-five pounds of spices (John 19:39–40). His corpse would have looked like a cocoon; it had been almost mummified.
- A stone weighing up to two tons had been fixed in place in front of the tomb (Mark 6:4).
- Roman soldiers were placed on guard (Matthew 27:65). Rumours of the resurrection led to the authorities taking this precaution. This 'guard' was a team of highly disciplined men representing one of the world's super-powers. They were heavily armed and trained to carry out their orders to the death.
- A Roman seal was placed across the stone (Matthew 27:66). This was the ultimate 'No Trespassing' sign. You mess with this seal, you die.

✨ QUOTATION

For the New Testament and Acts, the confirmation of historicity is overwhelming. Any attempt to reject its basic historicity, even in matters of detail, must now appear absurd. Roman historians have long taken it for granted.

A. N. SHERWIN-WHITE, CLASSICAL ROMAN HISTORIAN

Up to this point, almost everyone who takes history even pseudo-seriously agrees: The body of Jesus is sealed in a tomb and is beginning the process of decomposition. It looks like 'Game Over', 'The End', 'Do not pass "Go"; do not collect £200.'

But... But maybe that wasn't the end. Maybe that was just the night before the dawn... Maybe; just maybe he was *resurrected...* Do you believe that he rose on the third day? If you call yourself a 'Christian' you probably answer 'yes' to the resurrection question... But in my mind, it's not enough just to have the 'right' answer. We need to know *why* this is believable.

I had to take algebra in high school and I struggled terribly. Every once in a while, however, the most amazing thing would happen – call it a miracle if you want – evidence that an almighty loving Father was intervening in my little mathematical world: With no natural explanation, I would come up with the right answer to a problem without going through the proof correctly.

There was only one problem: The teacher wouldn't give credit for this. I would argue that the answer was right, but she always said I had to show *why* the answer was right. *I had to prove it.*

Most Christians can spout off at least a few right answers when it comes to *what* they believe. But how many of us can defend *why*? What do you say? 'Ummmm, I believe a dead guy came back to life just, ummmm, because I do.' A sceptical world won't accept empty answers like that. They want proof. In order for us to reach them, we need to be able to articulate both *what* we believe and *why* we believe it.

? QUESTION

Which do you think is more important, faith *or* fact? *Defend your answer.*

In order to do the proof and get credit for our claim that Jesus rose from the dead, we need the F.A.C.T.S. That stands for *Facts, Alternative, Change, Testimony,* and *Significance.*

✿ QUOTATION

Positive and conclusive proof of the resurrection by scientific, historical or other scholarly means is not to be had. But we may believe that Jesus was raised from the dead without in any way violating our intellectual and moral integrity.

C. E. B. CRANFIELD

Facts

Let's start with the facts, and nothing but the facts. These facts are not just biblical, but historical as well. Anyone who applies the normal rules of historical investigation will most likely agree that the evidence is as follows:

Fact 1: The dead body
The Apostle John personally confirmed the death of Christ. John was there; he recorded the soldier's confirmation that he was dead, and he saw them jab him in the side with a spear, causing water and blood to flow from his heart (John 19:33–35).

Fact 2: The stone rolled away
All four of the Gospel writers record that the stone had been moved. According to Matthew, on that first Easter morning a severe earthquake had occurred and an angel had rolled away the stone. The angel looked 'like lightning, and his

garments as white as snow'. He terrified the soldiers, who froze with fear 'as dead men' (Matthew 28:4).

Fact 3: The empty tomb

(This is when the plot really thickens.) When they looked in the tomb, the body was missing. The women couldn't find it; the disciples couldn't find it; the Jews never came up with it... no one was able to find the remains of Jesus Christ that had been sealed and guarded so carefully by the Romans (Luke 24:2–3).

Fact 4: The AWOL guards

The ancient historian Justin lists the reasons why Roman guards can be executed. Two of these reasons are falling asleep on duty and deserting your post. Specifically, a guard who was AWOL (absent without leave) was stripped down in public and burned alive with his own clothing. (Let's just say there was no incentive for sleeping on the job or taking a long lunch.) Dr George Currie, a student of Roman discipline, wrote that fear of punishment 'produced flawless attention to duty, especially in the night watches.'

And yet, amazingly, the guards were not at their post...

Fact 5: The grave clothes

The women who discovered the missing body were met by an angel who said:

> Do not be afraid, for I know that you are looking for Jesus, who was crucified. He is not here; he has risen, just as he said. Come and see the place where he lay.
>
> MATTHEW 28:5–6

> They ran to tell the disciples. Peter ran to the tomb and found it empty just like they said... but he also saw strips of linen lying where the body should have been.
>
> LUKE 24:12; JOHN 20:6–7

Fact 6: The witnesses

Jesus had died and his body was now missing. That was irrefutable. But this is where it starts to get good... because people started seeing him alive.

The Apostle Paul recorded that the living Christ appeared to Peter, and then to the disciples and more than 500 other people (1 Corinthians 15:3–8). Hundreds of these first-hand witnesses would still have been alive at the time that Paul wrote this letter. Dr Edwin Yamauchi, Associate Professor of History at Miami University, said, 'What gives special authority to the list [of witnesses] as historical evidence is the reference to most of the five hundred brethren still being alive. St Paul says in effect, "If you don't believe me, you can ask them."'

If you took the resurrection to court and each witness had only six minutes of testimony and cross-examination, that would be over fifty hours of first-hand eyewitness accounts confirming that Christ was alive. The list of witnesses also included those who were hostile towards Christ before their encounters with him. The most notable of all these was the Apostle Paul himself:

> Then he appeared to James, then to all the apostles, and last of all he appeared to me also, as to one abnormally born. For I am the least of the apostles and do not even deserve to be called an apostle, because I persecuted the church of God. But by the grace of God I am what I am, and his grace to me was not without effect.   1 CORINTHIANS 15:7–10

ᔛ QUOTATION

Positive evidence from a hostile source – which is the strongest kind of historical evidence – this means that if a source admits a fact decidedly not in its favor, then that fact is genuine.   PAUL MEIR

The writers who documented the resurrection also included the testimony of *women* witnesses. According to Luke 24:10, 'It was Mary Magdalene, Joanna, Mary the mother of James and the others with them who told this to the apostles.' This might not seem odd today, but at that time in history a woman's word wasn't worth much (sad but true) – nor was her testimony acceptable in a court of law. If the writers were trying to fabricate this story, why would they have made their first witnesses of the resurrection women? You probably wouldn't do that if you were making things up...

? QUESTION

How might your life be different if you had personally witnessed both the crucifixion and the resurrection of Jesus?

Fact 7: The Sunday worship

The traditional day of worship for the Jew has always been Saturday. Christian churches are notorious for resisting change, saying, 'We've always done it this way.' Jewish tradition beats us by several thousand years when it comes to worship customs... yet for some strange inexplicable reason, right after the death of Jesus Christ, this band of Jews started meeting on Sunday. Why such a massive change in the gathering practice? A celebration of the Sunday resurrection is the most likely reason.

Fact 8: The growing church

The Christian church started growing right away and has been growing ever since. Thousands of these first-generation believers chose to believe in the resurrection – an event which happened within their own lifetimes in their own back yard. That says a lot.

❧ QUOTATION

> I have been used for many years to study the histories of other times, and to examine and weigh the evidence of those who have written about them, and I know of no one fact in the history of mankind which is proved by better and fuller evidence of every sort, to the understanding of the fair inquirer, than the great sign which God hath given us that Christ died and rose again from the dead.
>
> PROFESSOR THOMAS ARNOLD, AUTHOR OF *THE HISTORY OF ROME*,
> CHAIRMAN OF MODERN HISTORY, OXFORD

Alternatives

What do you do with these facts? Are they convincing to everyone? That depends on your worldview. Each and every one of us has *presuppositions* (general beliefs that we use to organize and filter out information). The *rationalist* worldview presupposes that there is no God (or that if there is a god, it isn't involved in the real world). According to this view, the universe is a 'closed system'; physical laws govern everything that happens. There are never any exceptions to these basic laws.

Please understand: If you start with this rationalistic presupposition, you will be forced into rationalistic conclusions regardless of what the evidence might say to the contrary. *If you do not believe in a personal Almighty God, your decision about the resurrection has already been made.* It is naturally impossible for a dead body to come back to life on its own. But if you believe in a *relational* God, then at least the possibility exists that God did a miracle.

If you're coming from a rationalistic worldview, you're going to need to come up with some natural explanations of the facts. You'll need some sort of theory that keeps Jesus dead. Here are a few alternatives to the resurrection that have endured throughout the years:

✹ QUOTATION

I was raised with the notion that it was OK to ask questions, and it was OK to say, I'm not sure. I believe, but I'm not quite so certain about the resurrection.

PETER JENNINGS

Alternative 1: The wrong tomb

This is commonly known as 'the Kirsopp Lake Theory' (I call it the 'Yeah, Right' theory). Kirsopp argued that the women simply went to the wrong tomb – an empty tomb – while Jesus' body still lay dead as a doornail in a similar tomb nearby. Could be, maybe, sort of... but that means that *everyone* got the tombs mixed up. The Jews, the Roman guard... even the owner of the tomb, Joseph of Arimathea and his friend Nicodemus who had placed Jesus' body in there (John 19:39–40).

Alternative 2: Hallucinations

I call this 'the Woodstock Theory'. One survivor of the 1960s said, 'Anyone who says they remember the sixties clearly wasn't there.' The implication is that *everybody* was so messed up by the drugs and the culture and the music that *nobody* can truly recall what happened. The hallucination theory says that *all* of the witnesses to the resurrected Christ were deluded or high or something. They all saw a Jesus who really wasn't there. (I won't insult you by trying to explain the problems with this theory.)

Alternative 3: The Swoon Theory

I call this one 'the Snooze Theory'. It was put forth by H. E. G. Paulus in 1828. The basic idea is that Jesus didn't really die. After all the beatings, after hanging on the cross, after his heart was pierced, after being wrapped in all the spices and burial cloths, and after being locked in a tomb sealed with a huge stone and guarded by Roman soldiers, Christ wasn't dead – he was really just unconscious. In the coolness of the cave he was revived, unwrapped himself, pushed the stone over, overpowered the guard and then went back to work. Do you think that's a probable interpretation of the facts? (Not even if you went to Woodstock!)

✹ QUOTATION

You must be open-minded... but not so open-minded that your brain falls out.

JOSH MCDOWELL

Alternative 4: The body was stolen

I call this 'the Whodunit Theory' because we must answer the question, 'Who in the world had anything to gain by stealing the body?' (And this doesn't even consider the reality that anyone who did steal the body would have to get past the Roman guard first.)

The Romans had no motive; they just wanted him removed from the scene. The Jewish leaders had no motive; they were the ones who wanted him dead in the first place. And what about the disciples? Supposing that they could get past the guard, would they have any motive for faking the resurrection? It's possible, I suppose – but if they were whodunit, they weren't just thieves; they were idiots! That would mean that from that day forward, they intentionally and passionately lived and died for a lie.

If you're going to start with a rationalistic worldview that presupposes that there is no God, you'll have to embrace one of these alternatives or make up one of your own.

If you presuppose that a personal God exists, on the other hand, then anything could have happened that day. I call this the *relationalist* worldview. It starts with a belief in a God who is an active and relational almighty being. He is the maker of heaven and earth – the one who designed the physical laws that govern the material world. Because of that, he has the ability and the prerogative to intervene in the world in ways that don't follow the rules. It's called a 'miracle' when he does this; it's *super*natural – beyond the normal mode of things.

A *relationalist* has another alternative to choose from: *Maybe God brought that body back to life...*

Changes

Belief matters because belief changes us. What we believe to be true is the basis for all decisions and reactions. But remember, *your decision to believe does not determine reality. It only determines what is real to you.* In order to have true belief you must believe in something that is actually true. (It doesn't matter how much you believe something or how much you don't believe something. If your belief doesn't match up with reality... well, you're out of luck, for the strength of true belief lies not in ourselves, but in that in which we believe.)

With that in mind, I want to share one of my favourite pieces of evidence for the resurrection: The changed lives of the disciples. Granted, this is only circumstantial evidence. People's lives get changed for all sorts of different reasons, but the transformation that we see in the disciples' lives is irrefutable evidence that they believed they had encountered the living Christ.

Remember the disciples back in the Garden of Gethsemane? At the first threat of real danger, 'everyone deserted him and fled' (Mark 14:50). When Peter was put under pressure by questions from some young girls, he disowned Jesus completely (Mark 14:66–72).

But then, 'Blam!' Just like that, something changed. These guys became radical and fearless, willing to give their lives in the name of Jesus Christ. What happened?

> *On the evening of that first day of the week, when the disciples were together, with the doors locked for fear of the Jews, Jesus came and stood among them and said, 'Peace be with you!' After he said this, he showed them his hands and side. The disciples were overjoyed when they saw the Lord.*   JOHN 20:19–20

This encounter with the living Christ completely transformed them from men who were hiding behind 'doors locked for fear of the Jews' into unstoppable evangelists. After Jesus had ascended, he sent the Spirit of God to indwell the disciples, and they immediately and confidently began speaking of Christ. Look at the contrast in Peter: 'Then Peter stood up with the Eleven, raised his voice and addressed the crowd: "Fellow Jews and all of you who are in Jerusalem, let me explain this to you; listen carefully to what I say..."' (Acts 2:14). What a change from the denying coward we saw earlier!... And they never let up. The change that began with their belief has changed the world.

❧ QUOTATION

And I tell you that the evidence for the life, the death, and the resurrection of Christ is better authenticated than most of the facts of ancient history...

E. M. BLAKLOCK, PROFESSOR OF CLASSICS, AUKLAND UNIVERSITY

Testimonies

History and tradition show us that the Twelve were tortured, exiled and killed for proclaiming the resurrected Christ:

James son of Zebedee	Beheaded in Judea, AD 44
Philip	Scourged and crucified in Greece, AD 54
Matthew	Martyred in Ethiopia, AD 60
James son of Alphaeus	Martyred in Jerusalem

Matthias	Stoned and beheaded in Jerusalem, AD 80
Andrew	Crucified on an X-shaped cross in Greece, mid to late first century
Peter	Crucified upside down in Rome, circa AD 64
Bartholomew	Flayed alive and crucified in Armenia
Thomas	Thrust with spears in India
Simon the Zealot	Crucified in Samaria or Persia
Thaddeus (Jude)	Martyred in Persia, AD 65
John	Exiled on Patmos

Today it's not just hundreds, or thousands, or millions who testify of their encounter with Jesus Christ and the changed life that he brings to those who bow the knee before him... we can truthfully say that *billions* of people can testify to the change that the resurrected Christ has made in their life!

? QUESTION

Is the resurrection an important aspect of your life? If Jesus hadn't been raised from the dead, would it change your life?

Significances

Let's back up a bit and ask, What difference does this make, anyway? Is it really important to believe that the resurrection really happened? Let's let the Apostle Paul answer that:

> *And if Christ has not been raised, our preaching is useless and so is your faith. More than that, we are then found to be false witnesses about God, for we have testified about God that he raised Christ from the dead. But he did not raise him if in fact the dead are not raised. For if the dead are not raised, then Christ has not been raised either. And if Christ has not been raised, your faith is futile; you are still in your sins. Then those also who have fallen asleep in Christ are lost. If only for this life we have hope in Christ, we are to be pitied more than all men.*
>
> 1 CORINTHIANS 15:14–19

If Christ *wasn't* raised from the dead, quite frankly, we are *liars* and we are *lost*. But what is the significance for us if he *was* raised? I can't answer that any better than Peter:

Praise be to the God and Father of our Lord Jesus Christ! In his great mercy he has given us new birth into a living hope through the resurrection of Jesus Christ from the dead, and into an inheritance that can never perish, spoil or fade – kept in heaven for you, who through faith are shielded by God's power until the coming of the salvation that is ready to be revealed in the last time. In this you greatly rejoice, though now for a little while you may have had to suffer grief in all kinds of trials. These have come so that your faith – of greater worth than gold, which perishes even though refined by fire – may be proved genuine and may result in praise, glory and honour when Jesus Christ is revealed. Though you have not seen him, you love him; and even though you do not see him now, you believe in him and are filled with an inexpressible and glorious joy, for you are receiving the goal of your faith, the salvation of your souls.   1 PETER 1:3–9

M.A.P.S.

✿ *Meditate*

Ask God to guide your thoughts as you consider these words from the Creed:

I believe... on the third day he rose again from the dead.

✿ *Apply*

Review the F.A.C.T.S. regarding the resurrection:

- *Facts*
    - Jesus' body was dead.
    - The stone was rolled away.
    - The tomb was empty.
    - The Roman guards were AWOL.
    - The grave-cloths were present.
    - The witnesses reported what they saw.
- *Alternatives*
    - The wrong tomb.
    - Hallucinations.
    - The Swoon Theory.
    - The body was stolen.
- *Changes*
- *Testimonies*
- *Significances*

Do you believe Jesus rose again from the dead?

⚉ *Plot the passages*

- Key word: *Risen*.
- Key passage: John 19:31 – 20:18.
- Supporting passages: 1 Corinthians 15:3–8, 14–19; 1 Peter 1:3–9; 3:18–19.

✸ *Speak*

Speak to self

I believe in a relationalistic God who can do anything in order to bring glory to Jesus Christ.

I believe that the best interpretation of the facts is that Jesus rose from the dead.

Speak to others

When talking to people about the resurrection, you'll want to focus on two central questions:

1. *Could it have happened?* If someone comes from a rationalistic worldview, the answer will be 'no'. If that's the case, you'll want to prayerfully encourage them to be open-minded and show how their presuppositions are dictating their interpretation of the facts.
2. *Did it happen?* This is your chance to share the F.A.C.T.S. and then let them decide what is the best explanation of the evidence.

I'd also encourage you to invite others to church on Easter Sunday. Many people will come and most will hear the gospel presented in a fresh way.

Speak to God

Living God,

　Facts are facts, but faith is faith. Please – by the truth of your Word and the power of the Holy Spirit – give me genuine faith in these facts. Allow me to move beyond superficial belief into the mystery of the resurrection and all of its implications.

　Amen.

*　*　*

On Sunday morning the disciples were still locked away in hiding. The body of Jesus was still sealed securely in the tomb... or so they thought.

At some point in the night or early morning, Almighty God the Father and God the Holy Spirit performed a miracle. Molecule by molecule, they defied the natural laws. They were restructuring cell walls, purging toxins, replacing decayed biochemicals, expelling the microscopic scavengers... until the body was ready once again. And with a breath the soul and Spirit of Christ came again. Emmanuel again. God in the flesh, alive!

Supernatural? By all means. But after all, this is God. This is his business – re-creating, reversing decay and destruction, giving new life...

In the resurrection we find a reflection and a direct connection... an undeniable mystery for certain, but a connection that brings the historical resurrection of Jesus Christ into your today – right here; right now.

As I write this chapter, it is the day after Easter Sunday – nearly 2,000 years after the first one. Is the resurrection of the living Christ still significant today? This email from a member of my church says it all:

> *Dear Pete,*
>
> *It was 7 years ago Easter weekend that I was at the end of my downhill spiral. I had just spent the weekend choosing drugs over life, and the custody of my first son, and felt as though I had nothing left to live for. I cannot describe the overwhelming peace and joy that I experience today! I was allowed to serve at two services and attended the third. It is like there is no other place I belong on Easter Morning...*

Chemical abuse, abortion, desperation – and then one day someone introduced her to the risen Christ. Today she walks with him in forgiveness and grace and shameless worship...

If you really want to see the resurrected Jesus, just look at people like her.

I believe in God the Father Almighty, maker of heaven and earth; and in Jesus Christ his only Son our Lord; who was conceived by the Holy Ghost, born of the Virgin Mary, suffered under Pontius Pilate, was crucified, dead and buried. He descended into hell; the third day he rose again from the dead. **He ascended into heaven, and sits on the right hand of God the Father Almighty.** *From thence he shall come to judge the quick and the dead. I believe in the Holy Ghost, the holy catholic church, the communion of saints, the forgiveness of sins, the resurrection of the body, and the life everlasting. Amen.*

CHAPTER 10

The Seat

I never met a Christian who sat down and planned to live a mediocre life.
HOWARD HENDRICKS

Living the good life is frequently dull, flat and commonplace. Our greatest need is to make life fiery, creative, and capable of spiritual struggle. NIKOLAI BERDYAEV

I collapsed into the cushions, hoping the couch would just absorb what was left of me. I was exhausted. The best I could do was watch some guys on TV swatting a little white ball into a little hole while earning millions of dollars from the little symbols on their caps.

It was Sunday afternoon – Sunday is never a day of rest for a pastor, and this Sunday had been even more demanding than most. It was Easter, the end of the so-called 'holy week' that always leaves me 'wholly weak'.

The build-up to the resurrection starts weeks in advance for a pastor. By the time we were done remembering Jesus' death on Good Friday, I was dead tired myself. Then there was tons of preparation on Saturday night and then I was back in the office by 4:30 on Sunday morning to finish up my sermon (this is an annual ritual). We added a fifth Easter service that year (and I love every one of them), but by the time I had been through five celebrations of Jesus' resurrection, I was done.

Back home with my feet finally up on the couch, I let out a deep and satisfied sigh. Before the exhale had dissipated in the air, one of my sons, Liam, ran up to the couch and yelled, 'Daddy's home! Will you throw the football with me? Daddy, it's really nice outside!' I told him 'no' and mumbled through an explanation of how tired I was, while in the back of my mind the lyrics to the song 'Cats in the cradle and the silver spoon' poked needles into my guilty conscience. Right on cue he said, 'That's okay. Someday I'm gonna be like you,' and then he added, 'You're such a couch potato!'

That's probably more than you wanted to know. But it brings up a related question that actually has some relevance: If that's what I did after last Easter, what did Jesus do after the *first* Easter?

We are all pretty familiar with what Jesus accomplished up to the resurrection. (The Apostles' Creed works as a great summary for that.) But what about today? What is Jesus doing now? The next portion of the Creed answers:

He ascended into heaven, and sits on the right hand of God the Father.

That's it? Jesus is *sitting*?! That's what Scripture says:

When [Christ] had offered for all time one sacrifice for sins, he sat down at the right hand of God.   HEBREWS 10:12

'Sitting at the right hand of God' is not a position of leisure. It's a position of power and authority. He's on a *throne*, a position of vibrant strategic involvement from which he directs everything in heaven and earth.

Soon enough he will return to earth, but not yet.

✍ CONTEMPLATION

I pray also that the eyes of your heart may be enlightened in order that you may know the hope to which he has called you, the riches of his glorious inheritance in the saints, and his incomparably great power for us who believe. That power is like the working of his mighty strength, which he exerted in Christ when he raised him from the dead and seated him at his right hand in the heavenly realms, far above all rule and authority, power and dominion, and every title that can be given, not only in the present age but also in the one to come. And God placed all things under his feet and appointed him to be head over everything for the church, which is his body, the fullness of him who fills everything in every way. EPHESIANS 1:18–23

Jesus has a job description. He's in charge and he's got work to do. Importantly, *his* job description affects *your* job description. Unless you have a clear perspective of what *he* is doing today, you will not have a clue about what *you* are supposed to be doing today.

Jesus' job description

Supporting the saved

My dear children, I write this to you so that you will not sin. But if anyone does sin, we have one who speaks to the Father in our defence – Jesus Christ, the Righteous One.   1 JOHN 2:1

Even after Christ becomes a part of our life, we wrestle with ongoing temptation and sin on a regular basis. When we blow it, Jesus who is sitting next to the

Father, leans over and says to him, 'No problem; I paid for that one.' And the Father says, 'Okay, then: I don't even see it.'

That's comforting, big time. When you are in trouble with the law you want the best defence possible. You have that in Jesus Christ. He is a continual defender of your forgiveness as well as the one who paid for that forgiveness. His defence allows you to stay in continual fellowship with the Father.

Sending the Spirit

> *God has raised this Jesus to life, and we are all witnesses of the fact. Exalted to the right hand of God, he has received from the Father the promised Holy Spirit and has poured out what you now see and hear.*   ACTS 2:32–33

The Bible teaches us that anyone who knows Jesus Christ receives the Holy Spirit... and Jesus is the one who sends the Spirit to us.

What a cool job! I have no idea how this really works, but I imagine Jesus Christ sitting up there watching people around the world inviting him into their hearts. When they do, he looks at the Holy Spirit, points in their direction and says, 'Ready? Go!'

Christ, more than anyone else, understands our weaknesses. He knows that we are 'but dust' (Psalm 103:14 NASB). Jesus knows that the Father has given us a job description that we can't fulfil on our own. By sending the Holy Spirit into us, he knows that we at least have the choice to do what's right and fulfil our mission. With his Spirit in us we have the *ability* to obey, and he will even conform our will to his if we will allow him to.

✍ CONTEMPLATION

Peter and the other apostles replied: 'We must obey God rather than men! The God of our fathers raised Jesus from the dead – whom you had killed by hanging him on a tree. God exalted him to his own right hand as Prince and Saviour that he might give repentance and forgiveness of sins to Israel. We are witnesses of these things, and so is the Holy Spirit, whom God has given to those who obey him.'   ACTS 5:29–32

Granting the gifts

> But to each one of us grace has been given as Christ apportioned it. This is why it says: 'When he ascended on high, he led captives in his train and gave gifts to men.'
>
> EPHESIANS 4:7–8

Not only does Jesus send us the Holy Spirit but he also gives us special gifts and abilities to use in our mission. Everybody has at least one and they're not thrown out randomly. We are encouraged to ask for these gifts but Christ is the one who chooses who gets which gift (Hebrews 2:4).

? QUESTION

Some people make a distinction between spiritual gifts and natural abilities. Do you think there is a difference? Why or why not?

Representing the redeemed

> Who will bring any charge against those whom God has chosen? It is God who justifies. Who is he that condemns? Christ Jesus, who died – more than that, who was raised to life – is at the right hand of God and is also interceding for us.
>
> ROMANS 8:33–34

An 'intercessor' is someone who speaks on the behalf of another. Every day we face different kinds of condemnation from the world, from other people. Satan, in particular, continually bombards us with half-truths. He looks at our actions and our failures and says 'Guilty! Damned! Worthless!' He never lets up; he accuses us before God 'day and night' (Revelation 12:10). Jesus gets in the middle of this, he intercedes. When the accusations come he speaks to God on our behalf, saying, 'Yes, Father, that's true, but I know that one. That one is forgiven, loved and valuable!' Right now, today, this interaction is taking place between the Father and Jesus who is sitting next to him.

? QUESTION

Consider some of your closer friends. Do you think they see God more as a condemner or more as a justifier? How would an understanding of Jesus' job as an intercessor affect this?

Speaking for seekers

> *... because Jesus lives forever, he has a permanent priesthood. Therefore he is able to save completely those who come to God through him, because he always lives to intercede for them.*   HEBREWS 7:24–25

Jesus intercedes for those who are approaching salvation too. As the moment of decision gets closer, Jesus speaks on behalf of those who are guilty and condemned. On his good word, he brings seekers to God through himself. Because he lives forever, he can always intercede for them, saving them completely. That's quite a job. Nobody else could do that but him. (So, if you're holding out on becoming a Christian because you feel like you *can't* approach a perfect and holy God, you're right! You can't! But Jesus *can* and he will do that for you if you simply humble yourself and ask him to.)

Sympathizing with our struggles

> *For we do not have a high priest who is unable to sympathize with our weaknesses, but we have one who has been tempted in every way, just as we are – yet was without sin.*   HEBREWS 4:15

I love this verse. I love the idea that when I come to Jesus I come to somebody who understands me. It's one of the awesome by-products of the incarnation.

For some reason it's uncomfortable to think about Jesus being tempted. I'm not sure why, but it is. Do you think Jesus was tempted with greed? Maybe he could have made some money by setting up a little show down by the lake and charging people to watch him walk on water. Why not establish a little community health clinic where people could get healed for a reasonable fee? There's good money in that, my friends... good business. How about lust? Let's be honest, the guy had prostitutes following him around... and he was a *guy*.

He was tempted in *every* way, so he sympathizes with our struggles. But he also never blew it. When we depend on him, his strength works through us. We don't have to get sucked into the sin any more... as long as we trust in him. And this passage ends up telling us where to go when the heat gets turned up:

> *Let us then approach the throne of grace with confidence, so that we may receive mercy and find grace to help us in our time of need.*   HEBREWS 4:16

Connecting the church

... speaking the truth in love, we will in all things grow up into him who is the Head, that is, Christ. From him the whole body, joined and held together by every supporting ligament, grows and builds itself up into love, as each part does its work.   EPHESIANS 4:15–16

I always get uncomfortable when someone talks about 'Pete Briscoe's church'. I'm proud and honoured to be a part of a local fellowship... and my job description does list me as 'Senior Pastor'. (I prefer the title that one of my staff members recently suggested for me: 'Resident Dreamer'. Sorry, I digress...) The fact is, it's *not* my church. Christians place people on pedestals all the time but it's really awkward when they stick you up there. The truth is that the church belongs to Christ.

The little churches and the big churches, all the believers around the world, are held together by the person of Jesus Christ. Any growth that occurs, any depth that is dug, any love that is demonstrated, anything that is of value is accomplished by the work of Christ in us. After all, it is supernatural work that we desire in people's lives. Only Jesus can do that. It's his work; it's his church; he gets the credit!

Preparing a place

Do not let your hearts be troubled. Trust in God; trust also in me. In my Father's house are many rooms; if it were not so I would tell you. I am going there to prepare a place for you. And if I go there and prepare a place for you, I will come back and take you to be with me that you also may be where I am...   JOHN 14:1–3

Scripture gives dazzling descriptions of heaven, but I still don't think we have a clue of what we are headed for. Jesus has been busy getting ready for us to come for almost 2,000 years, doing some serious celestial construction before our arrival... and then one day he's going to lead us into this place he's prepared. I'm glad I've got a reservation, aren't you?

Waiting to win

But when this priest had offered for all time one sacrifice for sins, he sat down at the right hand of God. Since that time he waits for his enemies to be made his footstool...   HEBREWS 10:12–13

When the Romans conquered a people, they did so decisively. They didn't do anything halfway; they obliterated their enemies. To display their dominance in victory, they would bring the leader of the defeated army to the throne of the conqueror and make him kneel on all fours. In a symbolic and humiliating gesture, the conqueror would place his foot on the neck of the conquered, sometimes pushing his face to the floor... There were no questions about who was in charge and who had won.

Jesus is waiting for this moment. His enemies (Satan, sin, death, hell...) are still on the prowl, but not for long. In the future they will all bow the knee in submission and humility to his power and authority. But not yet... for now he waits and we wait.

Ruling the roost

> *... and put everything under his feet. In putting everything under him, God left nothing that is not subject to him. Yet at present we do not see everything subject to him...*   HEBREWS 2:8

Fifteen years ago, when I was a fledgling pastor, I took an emergency call and drove to the hospital. A baby girl had recently been born to one of the families in our church. Joy turned to pain, however, when she was diagnosed with Trisomy 13, a wretched disease that steals the lives of infants shortly after they enter the world.

As I entered the room my brain was seared with an image of grief I have never forgotten: A mother sitting alone in dim light, soaked in a river of tears, rocking back and forth, tightly holding and caressing the lifeless body of her baby in her arms...

The hospital staff had been gently trying to get her to let go of the child, now dead for more than thirty minutes. They asked if I could help... We talked; we cried; we tried to pray... Forty-five minutes later she was somehow able to loosen her hold and carefully place the baby in my arms.

Dear Jesus, are you really in charge... Are you in charge of this?! How can you allow such suffering in the hearts of those you love so much?

As I held the child, these questions swirled in my mind... then the mother looked me in the eye and asked the same questions. I didn't know what to say. There are few good answers to such questions when you are staring agony in the face.

If I were to translate Hebrews 2:8 into my own words, it would read something like this: 'Jesus is in control. The Father has left nothing outside his authority... But sometimes, we can't see it. Sometimes – like when the tiniest of hearts stop their beating – we can't see it at all... so we must trust, trust that Jesus (whose battered and lifeless body was also held by a weeping mother) is somehow working his purposes behind it all.'

From our perspective, some things just don't seem to fit into the big plan. Other things seem to be spiralling out of control. When we look at our neighbourhoods, when we watch the evening news or pick up the morning paper... it so often seems like evil has the upper hand and that chaos is the disheartening norm. But that's only from our limited point of view.

Pastor Bill Hybels was sailing his boat across Lake Michigan one summer when he was engulfed in a terrifying storm. The waves and the winds pounded from every side. He arrived unscathed physically but emotionally exhausted. A few days later he returned home but this time via commercial airline. As they passed over Lake Michigan another large storm was pounding below. As he viewed it from thousands of feet above the fray, he was struck by how different the storm seemed from that perspective – and how impossible it is to gain true perspective of a storm when one is in the middle of it...

From where Jesus is seated in heaven, he sees everything from the vantage-point of eternity. He sees the past; he sees the present; he sees the future – and there is no question about who is in control or what is going to happen. Jesus is good and he is in complete charge of the universe. But for some reason, we don't always see that. That's when we walk in true faith that is built on solid beliefs based on God's Word. What other option is there?

> ... Jesus Christ, who has gone into heaven and is at God's right hand – with angels, authorities and powers in submission to him.   1 PETER 3:21–22

Your job description

Yes, Jesus has a job description and he is fulfilling it perfectly. In light of that, *our* job description begins with some very interesting twists. Understanding Christ's position (what it means for him to be seated at God's right hand in the heavenly places) gives us an essential perspective from which we can understand our job description as one of his followers. Don't make any assumptions about this position. When you took on this job, you more than likely missed at least one or two of the indispensable and absolutely critical priorities of your job:

Seeing self seated

> But because of his great love for us, God, who is rich in mercy, made us alive with Christ even when we were dead in transgressions – it is by grace you have been

12

*saved. And God raised us up with Christ and seated us with him in the heavenly
realms in Christ Jesus, in order that in the coming ages he might show the
incomparable riches of his grace, expressed in his kindness to us in Christ Jesus.*

EPHESIANS 2:4–7

We've already seen that we have been crucified with Christ (Galatians 2:20), and that we have been resurrected with Christ (Romans 6:5). Now we find out that we are also *seated* with him. This is every intern's dream! We aren't just doing grunt work for some manager. We are actually with Christ in the throne-room where all the action is taking place. Because of what Christ did, God promoted us with Christ so that he can show us the 'incomparable riches' of his grace and kindness in Christ.

Unbelievable. But true.

In order to understand what God asks of us, we must understand that God *doesn't* operate like any other boss in the entire world (where position is always tied to performance). God operates on the basis of grace and mercy and love. Because of what Christ did (by no works of our own), we are seated at the top.

Resting relentlessly

*Come to me, all you who are weary and burdened, and I will give you rest. Take
my yoke upon you and learn from me, for I am gentle and humble in heart, and
you will find rest for your souls. For my yoke is easy and my burden is light.*

MATTHEW 11:28–30

Doing it the world's way wears you out, but living the righteous way leads to rest and peace and strength.

Here's the deal: When most of us became Christians we simply Christian-ized the world's model of performance. The only difference is that instead of living for the things of the world we are trying to live for God – but we are still *trying* to do it through our own self-sufficiency and self-effort. God is calling us to an intimate relationship that is based on *Christ's* sufficiency and *Christ's* effort working through us. This is a huge paradigm shift that must continually be applied, or you will eventually burn out.

It's to those of you who are 'weary and heavy laden' that Jesus calls out and says, 'I will give you rest.' A great example of this is found in Luke 10. Jesus and the disciples were on their way back from a big outreach event where crowds of people had committed their lives to Jesus. He and the disciples spent the night at the home of two sisters. One of them, Martha, was running around like crazy trying to get things done. Her sister Mary, on the other hand, 'sat at the Lord's feet listening to what he said' (Luke 10:39). Martha complained, but Jesus answered, 'You are worried and upset about many things, but only one thing is needed. Mary has chosen what is better and it will not be taken away from her' (verses 41–42).

Do you want to know what is at the *top* of your job description? *Sitting at the feet of Jesus and listening to him.* Because of the blood of Jesus, we can confidently enter the throne-room where Jesus and the Father sit in complete authority (Hebrews 10:19). But we aren't just to drop in once in a while. We need to realize that in some mystical way, that's where we *live*, seated with Christ. Moment by moment, hour by hour, we *are* seated with Christ. We need to recognize that and take full advantage of his position – *our* position – that was bought at the cross.

❧ QUOTATION

Sitting is an attitude of rest. Something has been finished, work stops, and we sit. It is paradoxical, but true, that we only advance in the Christian life as we learn first of all to sit down... to sit down simply means to rest our whole weight – our load, ourselves, our future, everything – upon the Lord. We let him bear the responsibility and cease to carry it ourselves.   WATCHMAN NEE[37]

Trusting totally

Do not let your hearts be troubled. Trust in God; trust also in me.   JOHN 14:1

The command 'Do not be afraid' appears in various forms 365 times in the Bible... that's one for every day of the year.

Once you see yourself seated and find yourself relentlessly resting, God can begin to work in you and through you in amazing ways... if you trust him totally. From your position seated next to Christ, a great many adventures of faith await. From this position of fellowship, a grand eternal exploration begins.

? QUESTION

Is this the kind of job description that you expected? What kind of things do you normally hear should be at the top of your priority list as a Christian?

M.A.P.S.

✹ Meditate

Ask God to guide your thoughts as you consider these words from the Creed:

> *I believe... he ascended into heaven and sits on the right hand of the Father Almighty.*

✹ Apply

Review the main areas of Jesus' job description. How should the things he is doing change the things you are doing?

Review your job description. What would you do differently if you *really* believed that these are primary priorities of the Christian life? How would all other activities begin to flow as an extension of the fact that you are seated with Christ?

✹ Plot the passages

- Key word: *Seated*.
- Key passage: Hebrews 12:2–3.
- Supporting passages: Hebrews 10:19–20; Ephesians 2:4–7; Colossians 3:1–4; Matthew 11:28–30.

✹ Speak

Speak to self

I believe that Jesus Christ is now seated at the right hand of God the Father. From this position, I believe that his job description includes:

- Supporting the saved.
- Granting the gifts.
- Representing the redeemed.
- Speaking for seekers.
- Sympathizing with our struggles.
- Connecting the church.
- Preparing a place.
- Waiting to win.
- Ruling the roost.

Because I am seated with Christ, my primary job description includes:

- Seeing self seated.
- Resting relentlessly.
- Trusting totally.

Speak to others

The truth about Jesus being seated in a position of authority is only relevant to two types of people: Those who believe in Jesus and those who don't.

Followers of Christ who aren't aware of what Christ is doing will try to do it all for him, resulting in frustration and/or burn out. Those who don't believe in Jesus will often look at an impossible religious job description and say 'no thanks'.

Prayerfully consider the people you know who fall into one of these two categories. How is God leading you to share the truth with them?

Speak to God

God in heaven,

Open the eyes of my heart, Lord. I want to absorb the full impact and implications of Jesus Christ being seated at your right hand. Give me a practical and even emotional understanding of how his job description changes my job description today.

There comes a point where my belief needs to lead to worship in obedience to you. Let that obedience begin in full awareness of my position beside you. I want to be one who sits at your feet, enjoying your presence, listening to your voice.

And then, when I am sitting and resting in you, give me ears to hear what it is that you specifically want to do through me today.

Amen.

*   *   *

Even if you are on the right track, you will get run over if you just sit there.

Will Rogers

Several years ago I was asked to perform a drama at a summer training conference for Campus Crusade for Christ. It was a theatrical interpretation of 2 Corinthians and the judgment seat that I had already performed at our church. I was excited to share it as an encouragement in front of 5,000 Campus Crusade staff. I could never have imagined the experience that awaited me.

As I arrived in Colorado I was told that Dr Bill Bright, the founder of Campus Crusade, was dying at his home after a long illness. Tens of thousands of staff and volunteers around the world were grieving his loss; many of them were connected by satellite to the conference. As I was preparing to go on stage, it was announced that Vonnette Bright, Bill's wife, was going to address the conference by phone. I sat in stunned silence as she ministered to the people, sharing stories of Bill's last days, rejoicing that he would soon be with his Father in heaven and challenging everyone to keep their eyes on Christ even though it was a time of great sorrow. There wasn't a dry eye in the place and then... I was up...

I was terrified. I felt like an outsider incongruously inserted into a family gathering. And then the entire two-hour script disappeared from my frontal lobe; I couldn't remember a thing. As I walked up on stage I prayed, 'Jesus, I simply can't do this; I rest in you; rescue me, *do this through me!'*

I opened my mouth and the first words came out... and off I went, resting in Jesus as he powerfully worked through me.

A picture of the Christian life: *Jesus, I can't do this. Rescue me, do this through me. I rest in you...* and then taking the first step.

Let there be no mistake: Christianity is no couch-potato religion. We aren't spectators of someone's sport; we aren't 'taking the afternoon off'. We are to be fully engaged, fully focused and full speed ahead.

But the starting-point and ending-point of all we do must be a position of sitting with, resting in and trusting in Jesus. Through our position in him, we will have the authority and power to be effectively unleashed in the world to the glory of Jesus Christ.

May God propel us all from this new perspective. May we always be stunned by these spiritual realities as we navigate with him through what remains of this earthly life:

Let us fix our eyes on Jesus, the author and perfecter of our faith, who for the joy set before him endured the cross, scorning its shame, and sat down at the right hand of the throne of God. Consider him who endured such opposition from sinful men, so that you will not grow weary and lose heart.   HEBREWS 12:2–3

Since, then, you have been raised with Christ, set your hearts on things above, where Christ is seated at the right hand of God. Set your minds on things above, not on earthly things. For you died, and your life is now hidden with Christ in God. When Christ, who is your life, appears, then you also will appear with him in glory.   COLOSSIANS 3:1–4

*I believe in God the Father Almighty, maker of heaven and earth; and in Jesus Christ his only Son our Lord; who was conceived by the Holy Ghost, born of the Virgin Mary, suffered under Pontius Pilate, was crucified, dead and buried. He descended into hell; the third day he rose again from the dead. He ascended into heaven, and sits on the right hand of God the Father Almighty. **From thence he shall come to judge the quick and the dead.** I believe in the Holy Ghost, the holy catholic church, the communion of saints, the forgiveness of sins, the resurrection of the body, and the life everlasting. Amen.*

CHAPTER 11

The Sure Return

It ain't over till it's over.   YOGI BERRA

I'll be back.   ARNOLD SCHWARZENEGGER IN *THE TERMINATOR*

Warm water filled his boots as he left the dry sands of the beach and waded out to the boat floating in the Filipino bay.

It was March 1942. Pearl Harbor was still in ruin and Japanese forces were tightening their grip on the Philippines. General Douglas MacArthur was following orders from President Roosevelt to 'relocate' (translation: 'retreat') to Melbourne, Australia.

As a soldier and as the Allied commander, orders like this were not easy for him to follow. He had seriously considered resigning his commission and fighting with the Filipino resistance. But it was the war (and not this battle) that he knew must be won. So MacArthur and a select group of advisers and subordinate military commanders chose to obey. Fighting the instincts of true soldiers, they left the Philippines in their wake.

Perhaps trying to convince himself of the necessity of the move, he would later write, 'We are not retreating; we are advancing in another direction.' The men arrived in Australia on 20 March and through clenched teeth MacArthur uttered the now-famous words: 'I came through and I shall return.'

Nearly 2,000 years before that day in the Philippines, another man had made a similar promise. He was leaving for good reason and his promise to come again was equally certain.

That man was Jesus Christ. When we recite the Apostles' Creed we lay claim not only to what Christ *has* done but to what he said he *will* do:

I believe... he ascended into heaven, and sits on the right hand of God the Father Almighty. From thence he shall come to judge the quick and the dead.

No one knew at the time if MacArthur had told the truth; history had yet to take its course. The Word of God, however, confirms ahead of time the truthfulness of Jesus' words. Approximately 300 passages in Scripture allude to Christ's second coming – a return that will be swift, righteous and unexpected for many... And this time he will come to judge and to rule.

What does this all mean to us today? In the pages ahead we will look at five principles that will give us the answers.

The Promise Keeper Principle

If one with complete integrity makes a promise, consider it done.

'Integrity' means more than sincere intention. The person who makes the promise must have the ability to follow through. In order to have true integrity, one must be both honest *and* capable. Jesus Christ is both of these things! Here is his promise:

> *Do not let your hearts be troubled. Trust in God; trust also in me. In my Father's house are many rooms; if it were not so I would have told you. I am going there to prepare a place for you. And if I go there to prepare a place for you, I will come back and take you to be with me that you also may be where I am.*   JOHN 14:1-3

This promise was confirmed by angels that stood beside the disciples when Christ ascended into heaven. The apostles were just standing there looking up into the clouds with their mouths open, and the angels asked them one of the most outlandish questions I've ever heard: 'Men of Galilee,' they said, 'why do you stand here looking into the sky?' (Angels, I guess, are used to seeing beings zipping around in the air. I'm thinking that didn't happen every day for the disciples!) The angels got right to the point, though: 'This same Jesus, who has been taken from you into heaven, will come back in the same way you have seen him go into heaven' (Acts 1:11).

In other words, they were saying, 'Quit standing there like a bunch of baby birds waiting for a worm. Jesus came; he saw; he gave it all; he's coming again. Now get back to it.'

Like MacArthur, Christ said, 'I came through and I shall return.' MacArthur, however, was facing a war that was ultimately out of his control. Jesus is one with Almighty God. Anything that he chooses to do he does. The promise has been made. Jesus is a keeper of promises. His return is not a matter of *if*; it's only a matter of *when*.

... And that places us smack dab in the middle of a very interesting little sliver of history.

You are already familiar with eternity past, creation and the birth, ministry, death and resurrection of Jesus. Now, notice that little circle on the timeline. That's the 'second coming' of Christ, the time when he will return to earth to judge the quick (those who are alive) and the dead (those who aren't quite so quick any more).

A missionary friend of mine told me the story of a huge snake – an anaconda, I believe – that made its way into his house. He was new to the field and was understandably terrified. He quickly gathered his family and ran out the back door calling for help. A group of men from the village came to the rescue, sliding up to the open window and shooting the massive serpent in the head. The snake started to thrash about violently, taking out coffee-tables, dishes, decorations and lamps. The racket lasted for what seemed like an eternity – until finally the slithery thing gave up the fight. Everyone waited for a few minutes just to be sure. Inside the home was a complete mess... but the snake was finally dead.

At the cross the death-blow to Satan was levied by Christ. Jesus has won the victory – but the serpent is still thrashing around destroying anything he can before the end of his miserable existence.

That's were we are in human history: Between victory (the cross and resurrection) and the end of the game (the second coming). Complete triumph *is* coming... But when?

The Time-Keeper Principle

Only the Referee knows when the game will end.

Soccer was my sport as a kid. Growing up in England, that was normal, of course. But there is one thing that isn't normal about soccer: No clock on the scoreboard. The ref keeps the time. He starts and stops the clock as he decides; he's the only one who knows when the game will end. *No one else does.*

See the parallel? We don't know when *this* period in history will end either. If you own this principle, you will save yourself many a headache. Matthew 24:36 clearly says, 'No one knows about the day or the hour, not even the angels in heaven, nor the Son, but only the Father.'

Only the Father. That's the Time-Keeper Principle... But a lot of people don't get that. When they don't, it leads to some rather comical behaviour.

Deriders will deride
Even before the Bible was finished being written, people were sceptical about Christ's return.

First of all, you must understand that in the last days scoffers will come, scoffing and following their own evil desires. They will say, 'Where is this "coming" he promised? Ever since our fathers died, everything goes on as it has since the beginning of creation.'   2 PETER 3:3–4

Plenty of us feel the same way. It's been almost 2,000 years and none of us regularly check the skies to see if his return flight is coming in. Peter responds to the scoffers with a reminder and a warning: 'Remember the great flood?'

✍ Contemplation

But they deliberately forget that long ago by God's word the heavens existed and the earth was formed out of water and by water. By these waters also the world of that time was deluged and destroyed. By the same word the present heavens and earth are reserved for fire, being kept for the day of judgment and destruction of ungodly men.   2 PETER 3:5–7

Before the flood, even though Noah had given warning, everybody just kept on doing their own thing... then a wall of water, *WOOSH*. Today it's the same thing; Jesus has warned, but the masses go about their merry way either indifferent or unaware that God will again intervene with judgment and fire (gulp).

? Question

Scoffers live on today, thumbing their noses at the promise of Christ's return. Why do you think that is? A lack of information? A lack of faith? Something else?

Daters will date

Trying to pin an exact date on the return of Christ is an ongoing hobby in the church. Throughout the centuries, dozens of predictions have been made and they all have one thing in common: They were all wrong.

My favourite example was a little book entitled *88 Reasons Why Christ Will Return in 1988*. By carefully manipulating numerous prophetic verses in the Bible, the author concluded that Jesus would come back during the Jewish feast of Rosh Hashanah on a weekend in September 1988. He sold about a zillion copies of this book. Everybody was trying to get their hands on one. I was attending my home church where my Dad was the pastor at the time. We were constantly getting calls requesting copies from our bookstore. As September drew near, the callers kept asking my Dad's secretary why he wasn't carrying the book. 'Just tell them to call me back in October,' he said.

Nobody called.

Did the author give back all the royalties? No. He said he made a slight miscalculation, switched the date to 1989 and sold a billion more booklets. But when I watched the news that September, there was still no mention of Jesus.

Debaters will debate

The Scripture verses dealing with the dating of the second coming come from 'apocalyptic literature', including books like Daniel and Revelation. These books are beautiful and fascinating to read – full of wild imagery and amazing snapshots of future history – but they are very difficult to interpret. Very few of the passages are presented in a clear sequence, so it's a challenge to determine the order of events (let alone a specific date).

The four main events under question are:

- *The rapture:* A mass 'lifting up' of all Christians, who will go to heaven without having to die (1 Thessalonians 4:16–17).
- *The tribulation:* A seven-year period of brutal hardship and destruction (Revelation 7:14).
- *The millennium:* A 1,000-year period of peace and harmony on earth (Revelation 20).
- *The second coming:* The return of Jesus Christ to earth (there are 300 references to this).

These are the four big pieces of the puzzle (although many consider the rapture and the second coming to be one and the same event)… but it's not entirely clear how they fit together, and that's when the debaters start debating. There are about three popular options with a couple of variations thrown in to spice it up.

1. Pre-millennial return

Jesus returns to earth, raptures all believers in Christ, and than establishes his kingdom on earth for a thousand years.

Proponents of this view believe that the tribulation will happen before the millennium. So if you hold to a pre-millennial kingdom view, you have three more choices to make: (a) pre-tribulation rapture; (b) post-tribulation rapture; or (c) mid-tribulation rapture.

This 'pre-millennial pre-tribulation' view has been pretty popular for the last fifty years. It does allow the believer to escape the tribulation, which is something we can hope for. Dr Walter Martin, on the other hand, was one of the great defenders of the faith of this generation. He took a pre-millennial post-tribulation view of things (meaning that he expected that he would have to live through that seven-year period of difficulty and destruction). But he also often joked that he really, really hoped he was wrong. (He's in heaven now, so I guess he doesn't really have to hope either way!)

2. Post-millennial return

Things get better and better until we arrive at a harmonious state of affairs in our world; then Christ comes back. That one doesn't have as much scriptural support in my mind – and it certainly doesn't seem to be the trend. When I look at where we are headed as a planet, I don't see *any* solution to our problems short of Jesus coming back.

3. A-millennial return

This view says that there *won't* be a literal thousand-year reign of Christ. Many of the things we see in the book of Revelation are figurative, and not literal. Those who hold to this view say that Christ's reign is figurative as well. They believe that the millennium is going to be a spiritual reign in the hearts of people, not a physical reign by Christ in person.

I have to admit, I've always liked a good debate. But my concern is that we get so caught up in dating and debating that we forget the point. Imagine watching a World Cup soccer match. It starts getting pretty intense but all of a sudden the guys from one team sit down in the middle of the field and start debating about when the game is going to end:

'I think it's going to end in about ten minutes.'

'No, I think we need to score again.'

'No, it doesn't matter what we do – the ref chooses, no matter what the watch says...'

Meanwhile the enemy scores again, and again, and again...

❧ QUOTATION

> *We are living, then, in an interim period, the period between the Ascension and the return of Christ. We are living in the age of the Church. It is an age of Grace and an age of the Spirit in which we have, by God's mercy and love, opportunity to proclaim to the world the good news about Jesus Christ.*   RON JAMES[38]

Jesus said in Revelation 22:7, 'Behold, I am coming soon!' He repeats it in verse 20: 'Yes, I am coming soon.' 'Soon' could mean in ten seconds or it could mean ten centuries. Just remember the Promise-Keeper Principle and the Time-Keeper Principle, and you'll remember what to do.

> *'Wake up, O sleeper, rise from the dead, and Christ will shine on you.' Be very careful, then, how you live – not as unwise but as wise, making the most of every opportunity, because the days are evil. Therefore do not be foolish, but understand what the Lord's will is.*   EPHESIANS 5:14–17

? QUESTION

When it comes to your beliefs, where to you draw the line between things that are 'debatable' and things that are 'non-negotiable'?

The Mind-Sweeper Principle

Explosive mines destroy seafaring vessels. Corrosive minds destroy living vessels.

Have you ever watched a ship being taken out by a mine? Not a pretty sight. A plume of water – a shuddering throughout the skeleton of the vessel – a chaotic descent into the depths...

The same thing can happen in the human mind. Certain philosophies drift just under the surface of life. If they go undetected they can sink you without warning. Jesus is coming back, but never forget that he is coming back to judge. Many will be found wanting because of philosophical bombs that sank them some time before. In my Dad's book on the Apostles' Creed he describes three such bombs to avoid:[39]

Utopianism: A misplaced optimism
Applied technology and exploding amounts of information are giving rise to incredible accomplishment in certain areas of humanity. There is no question that we are experiencing things that our ancestors couldn't even have dreamed possible. But is it resulting in an improvement in the overall human condition? Given enough time, could we possibly create our own utopia?

The honest answer is 'no'. With all our accomplishments, we have yet to come up with our own solution to the sinful and selfish soul of man. Our world will not end in paradise. Our accomplishments are really just fuelling our demise. This period of history will end in the fair and righteous judgment of Christ. Full stop.

Universalism: A misguided dream

One of the dominant mottos of our generation goes like this: 'It doesn't matter what you believe as long as you believe it sincerely.' That's called *universalism*, the dream that everyone will be saved regardless of the choices and decisions they make. Universalists cling to the truth about God being a loving God, but they ignore (or are ignorant of) the fact that he is also righteous and holy.

The Creed reminds us that Jesus is coming back to judge. Matthew 25:46 talks about that hour when he will separate those who believe in him (and have been made righteous in him) and those who do not: '... they will go away to eternal punishment, but the righteous to eternal life.'

Utilitarianism: A mistaken philosophy

Utilitarianism can be summed up in another of our favourite mottos: 'If it feels good, do it!' According to this philosophy we should always pursue the greatest happiness for the greatest number of people. (Sounds like our political 'democracy', doesn't it?) It doesn't matter what's *right*; it only matters what *works*. That's what drives our society.

The problem, of course, is that trying to find happiness in circumstances is contrary to finding joy in Christ. I've already brought up the idolatry issue, but it shows up again in utilitarianism when we pursue pleasure and 'happiness' *instead* of God rather than *in* God. Those idols just can't stand on their own and Jesus won't stand for them when he returns.

? QUESTION

To what extent do you find these false '-isms' in your own beliefs? Where did they come from? How do they affect your perspective on life and the decisions you make?

The Book-Keeper Principle

You can't judge a book by the cover unless the Judge has the book.

After my family moved to the United States from England, I tried out for the basketball team. I was in ninth grade and while I had been a string-bean up to that point, the summer before my freshman year I grew six inches. That's no joke; six inches in one summer!

But no matter how tall I was, basketball didn't come easy for a soccer player. I tried my best but when 'cut-day' came, my best just wasn't good enough. The list posted on the locker-room door didn't have my name on it. I had been cut from the team – one of the last two ousted. My friends whose names were on the list jumped, hollered and walked away arm in arm, laughing and dreaming of a great season ahead... I stood there with the other 'cuttee', not really knowing what to say, trying not to cry. Ouch. Has anything like that ever happened to you? It stinks!

Now take that feeling and multiply it times eternity.

> *Then I saw a great white throne and him who was seated on it. Earth and sky fled from his presence, and there was no place for them. And I saw the dead, great and small, standing before the throne, and books were opened. Another book was opened, which is the book of life... If anyone's name was not found in the book of life, he was thrown into the lake of fire.*   REVELATION 20:11–12, 15

It's 'cut-day' in heaven and, to be honest – even though you might be trying your best – your best just isn't good enough to make the team. The criterion that Jesus will use to make the cut is very clear:

> *Whoever believes in him is not condemned, but whoever does not believe stands condemned already because he has not believed in the name of God's one and only Son... Whoever believes in the Son has eternal life, but whoever rejects the Son will not see life, for God's wrath remains on him.*   JOHN 3:18, 36

These passages aren't all that popular in our pluralistic culture, but they are there and they are true. Do we choose to avoid them because they make us uncomfortable? Do we refuse to speak of them because our God happens to be less tolerant than our contemporary culture requires? What's the moral of the Book-Keeper Principle? Jesus is coming. Jesus will judge. And belief matters, so please make sure you are in the book.

The Good Housekeeper Principle

There is nothing like an unexpected guest to get everyone cleaning up the mess.

Our home was rarely messy when we were growing up. But sometimes 'messy' depends on who is in the house. One Saturday afternoon, when Billy Graham was doing a crusade in Milwaukee, we got a call from one of his staffers:

'Would it be possible for Dr Graham to retreat to your home for a few hours to get away from the relentless nature of his public life?'

My mother said, 'Why, of course! We'd love to have him. What day would he like to come?'

'How about in two hours?'

Minor panic. Mum hung up the phone and immediately assembled all the children. Our home was clean enough for us but it certainly wasn't ready for Dr Graham. We scrubbed and scoured every inch of the home. Then we were sent upstairs to shower and dress 'appropriately' (our wardrobe choices demonstrated the fact that we weren't clear on the definition of that term).

When the great preacher finally arrived, we were summoned into the living-room where we all sat staring at him. My Mum sat down next to him, crossing her legs and leaning in to show interest and concern. We had pulled it off, almost. A few minutes later the doorbell ring and my Mum popped up to answer it – not realizing that her leg had fallen asleep. As she stepped on it the numb leg gave way, sending her onto the lap of Dr Graham. It was the highlight of the day – a moment we never let her forget. The frenzied preparation for the arrival of Dr Graham literally had us 'falling all over him'!

? QUESTION

If Jesus returned today... (You know the rest!)

The scriptural support for this 'Good House keeper' principle is so clear that it really requires very little explanation. Scripture speaks for itself. I have to admit that when I am reading books I sometimes skip over the Bible part to get to the good stuff. Think about that for a second. If you do likewise, please resist the temptation here. These passages come from the very heart of God and he wants you to hear what he has to say to you. Read them slowly and carefully, asking God to speak to your heart as you do.

Be ready

> *Therefore keep watch, because you do not know on what day your Lord will come. But understand this: If the owner of the house had known at what time of night the thief was coming, he would have kept watch and would not have let his house be broken into. So you also must be ready, because the Son of Man will come at an hour when you do not expect him.* MATTHEW 24:42–44

Be holy

> *For the grace of God that brings salvation has appeared to all men. It teaches us to say 'no' to ungodliness and worldly passions, and to live self-controlled, upright and godly lives in this present age, while we wait for the blessed hope – the glorious appearing of our great God and Saviour, Jesus Christ.* TITUS 2:11–13

Be hopeful

> *Therefore, since we have been justified through faith, we have peace with God through our Lord Jesus Christ, through whom we have gained access by faith into this grace in which we now stand. And we rejoice in the hope of the glory of God. Not only so, but we also rejoice in our sufferings, because we know that suffering produces perseverance; perseverance, character; and character, hope. And hope does not disappoint us, because God has poured out his love into our hearts by the Holy Spirit, whom he has given us.* ROMANS 5:1–5

Quotation

In the Creed we say that we believe in Jesus, who is the future both for us and for the world. In the face of all terror and uncertainty and illusion about the future we gladly point to Jesus and say that he is the future. THEODORE W. JENNINGS, JR[40]

Be helpful

> And we urge you, brothers, warn those who are idle, encourage the timid, help the weak, be patient with everyone. Make sure that nobody pays back wrong for wrong, but always try to be kind to each other and to everyone else. Be joyful always; pray continually; give thanks in all circumstances, for this is God's will for you in Christ Jesus. Do not put out the Spirit's fire; do not treat prophecies with contempt. Test everything. Hold on to the good. Avoid every kind of evil. May God himself, the God of peace, sanctify you through and through. May your whole spirit, soul and body be kept blameless at the coming of our Lord Jesus Christ. The one who calls you is faithful and he will do it.   1 THESSALONIANS 5:14–23

The one who calls you is faithful and he will do it... Be ready. Be holy. Be hopeful. Be helpful... Because Jesus Christ is coming to judge the quick and the dead. Who will do this? 'He will do it.' Our job is to sit, rest and trust. Be willing and he will move through you.

✌ QUOTATION

> Build me a son, O Lord, who will be strong enough to know when he is weak, and brave enough to face himself when he is afraid, one who will be proud and unbending in honest defeat, and humble and gentle in victory.
>
> GENERAL MACARTHUR

It is time to stand back and take a good look at the big picture. Days, months, years, decades... your entire life can be swallowed up by the demanding moment-by-moment details of life. Don't let that happen. These are unprecedented days and they will not go on forever. Between today and the second coming of Jesus, a great opportunity exists to make an eternal impact in the lives around you. God is calling. God is faithful... and if you allow him to move through you, he himself will make this happen.

> May your whole spirit, soul and body be kept blameless at the coming of our Lord Jesus Christ. The one who calls you is faithful and he will do it.
>
> 1 THESSALONIANS 5:23–24

M.A.P.S.

✌ Meditate

Ask God to guide your thoughts as you consider these words from the Creed:

I believe... From thence [heaven] he shall come to judge the quick and the dead.

Apply

Take as much time as you need to ponder the verses in the 'Good Housekeeper Principle' section above. Ask God to reveal specific action points to you as you pray through these passages from his Word.

- Be ready.
- Be holy.
- Be hopeful.
- Be helpful.

Plot the passages

- Key word: *Return*.
- Key passage: John 14:1–4.
- Supporting passages: Matthew 24:43–44; John 14:1–4; 3:18–36; 1 Thessalonians 5:24.

Speak

Speak to self

I believe that Jesus Christ is returning to judge and rule this earth. Because of this:

- *If one with complete integrity makes a promise, consider it done* (the Promise-Keeper Principle).
- *Only the Referee knows when the game will end* (the Time-Keeper Principle).
- *You can't judge a book by the cover unless the Judge has the book* (the Book-Keeper Principle).
- *Explosive mines destroy seafaring vessels. Corrosive minds destroy living vessels* (the Mind-Sweeper Principle).
- *There is nothing like an unexpected guest to get everyone cleaning up the mess* (the Good Housekeeper Principle).

Speak to others

Think about specific people you know who have fallen victim to one or more of these false '-isms':

- Utopianism.
- Universalism.
- Utilitarianism.

How could you guide a conversation in a way that shows them respect and understanding, while sharing the truth about your belief in the second coming of Jesus as our only hope?

Speak to God

> *My Dear God,*
>
> *Through the power and presence of your Son who lives in me, use me to warn those who are confused, to encourage the timid and to help the weak.*
> *Give me the willingness to be joyful, to pray and to give thanks according to your will. Give me the wisdom to test everything and to embrace that which is good.*
> *Thank you that my body, soul and spirit will be found blameless in Jesus when he returns because of his work in me.*
>
> *Father, I know that you are faithful; I'm trusting you to do this through me, for I know that I cannot do this on my own.*
>
> *For the glory of Jesus, Amen.*

* * *

On 20 October 1944, General MacArthur again felt the warmth of the Philippine waters in his boots. This time, however, he was wading from boat to beach.

Two and a half years had passed. The blood of thousands from both enemy and ally stained the waters and the shores, but through the Battle for Leyte Island he made good on his famous words.

He had returned.*

Today we stand and fight on a small island of time between the ascension of Jesus Christ and his promised return. Victory is assured, yes. But there is much to do between now and then. We live in a brief window of history that will soon pass – yet one that has eternal consequences.

Let us praise Jesus that he still waits patiently, allowing this short season for others to turn to him... but let us also pray the final prayer of the Bible – 'Come, Lord Jesus, come' – knowing that when he does it will all be made right.

---

*   Image available from:
    http://en.wikipedia.org/wiki/Image:Douglas_MacArthur_lands_Leyte1.jpg

*I believe in God the Father Almighty, maker of heaven and earth; and in Jesus Christ his only Son our Lord; who was conceived by the Holy Ghost, born of the Virgin Mary, suffered under Pontius Pilate, was crucified, dead and buried. He descended into hell; the third day he rose again from the dead. He ascended into heaven, and sits on the right hand of God the Father Almighty. From thence he shall come to judge the quick and the dead. **I believe in the Holy Ghost**, the holy catholic church, the communion of saints, the forgiveness of sins, the resurrection of the body, and the life everlasting. Amen.*

CHAPTER 12

The Sanctifying Spirit

Who has seen the wind? Neither you nor I. But when the trees bow down their heads the wind is passing by.　　　　　　　CHILDREN'S POEM

The wind blows wherever it pleases. You hear its sound, but you cannot tell where it comes from or where it is going. So it is with everyone born of the Spirit.

　　　　　　　JOHN 3:8

No one turned me in. I was getting away with it.

I slouched low on the green vinyl seat as the yellow school bus pulled away, removing me from the scene of the crime. A minute of relief. But as we bumped along toward home a lump grew in my throat... I felt the warmth of a tear trickle down my cheek. A wave of intense sadness welled up from deep inside. A cloud of depression had descended on my soul by the time I got home. I retreated directly to my room and sat in quiet despondency, until my Mum sat down next to me. I broke down and told her the whole story:

I was standing in the hallway of Tonawanda Elementary School waiting for the bus, my hands behind my back, leaning against the wall. I was skinny in those days, long and slim and sensitive about it. A boy directly across from me started to poke fun at me – his comment having something to do with the negligible circumference of my thighs.

I ignored the first comment, pretended not to hear the second and verbally rebuffed him on receipt of the third... But as the fourth hurtful statement registered in my mind, I instinctively lunged across the hall and kicked him full force, square in his straightened knee. His knee doubled backwards. The leg hyperextended, bending in the wrong direction. He crumpled to the floor, screaming in agony. I quickly pulled back to my side of the hall, hands behind my back, leaning against the wall, innocently watching in horror as they carried him down the hall to the nurse's office.

No one turned me in. I was getting away with it... So why did I feel so wretched?

Mum listened carefully before speaking. 'Peter, the Holy Spirit lives within you. When you walk into sin, you take him with you. You know how much God hates sin. Can you imagine how difficult it is for him to be carried into the heart of it? The Holy Spirit is grieving because of what he just experienced – and because you are one with the Spirit you are grieving too.'

There was a long pause.

'This is a good thing, Pete. It is one of the ways we know we are redeemed – this misery we feel after we have sinned.'

God bless that woman!

The Greek word for 'spirit' is *pneuma*. It's the same as the Hebrew word *ruach*. They both mean 'wind, breeze, breath'. I learned that day that the holy wind, breeze and breath of God was blowing through my spirit.

Who is this Spirit? And what is our relationship to him? What do we proclaim when we say: *'I believe in the Holy Ghost'*?

The Spirit is instrumental

> *Now I am going to him who sent me, yet none of you asks me, 'Where are you going?' Because I have said these things, you are filled with grief. But I tell you the truth: It is for your good that I am going away. Unless I go away, the Counsellor will not come to you; but if I go, I will send him to you.*   JOHN 16:5–7

Jesus had just informed the disciples that the end of their earthly journey together had come. There were tears and there was disillusionment, but Jesus told them, 'This is a good thing, men.'

Jesus, while fully God, was also fully man; he was subject to the limitations of a man. He could only be in one place; he could only engage in one conversation at a time; his loving touch was limited by the length of his arm...

Not so with the Holy Spirit, who moves like the wind, freely, all at once, everywhere and anywhere. He may come as a gentle breeze or with the torrent of a tornado. Like the wind, we can't see him, but we can see his work – sometimes we can even feel his touch.

Whenever God does something big, the Holy Spirit is involved:

- *Creation:* The 'Spirit of God was hovering over the waters' as God began to separate his creation into recognizable parts (Genesis 1:2).
- *Incarnation:* When Mary became pregnant, the angel made it clear to Joseph that 'what is conceived in her is from the Holy Spirit' (Matthew 1:20).
- *Crucifixion:* '... the blood of Christ, who through the eternal Spirit offered himself unblemished to God' (Hebrews 9:14).
- *Revelation:* 'All Scripture is God-breathed and is useful for teaching, rebuking, correcting and training in righteousness' (2 Timothy 3:16).

- *Regeneration:* 'The wind blows wherever it pleases. You hear its sound, but you cannot tell where it comes from or where it is going. So it is with everyone born of the Spirit' (John 3:8).
- *Resurrection:* 'And if the Spirit of him who raised Jesus from the dead is living in you, he who raised Christ from the dead will also give life to your mortal bodies through his Spirit, who lives in you' (Romans 8:11).

... and whenever God does something in your life, the Holy Spirit is involved there too.

✑ CONTEMPLATION

I tell you the truth, anyone who has faith in me will do what I have been doing. He will do even greater things than these, because I am going to the Father. JOHN 14:12

The Spirit is interpersonal

But when he, the Spirit of truth, comes, he will guide you into all truth. He will not speak on his own; he will speak only what he hears, and he will tell you what is yet to come.   *John 16:13*

Star Wars hit the cinemas about the time I hit high school. Wow. I don't think there was a boy in America who didn't imagine himself gallivanting throughout the universe with a light-sabre in his hand. *May the Force be with you, Pete! Use the Force, Pete!*

'The Force' was a mystical energy that permeated the universe, a nebulous strength that flowed through the galaxy. While there was some confusion in my mind at the time, it's clear now that the fictional Force is nothing like the reality of the Holy Spirit. The Holy Spirit is not *something* we tap into, but *someone* we relate to.

Look at the verse above. There is a word that is repeated several times. Do you see it? It's the word 'he'. That's a *personal* pronoun (not the impersonal pronoun 'it'). The Holy Spirit is a personality, able to relate to us in a personal way.

? QUESTION

In your opinion, who is easier to think of as being 'personal': The Father, the Son or the Holy Spirit? Why do you feel that way?

The Spirit is intertwined

Therefore go and make disciples of all nations, baptizing them in the name of the Father and of the Son and of the Holy Spirit...   MATTHEW 28:19

It's interesting that Jesus used the word 'name' here. We've got three different names there; shouldn't he have said 'in the names'? No. Jesus is intentionally communicating something important: We have one God in three persons – that's the basic concept of the Trinity. Throughout Scripture we find this reflected in the grammar that God used to describe himself.

It's difficult to comprehend (yet another example of the almighty ability of God that surpasses our understanding), but what's the bottom line? The Holy Spirit is fully God, just as Jesus and the Father are.

✐ CONTEMPLATION

He [the Holy Spirit] will bring glory to me by taking from what is mine and making it known to you. All that belongs to the Father is mine. That is why I said the Spirit will take from what is mine and make it known to you.'   JOHN 16:14–15

The Spirit is involved

Believing that the Holy Spirit is God is good theology. But how does that impact your biography? The Spirit is *instrumental*, *interpersonal* and *intertwined*... that all adds up to an *involved* Holy Spirit. In each of the areas below, you'll first see the uncomfortable truth about who you are *without* Christ and the Holy Spirit. Then you'll see the all-important 'but' that reveals who you are *because* of the Holy Spirit.

(Please, avoid the temptation to simply superficially skim over these truths. As you learn about the Holy Spirit, you have an opportunity to really relate to him *right now*. If you believe in the Holy Ghost, you can believe that he is willing and able to speak to you as he reveals himself to you through the Word and his personal stirring in your soul *right now*.)

Jesus left. The Holy Spirit has come. This is a good thing.

Pray right now that God will open your mind to how good this is for *you*.

I'm corrupted... but he changes me

> *I will give you a new heart and put a new spirit in you; I will remove from you your heart of stone and give you a heart of flesh. And I will put my Spirit in you and move you to follow my decrees and be careful to keep my laws...*   EZEKIEL 36:26–27

One of the great hymns of old asks, 'Were you there when they crucified my Lord?' The first time I heard this song I was a small boy and thought, 'What a silly question! I wasn't even born yet.' But an adult reminded me that Jesus took my sins to the cross and they hadn't even been committed yet. (God is obviously capable of working outside the boundaries of time.) And Romans 6:6 says, 'For we know that our old self was crucified with him.' That's the fulfilment of the Ezekiel prophecy! I've been changed by the presence of the Holy Spirit in my spirit and he now moves in me toward obedience.

I'm weak and alone... but he comes beside me

> *If you love me, you will obey what I command. And I will ask the Father, and he will give you another Counsellor to be with you forever – the Spirit of truth...*
> JOHN 14:15–17

I have to admit, this passage makes me nervous. It forces me to face a continual inner struggle that I have with God: *I want to obey you, Lord; but quite honestly, I also don't want to... But don't think I don't like you. I do. It's just that I, well...*

Jesus puts an end to my babbling self-justifications. He simply says: *If you love me, you will obey. So I'm sending the Counsellor to be with you.*

🐚 DEFINITION

counsellor (koun's[e]-l[e]r, -sl[e]r) n. From the Greek word *parakletos*, meaning *para* ('alongside') and *kletos* ('to call'). So a counsellor is 'one who is called to our side'.

comforter (kŭm'f[e]r-t[e]r) n. From the Latin term *con fortes*, meaning 'to strengthen from within'.

Jesus also described the Holy Spirit as our comforter. As both our counsellor and comforter, the Holy Spirit can be described as 'the one who comes alongside to strengthen and encourage from within'.

The Holy Spirit *enables you to obey*. Equally important, he is there to encourage you and support you as you make these often difficult decisions to obey.

I'm incomplete... but he indwells me

> *... for he [the Holy Spirit] lives with you and will be in you. I will not leave you as orphans, I will come to you. Before long, the world will not see me any more, but you will see me. Because I live, you also will live. On that day you will realize that I am in my Father, and you are in me, and I am in you.*   JOHN 14:17–20

These are clearly amazing words. Jesus is comforting his disciples, telling them that not only is the Holy Spirit *with* them right now, but soon he will be *in* them.

Consider some of the creative geniuses of the world: Michelangelo, Brahms or Beethoven... there is no way that I could create the sort of things that they created... *not unless their genius somehow lived in me*. Then I could do what they did. This passage says that we have the genius of the Holy Spirit of God inside of us.

When I was illustrating this during a sermon one morning, I took a golf club and glove onto the platform. I propped the club up, placed the glove on the handle and crumpled up a piece of paper for the ball. Then I instructed the glove to swing when ready. We all waited. Nothing happened. I repeated my instruction but still nothing. Then I slowly placed my hand in the glove, grabbed the club and swung at the paper ball, sending it flying... right into the face of a first-time visitor sitting in the front row. Let's just say that the analogy was quite a hit with the congregation and made quite an impact on the visitor who, for some odd reason, has yet to return. (He never even thanked me for not using a real ball. Humph.)

After we were done with first aid, I got back to my point: *The glove is useless by itself, but indwelt by the hand, the glove is now capable of anything the hand can do.* Because the Holy Spirit is in us, we are filled with the hand of God. With him inside of us we are enlivened, energized and enabled to experience life as it was intended to be.

✌ QUOTATION

> *He is asking us to be the chief bearers of His likeness in the world. As spirit He remains invisible on this planet. He relies upon us to give flesh to that spirit, to bear the very image of God.*   PAUL BRAND[41]

I'm ignorant... but he instructs me

> *All this I have spoken while still with you. But the Counsellor, the Holy Spirit, whom the Father will send in my name, will teach you all things, and will remind you of everything I have said to you.*   JOHN 14:25–26

The Holy Spirit *teaches* us through the Word of God (which comes to us through teachers, pastors, books, and our own personal studies of the Scriptures). When we hear the Word of God and the Holy Spirit of God instructs us, we grow and we learn. Then, in times of need, the Holy Spirit *reminds* us of what we have learned. *But you cannot be reminded of something you never learned.*

That's why the work that you are doing now is so vitally important. Through this study of the Apostles' Creed, you're absorbing a tremendous amount of truth into your mind. So keep it up! Be encouraged! When it's time to speak the truth to yourself or someone else, the Holy Spirit will *remind* you of what he *taught* you.

? QUESTION

If the Word of God and the teaching and reminding of the Spirit were to become your primary and final authority in life, think of one thing that would change for you.

I'm wayward... but he alerts me

> *And do not grieve the Holy Spirit of God, with whom you were sealed for the day of redemption.*   EPHESIANS 4:30

With the Holy Spirit living in our spirit, it gets uncomfortable when we sin. The Holy Spirit doesn't like sin... and I think we can sense that. We get this feeling in our guts, an awareness that things are out of whack. His grief becomes our grief (like when you shatter the knee of a fellow schoolboy). This is God's way of reminding us that we are walking in a way contrary to his nature – and because we are in Christ, it's now contrary to *our* nature as well. The grief is a reminder that we are a new creation. It is his early warning system – his fog-horn in our ear protecting us from further missteps and alerting us to his grief and sadness. In *his* grief *we* are drawn into repentance and reconnection with our Father.

I'm immature... but he sanctifies me

But the Counsellor, the Holy Spirit, whom the Father will send in my name...
JOHN 14:26

Notice the word 'Holy' from this passage. If it wasn't for the *Holy* Spirit, there would be nothing holy or spiritual about us. Because the Spirit of God is holy, and because he is in us, we are now holy as well!

✎ DEFINITION

sanctify (sāngk't[e]-fī') *tr. v.* 1. To set apart for sacred use. 2. To make holy; to purify. 3. Just one of the absolutely incredible things the *involved* Holy Spirit does in our life.

How does that work?

- We are born with a sinful heart, a dead spirit, and sinful flesh (our desire to do things in our strength instead of his power).
- When we are born again, we get a new heart and the Holy Spirit comes into us.
- Our ongoing struggle with sin is between our spirit (which is holy because of the Holy Spirit), and indwelling sin – the conduit through which the evil one tempts us from within.
- Because the Holy Spirit is in us, he can enable, empower and direct us by being holy *through* us *when we choose to allow him to do so*.

Galatians 5 is one of the many places where the Bible talks about 'walking in the Spirit' rather than living by the 'flesh'. The difference isn't just what you do; the difference is also in how you do it.

Most of the time, when we are tempted, thoughts like this run through our head: '*I'm* not going to do this. *I'm* going to resist. *I'm* going to keep myself pure...'

Well, good luck to *you*, because *you* are going to need it. In your flesh you are not designed to live a holy life – you are just an empty glove, remember? You are designed to have the Holy Spirit live his holy life through you. Huge difference. When you trust in your own strength (the flesh), you're going to fail. When you trust in him, you'll find him overcoming things in your life that you never thought possible.

This is the key: *We must rely on the sanctified Holy Spirit within us to live through us to set us apart in holiness.*

Are you fighting with sin and temptation on your own? It's time to give up and let God into this area of your life.

- Identify the specific area of struggle.
- Tell Jesus, 'I love you and I want to obey...'
- Pray, 'By the power of your Holy Spirit in me, I am choosing to give up and let him be holy through me in this situation.'
- ... And then go do what he prompts you to do. (By the way, he will always tell you to do what God has asked you to do in his Word. He will *never* lead you to do something contrary to biblical principles... That's what Satan and the flesh do.)

It's a continual process of listening to the Holy Spirit, surrendering to the Holy Spirit, and then relying on the Holy Spirit to do what he has told you to do. Get used to this pattern and you'll start to see the Holy Spirit sanctify your life in ways you never thought possible.

? QUESTION

If the Holy Spirit is available and willing to live through us, why doesn't everyone let him do so? What holds you back?

I'm confused... but he illuminates me

But when he, the Spirit of truth, comes, he will guide you into all truth. He will not speak on his own; he will speak only what he hears, and he will tell you what is yet to come.   JOHN 16:13

What is 'Truth'? Jesus is Truth (John 14:6); the Word of God is Truth (John 17:17). The Holy Spirit will guide you into that truth. When you need to see Jesus, when you need illumination from the Scriptures, the Holy Spirit is there leading you where you want to go, lighting the way through the confusion, showing you the next step to take.

I'm distracted... but he models for me

He will bring glory to me by taking from what is mine and making it known to you.

JOHN 16:14

One of my seminary professors was always drilling this into our heads. (When he loosened his tie, we knew that he going to talk from the heart.) One day he said, 'One of the biggest temptations for the Christian is that you want the people to look at you rather than at Christ.' Ouch. That nailed me. It still does. I like it when people compliment *me*. I like it when people come up and say that they enjoyed *my* message. I like it when people look at... *me*. It makes *me* feel good.

I'm not alone here, am I? We are all continually distracted by the temptation to bring glory to ourselves rather than to Jesus.

Now, if anyone has the right to say 'Glorify me', it's the Holy Spirit. He is God. He is instrumental, intertwined and all that... but he doesn't let that go to his head. He knows his purpose: *To bring glory to Jesus*... and, without exception, he always does so. When we get distracted with ourselves, the Holy Spirit's focus on Christ is a powerful role-model for us.

I'm doubtful... but he assures me

Now it is God who makes both us and you stand firm in Christ. He anointed us, set his seal of ownership on us, and put his Spirit in our hearts as a deposit, guaranteeing what is to come.   2 CORINTHIANS 1:21–22

The light of faith only exists in the shadow of doubt. Let's be honest, we believe in some pretty extreme things. God's way of doing things is almost always 180 degrees off from what the world says. Day after day we are bombarded with lies and in the stillness of the evening it's natural to ask, 'Is this really true?'

Last night at dinner I was sharing with my kids how grateful I am that they are all Christians. Our daughter, Annika, piped in, 'I was so young when I trusted Christ for salvation. Sometimes I wonder if I really meant it. Am I really saved?' Libby and I can relate to that. We both received Christ at a very young age too. I had a chance to tell her that it's not our feelings or an amazing 'testimony' that confirm our salvation... It's the Holy Spirit who affirms that we belong to Christ.

❦ QUOTATION

Anyone who says they don't turn out the light at night and sometimes stare at the ceiling wondering if this is all really true, lies.   TONY CAMPOLO

Evidence of the Holy Spirit's work in your life is a reflection of the seal of Jesus' ownership on your life... a security deposit or guarantee of what awaits you in eternity. Doubts are part of the Christian life, but don't leave them to fester – and don't be swayed (either way) by feelings.

Are you walking with Christ? Take a look again at the list of things the Holy Sprit is and does. Do you see his fingerprints on your life? If not, you may want to rethink your journey with him or you may need to re-evaluate if you are allowing him to live through you – perhaps you are trying to live the Christian life in your own strength.

Either way, it's important to ponder this critical phrase of the Apostles' Creed, because it matters when you say: *'I believe in the Holy Ghost.'*

M.A.P.S.

✺ *Meditate*
Ask God to guide your thoughts as you consider these words from the Creed:

I believe in the Holy Ghost.

✺ *Apply*
Review the different ways that the Holy Spirit is involved in your life:

- I'm corrupted... but he changes me.
- I'm weak and alone... but he comes beside me.
- I'm incomplete... but he indwells me.
- I'm ignorant... but he instructs me.
- I'm wayward... but he alerts me.
- I'm immature... but he sanctifies me.
- I'm confused... but he illuminates me.
- I'm distracted... but he models for me.
- I'm doubtful... but he assures me.

Pray that the Holy Spirit would show you just one or two things that he would like to change because of this involvement. Then give up your self-effort and place your total dependence on him to make this change.

✺ *Plot the passages*

- Key word: *Spirit*.
- Key passage: John 16:5–15.
- Supporting passages: Ezekiel 36:26–27; John 14:15–27; Ephesians 4:30.

✳ *Speak*

Speak to self

I believe that the Holy Spirit is:

- *Instrumental* in everything that happens.
- *Interpersonal* and knowable to me as an individual.
- *Intertwined* with the Son and the Father as one God.
- *Involved* in every aspect of my life.

Speak to others

Misunderstandings about the Holy Spirit are causing many believers in Jesus Christ to burn out and become disillusioned in their faith. So many are trying so hard to live the Christian life in their own strength rather than resting and relying on the Holy Spirit.

Who do you know who falls into this category? What creative and caring ways could you use to communicate these truths about the Holy Spirit to them?

How could you be praying for God to reveal his involvement in their lives as the Holy Spirit?

Speak to God

Holy God,

By the power of your Holy Spirit, take these things that you have taught me and make them a reality in my day-to-day life. I know that the work of your sanctifying Spirit is ongoing and continual. Give me the willingness to allow the Holy Spirit to be involved in my life, moment by moment.

I love you, Lord, and I want to obey. But I give up trying in my own strength. In my own power I cannot do what you command, and I cannot resist what you have forbidden. I place my dependence on the Holy Spirit to live this life through me, because I believe he is in me.

Lord, thank you for keeping these truths alive in my mind. Remind me, Holy Spirit, a thousand times a day who you are and what you are doing. I am the glove; you are the hand. Work through me so that together we might bring glory to the name of Jesus Christ.

Amen.

*   *   *

Wes stood in the bedroom, pistol in his mouth, hammer cocked, finger twitching on the trigger.

He had just arrived home and had found an empty house. His wife was gone, so were the kids, the furniture, her clothes...

Empty.

Empty like the day his first wife left. Empty like his heart and life.

Leaving home at sixteen, Wes had been slugging his way through life and school. He learned the hard way how to care for himself, defend himself and promote himself. He also had learned how to numb his pain. He was self-made and self-sustained. But now, two failed marriages later, with multiple addictions overwhelming his soul, he found himself at the end of the road. He had nowhere to turn. He was out of ideas... and he didn't even care.

Maybe it was out of indifference, maybe it was second thoughts, but Wes pulled the gun from his mouth... for the moment. He spent the rest of the evening 'getting his affairs in order'. He woke up the next morning, went to work and settled into his desk.

That day Eric walked by wondering if he should ask Wes one last time. He had asked before, each time receiving a grunt or an 'eye-roll'. Wes's pale and corpse-like complexion convinced Eric that Wes was in desperate need. It was time to ask again.

'Will you go to church with me this weekend? We have a new pastor and I think you'll like him...'

Much to his surprise, Wes agreed to go.

It was my first Sunday at the church. I can honestly say I was not distracted with bringing glory to myself (nor was I focused on bringing glory to Christ). I prayed only for survival; that somehow the flocks of butterflies in my stomach would start flying in formation.

Somewhere in the message that morning I stumbled through the gospel – sharing that Christ hears the desperate plea of someone who wants to make a new start. The Holy Spirit took that chunk of ill-presented truth and taught it to Wes... who said 'yes' to Jesus that day.

Then the Holy Spirit began doing his thing. Some changes came instantly. Other changes are ongoing (just as the process of sanctification continues for all of us). The cycle of alcohol addiction that had plagued the men in his family for generations was broken. His marriage was healed. His family is reunited. And for thirteen years he has been instilling the truth into a new generation of Sunday school kids.

His giving is hilarious. His encouragement is instantaneous. His journey is outrageous. His joy is contagious...

And he's one of my very best friends.

But when it comes down to it, Wes is really just a glove... just like you; just like me. Limp, lifeless, empty... were it not for the Holy Spirit living *in* us and *through* us.

*I believe in God the Father Almighty, maker of heaven and earth; and in Jesus Christ his only Son our Lord; who was conceived by the Holy Ghost, born of the Virgin Mary, suffered under Pontius Pilate, was crucified, dead and buried. He descended into hell; the third day he rose again from the dead. He ascended into heaven, and sits on the right hand of God the Father Almighty. From thence he shall come to judge the quick and the dead. I believe in the Holy Ghost, **the holy catholic church, the communion of saints,** the forgiveness of sins, the resurrection of the body, and the life everlasting. Amen.*

CHAPTER 13

The Saints

But you are a chosen people, a royal priesthood, a holy nation, a people belonging to God, that you may declare the praises of him who called you out of darkness into his wonderful light.   1 PETER 2:9

- *Don't let worry kill you – let the church help.*
- *A song fest was hell at the Methodist church on Wednesday.*
- *Remember in prayer the many who are sick of our church and community.*   CHURCH BULLETIN BLOOPERS

God's team

In the New Testament the church is described in several different word pictures:

- The *bride* of Jesus Christ (Revelation 21:9).
- A *building* where Christ is the cornerstone and we are the bricks in the mortar (Ephesians 2:19–20).
- The *body* of Christ (Romans 12:5).

Those are all great images, but I'd like to introduce a new one: The church as a 'team'. That's right, 'team'. This concept will help us discover what the Creed means and what we believe when we say: *'I believe in the holy, catholic apostolic church, and the communion of saints.'*

Every team has identifying *marks*, a *membership*, a *mission* and a special *mind-set* that sets it apart from all others. As God's team, the church has its own unique characteristics as well. In order to understand the team concept better, we're going to look at a letter that the Apostle Paul wrote to one particular church, the church at Ephesus.

The city of Ephesus was one of the great cultural and information centres of the ancient world. As a major seaport, the city was continually filled with travellers and foreigners... and sailors looking to fill their time with pleasure. No wonder that the goddess Diana was worshipped there. She was the goddess of sex and her worshippers were rather busy.

Into this corrupt mess came the Apostle Paul. He came to proclaim what he had experienced and believed through Jesus Christ. People listened; the Holy

Spirit moved; hearts were changed, then those with these new hearts began to gather together. The First Church of Ephesus had been founded.

Paul left Ephesus and was eventually thrown into prison in Rome. While he was there, his heart and his pen turned toward this fledgling little group of believers. From his dark and musty cell he wrote down words of reminder, instruction and encouragement. In this one letter Paul brings to light a beautiful picture of who the church is and what she is to be about. He is communicating a team vision for the church – a vision that is as necessary for us today as it was in the first century AD.

The marks of the church

The church is one

> There is one body and one Spirit – just as you were called to one hope when you were called. One Lord, one faith, one baptism; one God the Father of all, who is over all and through all and in all.   EPHESIANS 4:4–6

Wait a minute! *One* church? (Why do I always start off with the hard issues?!) I know what you're thinking: Most towns have several churches on one city block. How can we say that the church is one? Because the focus of the true church is not a building, the focus is God himself. Sure, we have dozens of denominations, thousands of buildings and we have different styles, tastes and doctrinal stances on many issues... but the central themes of the Creed are the glue that binds us together.

❦ DEFINITION

Church (chûrch) *n.* The worldwide company of true believers in Jesus Christ, both living and deceased.

We are *one* church. When we believe *in God the Father Almighty, maker of heaven and earth, and in Jesus Christ his only Son our Lord*, we can enter that focus of one.

One body. One Spirit. One hope. One faith. One baptism. One God.

When we lose that focus of *one* we immediately begin to make idols of *our*selves, *our* buildings, *our* statements of faith... and I believe Satan laughs. If we keep that focus of *one*, we tap into the amazing potential of all our gifts and talents and resources, and we can share them for our common mission.

❧ DEFINITION

---

congregation (kŏng′grĭ-gā′sh[e]n) *n*. 1. A group of believers who regularly meet together in one place at the same time. 2. A local squad of God's worldwide team.

Shortly after we relocated to our present site, Prestonwood Baptist Church, one of the largest churches in the world, moved in across the street. They built a magnificent facility and immediately started filling it with 20,000 people on a weekend. It would have been natural to see each other as competitors, but by God's grace he has kept us focused on the fact that the church is *one*.

I took the senior pastor, Jack Graham, to lunch some time ago because our congregation had a need.

'I'd like to ask you a favour,' I said.

'The answer is "Yes",' he responded.

'You don't even know what I'm going to ask!' I said.

'The answer is "Yes",' he said.

(For a second, I considered changing my question!) Our twenty-fifth anniversary as a church was coming up and we needed a large worship centre to get our whole church in for a special service. Jack instantly agreed to allow us to use their building. He even put his staff at our disposal for the event and then refused to charge us a penny!

That's what it means to be part of the team. That's *one*ness; that's 'the church'.

Several years ago our congregation went through a split. Some wanted us to be exercising the sign gifts in the worship service; when they met resistance, these people chose to leave. One of the founding members of our church became the pastor of the splinter congregation, Sojourn Church. Feelings were hurt; pain remained. But a few years later the leadership of the new church approached our elders asking for forgiveness for the disunity they had brought. It was an amazing meeting as the healing forgiveness of Jesus was shared back and forth.

Then, by God's providence (or maybe just his sense of humour), Sojourn Church bought the property directly across the street from us (on the opposite side of Prestonwood). Each Sunday morning their leadership team prays for our church, that God would move in a powerful way in our midst. (There's nothing like having a Charismatic church pray for you!)

Like the Baptists, they lent us their facilities while we were in the middle of a building project. Just a few weeks ago we gave them a tour of our new buildings. Terry, the senior pastor, stopped on the stage of our new worship centre and asked if he could pray for us. Off he went – a most remarkable moment of intercession on our behalf. (If God answers only half his prayer in the affirmative, we'll be busy for years!)

Then Terry pulled out an envelope and said, 'I know we can't help much but we want you to know that we love this church and feel that your ministry is in many respects our ministry too. We would like to contribute to your expansion fund.' He handed me a cheque for $8,000.

Bent Tree stands in North Dallas with one hand grasping the hands of our Baptist siblings to the north and the other grasping the hands of our Charismatic siblings to the south... One church – held together by Christ and our shared beliefs.

? QUESTION

If one of your co-workers said, 'I go to church', what would that mean to you? How do you think our Western concept of 'church' affects the way we practise our beliefs?

The church is holy

For he chose us in him before the creation of the world to be holy and blameless in his sight.
                                                              EPHESIANS 1:4

What does it mean to be 'holy'? The origin of this word means 'to cut, separate, and distinguish between'. The Scottish word for 'church' is *kirk*, which comes from the German word *kirche*, which comes from the Greek word *Kiriake*, which means 'Lord'.

To say that we are a 'holy church' means that we are a group that is 'separated unto the Lord'. He has made us distinct from other groups for the purpose of bringing glory to himself. And how has he done that? By infusing our individual and group lives with the power of his very own Holy Spirit.

? QUESTION

In your opinion, how does God's team differ from other teams? Would you say your local congregation is 'separated unto the Lord'? Why or why not?

The church is catholic

When we say that the church is 'catholic', we spell that word with a small 'c' and not a capital 'C'. The Creed isn't referring to the Roman Catholic Church; it's referring to the 'universal' church (that's what the word 'catholic' means). The word has changed its meaning over the centuries, so some of the most recent versions of the Apostles' Creed actually use the word 'universal' instead: '... *the holy, universal and apostolic church'.*

☙ DEFINITION

universal (yōō'n[e]-vûr's[e]l) *adj.* Of, relating to, extending to, or affecting the entire world or all within the world.

catholic (kāth'[e]-lĭk) *adj.* Including or concerning all humankind; universal.

How is the church universal?

- It responds to a *universal need* – for *all* have sinned (Romans 6:23).
- If tells of a *universal remedy* – Christ died for *all* (1 Peter 3:18).
- If follows a *universal mandate* – 'Go into *all* the world...' (Mark 16:15).
- It has a *universal* membership – If *anyone* opens the door of their life to Christ, he will come in, regardless of colour, culture, language etc. (Revelation 3:20).
- It looks forward to a *universal consummation* – the time is coming when *all* members of the church will worship together in the same place (Revelation 20).

The forgiving love of Jesus Christ is not restricted by national or political frontiers. The church crosses *all* boundaries of race, culture, social status... even *all* denominations. Tragically, however, there are plenty of people in every denomination who are simply going through the motions of 'church' (going to a building, dressing a certain way, singing, praying...), who are not a part of the universal church because they have not accepted the universal remedy for their universal need. They might know about Jesus; they might even be serving him to the best of their ability... but they've never taken that step of faith to know him personally.

✆ CONTEMPLATION

Many will say to me on that day, 'Lord, Lord, did we not prophesy in your name and in your name drive out demons and in your name perform many miracles?' Then I will tell them plainly, 'I never knew you. Away from me, you evildoers!'

MATTHEW 7:22–23

So don't criticize somebody else's denomination – and don't think that just because you belong to a certain denomination, you're good to go. The true church is *universal*; but you need to make a *personal* choice to join.

The church is apostolic

Here is an interesting thought: Almost every single one of us can trace our spiritual heritage back to one of the original apostles. (Throughout history, God has spoken directly to some people through dreams and visions. The vast majority of us, however, came to know Christ because of someone telling us what they had been told – and that person had been told by somebody else, who was told by somebody else...)

Whether it was the Bible placed in a hotel room by someone, or the words of a song on the radio sung by someone, or the written words on a small gospel tract given by someone, God's normal mode is to use *someone* to touch someone else. Likewise, this generation and the ones to follow will be touched by you and me.

The gospel and the foundational teachings of true Christianity can all be traced back to the Apostles. God used them to start the church and then preserve the message of the church through the written Word of God. That's why we are commanded to 'continue steadfastly in the faith and teaching of the first Apostles.' It's fine to debate, speculate and pontificate about spiritual issues, but the words and teachings of the Apostles in the New Testament must always be the central core of belief for the matters of the church.

The members of the church

Becoming a member of a professional sports team comes through intensely hard work, dedication and personal sacrifice. Even with passionate effort, the chances of playing the game at that level are very remote.

Becoming part of God's team is entirely different. It comes through *belief*. If we believe in the Lord Jesus Christ and that God raised him from the dead, we will be saved (Romans 10:9). That automatically gets us our membership card into the universal church. Because, again, our position is not dependent on what we have done but on what Christ has done on our behalf. Once we are in, we become a part of what the Creed describes as 'the communion of saints'.

🔖 Quotation

Jesus call[ed] to his side a roving band of followers and friends. And what an astonishing company it is! It included guerrilla fighters (Simon the zealot, Luke 6:15) together with tax collectors (Matthew 10:3). The guerrillas fought in the mountains to expel the Romans, the tax collectors collaborated with Roman rule... The company also included ignorant laborers and a number of women... Some of them had apparently been prostitutes, others, like Mary Magdalene, may have been healed of disease or demon possession (Luke 8:2), at least one was the woman of an official of Herod's court (Luke 8:3). THEODORE W. JENNINGS, JR[42]

'The communion of saints'. That sounds really official, considering we are such a group of misfits. The word 'saint' is translated from the Greek word *hagioi*, which means 'sanctified and holy'. No credit goes to us for this, of course. Our holiness comes only from the Holy Spirit's work in us and the work he does through us.

But we are a *communion* too. We have things *in common* that make us a powerful force *if* we work together as a team. Ephesians 4:11–12 says:

It was he [Christ] who gave some to be apostles, some to be prophets, some to be evangelists, and some to be pastors and teachers, to prepare God's people for works of service, so that the body of Christ may be built up...

Look at that verse carefully. Pastors are not supposed to be running around out there doing everything while everyone else sits and watches from a thing called a 'pew'. Their purpose is to 'prepare God's people for works of service'. Biblical pastors are more like coaches. They guide a team effort in the game that really matters.

That's why it is so, so vital that we are each connected in the 'communion of saints'. We each have gifts and skills that are needed to 'build up the body of Christ'. If we aren't integrated into the universal church through real communion with other believers, we all *universally* suffer.

If you're struggling with living together in a church, the whole book of Ephesians offers no-nonsense advice for those who heed the call to be connected in the communion of saints. It's worth reading and seriously considering.

? QUESTION

What holds you back from fully immersing yourself in the communion of saints?

The mission of the church

Let's be honest, being a part of any team has its costs. How many hundreds of gifted athletes have walked away from their coaches and teammates because it just didn't seem to be worth the hassle?

As part of God's team, you might feel the same way. You may very well be one of those faithful and devoted members who rarely misses a practice, who works out faithfully, and who stands as a faithful cheerleader.

But does it sometimes seem like something is missing? Have you ever wondered what the purpose is for the team? All athletic teams have a tangible goal in front of them at all times. They know the immediate goal is to make a certain number of points, shave critical seconds off their time, win a critical match to advance into the semi-finals... and it's all focused on working towards the *big* win – some sort of championship where the true victor gets their crown.

Does the universal 'church team' have such a goal or are we all just running around getting worn out playing some sort of never-ending religious game? There is a goal, there is a purpose and over the centuries, some have summarized it this way:

To know God and to make him known.

Does that sound too simple? Too 'fuzzy'? Too difficult to measure? It is for many people. (It sounds clichéd and open-ended – a nice motto but a really lousy *purpose* statement.)

A team vision needs to be S.M.A.R.T.: *Specific, Measurable, Attainable, Reasonable* and *Timely*. And the cool thing is that Christ gave a very S.M.A.R.T. mission to the church:

Then the eleven disciples went to Galilee, to the mountain where Jesus had told them to go. When they saw him, they worshipped him; but some doubted. Then Jesus came to them and said, 'All authority in heaven and on earth has been given to me. Therefore go and make disciples of all nations, baptizing them in the name of the Father and of the Son and of the Holy Spirit, and teaching them to obey everything I have commanded you. And surely I am with you always, to the very end of the age.'   MATTHEW 28:16–20

Specific

Jesus told us to go and make disciples of all nations. That's very specific, involving evangelism, training, teaching... the goal is to establish congregations of believers in every nation. But what is a 'nation'? Jesus isn't talking about *political* nations (like Canada, Zambia, or India). The word 'nation' is translated from the Greek word *ethnos*, from which we get our word 'ethnic'. An *ethnos* is sometimes called a 'people group' – a group of people with their own language and culture.

Measurable

Let's put some numbers to this. The statistics vary depending on your specific definition of 'nation', but the Joshua Project calculates that there are 16,291 distinct peoples in the world; 6,873 of these people groups have little or no current access to the gospel and have no extension of the church to be a part of. Of the 6.6 billion people on earth, 2.7 billion fall in this 'unreached' category.[43]

So, that's our goal: As a unified body of believers, according to our individual gifts and talents, in the enabling of the Spirit, we are to labour together to reach these nations with the message of Christ.

Attainable

Can this be done? First off, let me take my hat off to you right now. By working your way through this book, you are equipping yourself to be more effective in this mission. By learning the Apostles' Creed and learning to navigate through the scriptural support behind it, you are going to be far better capable and able to communicate the gospel to those around you... and maybe those who are a long way away.

But 6,800 nations? Yes, I know that sounds like a lot. Far more than any one person could attempt; far more than any single congregation could accomplish. But the *universal* church *can* do it.

Right now we are seeing a massive worldwide movement within the church to adopt and embrace this mission. Missionaries from all corners of the globe are beginning to mobilize their passions and their resources to reach this goal. The results are astounding. Technology is helping amazingly. Today the world is smaller, travel is faster, communication is instantaneous – even the internet is being used to reach these needy nations. (A group of computer geeks with Campus Crusade for Christ, for example, is making the gospel available to hundreds of millions of people with the click of a mouse.)

Actually, there's no question that the fulfilment of this mission will be attained. Read very carefully this passage from the book of Revelation:

After this I looked and there before me was a great multitude that no one could count, from every nation, tribe, people and language, standing before the throne and in front of the Lamb. They were wearing white robes and were holding palm branches in their hands. And they cried out in a loud voice: 'Salvation belongs to our God, who sits on the throne, and to the Lamb.'

All the angels were standing round the throne and around the elders and the four living creatures. They fell down on their faces before the throne and worshipped God, saying: 'Amen! Praise and glory and wisdom and thanks and honour and power and strength be to our God for ever and ever. Amen!'

REVELATION 7:9–12

Now, read that out loud, with *feeling*! Close your eyes and imagine yourself standing among this multitude. Hear the praise being raised to God in every language; see the rainbow of skin tones and hear the roar as we all stand together to worship our Saviour and God...

Attainable? Yes. But more than that, *it's promised*.

Reasonable

Consider this: There are *hundreds of thousands* of solid Bible-believing congregations in the United States alone. God only knows how many millions there are in the world. Realistically, there are *several hundred* existing congregations for *each* unreached people group. What could happen if we really started to work as a team to reach this goal?

How about money? Current giving by American churches toward mission efforts for unreached nations totals less than 2 per cent of income. Pretty pathetic; but also very hopeful. We could reasonably *triple* our financial resources by just giving 6 per cent of church income to missions to unreached groups.

If we look at the matter from a team perspective, the mission becomes *very* reasonable.

Timely

And this gospel of the kingdom will be preached in the whole world as a testimony to all nations, and then the end will come.   MATTHEW 24:14

The completion of the mission of Christ (to go and make disciples of all nations) will come at a critical time in end-times history: Just before 'the end'. What 'the end' means depends on your view about when Christ returns, and that can get a little complicated to figure out. (See Chapter 11 on 'The Sure Return' for more discussion.) But the main point is this: in time, the mission *will* be complete.

On that day, the holy, catholic and apostolic church will be complete and the communion of saints will be experienced in its full, eternal glory.

❧ Quotation

We are privileged to believe. We are privileged to put what we believe into practical application. And we are privileged to live among men and women in such a way that our beliefs will take root in their lives and will be a help and a blessing to them. But it all depends on what you believe, how thoroughly you believe it, and how the implications of that work out in your life.   STUART BRISCOE[44]

The Mind-set of the church

The 'church' and the 'communion of saints' must be defined in the context of the cause of Christ. Understanding our mission infuses purpose and vision into the church like nothing else. Good music, animated preaching, big buildings... nothing can substitute for a biblical understanding of the church and its mission, *nothing*.

When we see our place within the *marks, membership and mission* of the universal church, an unstoppable *mindset* begins to fuel our faith: God has us here for a reason and that reason is worth both living and dying for!

? Question

Consider the following statement carefully: 'If I am not living for a cause worth dying for, I am the greatest of fools, for certainly, one day, I will die.'
Do you agree or disagree? Defend your answer.

M.A.P.S.

❧ *Meditate*
Ask God to guide your thoughts as you consider these words from the Creed:

I believe in... the holy catholic church, the communion of saints...

❧ *Apply*
Consider ways in which your gifts and skills could synergize within the universal church to fulfil God's purposes. Don't be shy and don't limit the possibilities by

the past or the present! The Almighty God made you for a purpose and his Spirit fills you for a reason.

Pray that you will be willing to obey him in the next step of faith and obedience he has prepared for you.

❧ *Plot the passages*

- Key word: *Saints*.
- Key passage: 1 Peter 2:9.
- Supporting passages: Ephesians 4:4–11; Matthew 24:14; 28:16–20; Revelation 7:9–12.

❧ *Speak*

Speak to self
I believe…

- That the church is God's team.
- That the church is one, holy, universal and apostolic.
- That our mission is Specific, Measurable, Attainable, Reasonable and Timely.
- That believing in the church leads to a mindset of sacrificial devotion to the cause of Christ.

Speak to others
Sharing the vision for the marks, members, mission, and mindset of the church is something that God can do through you. Is God asking you to reach out to other believers with this message?

- Who do you know who is discouraged and unfocused in their faith?
- What prayers of healing can you offer for those who have been hurt by their involvement in churches in the past?
- How could you communicate the vision of the church and its mission in a way that would give them hope and direction?

Pray patiently and expectantly as God raises up his team!

Speak to God

Almighty Coach,

The church is your team and by your grace you have allowed me to be one of its members. Give me a clear understanding of what that means – what it means to be a part of the communion of saints, the holy, catholic and apostolic church. Hook my heart with a passion for the mission of sharing the gospel with every nation. Free me from any legalistic guilt or pressure. Give me an enthusiastic and engaged commitment to see the gifts that you have given me used in the context of the church you are building.

I lay myself before you again today as one who is weak and inadequate for the tasks ahead... yet you are the one who promises your Holy Spirit, who promises to work through me for your glory.

Amen.

*   *   *

You have to love the church. You *really* do.

Is it the perfect team? Of course not. Only the continual grace and forgiveness of God keeps the whole thing from going up in smoke. Local congregations can hand out plenty of headaches and hassles – as these church bulletin announcements reveal:

- The senior choir invites any member of the congregation who enjoys sinning to join the choir.
- The youth group is saving aluminium cans, bottles and other items to be recycled. Proceeds will be used to cripple children.
- The outreach committee has enlisted 25 visitors to make calls on people who are not afflicted with any church.

Yes, sometimes those are the marks we focus on... the sinning, the crippling, the afflicting... things which fester whenever we forget to focus on our true mission, whenever we forget that we are *one*, whenever we forget that the universal church is nothing more and nothing less than the very life of Christ flowing through each of our lives as we live together as a team.

When the church is functioning as the church was designed to, it is a beautiful and powerful thing. From around the globe we see a great kaleidoscope of blessings as Christ works through all of us to do what we could never do on our own. As I was writing this chapter, I received one snapshot of this from right inside our own congregation:

Dear Pete,

I am fairly new to the church family! I just wanted to share what God has done through the body in my own life with you.

In September of 2007 I found out I had a brain tumor the size of a tennis ball and had to have immediate surgery... I was in Nashville speaking at the time, so Tammy, a dear friend, flew to Nashville just to be with me. Then when I had surgery 2 weeks later, Sheryl and Maynard flew to Nashville to be with me for 30 minutes after my surgery. I kept thinking, 'Who are these people?' I had NEVER in all of my Christian life experienced this kind of 'body' before.

My life group and small group Bible study surrounded me with prayers, phone calls, emails, providing meals, driving me around, taking care of me and even financial support to help pay for medical bills (the list is too great to even say)... Again the body kept pouring out their love to me. Yet they hardly even knew me! But that didn't seem to matter.

Earlier this year, as the bills piled up and I was really hurting financially, it was the benevolence fund that paid all of my bills for Feb 2008! over and above all I could ask or imagine!

Now, the financial support has been overwhelming, but the love, acceptance, caring, I have received from this group of people has been far more than I could ever ask or imagine!

I still ask myself, 'Who ARE these people?', but I know the answer is: they are Jesus with skin!

I thank God every day that he brought me to this congregation. I have grown more in these months than I have in a very long time. There is no healing without relationship...

This type of thing happens all the time all over the world. It is called *the communion of the saints*. When we humbly and sincerely embrace the mission we have been given and allow God's Spirit to lead and work through us, then we become the holy, catholic and apostolic church, and there is no other team on earth like it!

*I believe in God the Father Almighty, maker of heaven and earth; and in Jesus Christ his only Son our Lord; who was conceived by the Holy Ghost, born of the Virgin Mary, suffered under Pontius Pilate, was crucified, dead and buried. He descended into hell; the third day he rose again from the dead. He ascended into heaven, and sits on the right hand of God the Father Almighty. From thence he shall come to judge the quick and the dead. I believe in the Holy Ghost, the holy catholic church, the communion of saints, **the forgiveness of sins,** the resurrection of the body, and the life everlasting. Amen.*

CHAPTER 14

Second Chances

Man is the only animal that blushes or needs to.   MARK TWAIN

Yet who of us is not ready to admit that there is a tragic flaw at the very heart and center of human experience?... There are tendencies within me that frighten me, pools of darkness I can neither understand nor explain.   RON JAMES

'Do you know what your problem is?' he asked. 'You don't really believe in grace!'

I could feel my gut tightening. I stayed calm on the outside, but inside I didn't like where this was going. The man across from me was a paid counsellor and I was shelling out good money to have him speak into my life... But this idea that I didn't believe in grace? I nearly laughed out loud.

'I do too!' I coolly shot back. 'I just finished preaching a whole series on it!'

He smiled. 'You could preach a series, write a book and tattoo the word on your forehead if you want, but I'm telling you that you haven't *owned* grace yet, Pete. Why would you refuse to forgive yourself when you have already been forgiven by God?'

... Long silence.

He picked up Phillip Yancey's book *What's so Amazing about Grace?* and began to read: 'There is nothing we can do to make God love us more... there is nothing we can do to make God love us less...'[45]

I heard the words but my mind began to argue with Yancey's statements. *Certainly I can increase or decrease God's love for me because of my efforts... Certainly I must try to deserve his acceptance...*

I bought Yancey's book on the way home and immediately started reading about a teenage girl from Traverse City who ran away from home and ended up on the cold, harsh streets of Detroit... As her story unfolded, tears began to well up in my eyes and I began asking a question that I thought I had long ago answered:

Do I believe in 'grace'? Am I being honest when I say, 'I believe in... the forgiveness of sins'?

Imprisoned

The evil deeds of a wicked man ensnare him; the cords of his sin hold him fast.
PROVERBS 5:22

Freedom, I think, is a God-given desire. No one likes to be tied down. We fight for national freedom and support political freedom, but the most important freedom – the one that is truly experienced in the soul – is most often overlooked. Whether we fully realize it or not, we can be bound up by our sin and the sins of others in the deepest part of our being. We get so used to the burden that we aren't even aware of the ways it destroys, decays and shreds our life. It's like a string tightly wound and woven through our body and mind... crippling us, cutting off our circulation, immobilizing us.

Throughout the Bible several words are used to describe it:

- **S**in (*hamartia*): An archery term for falling short of the target.
- **T**ransgression (*parabasis*): It means going out of bounds or trespassing.
- **R**ebellion (*adikia*): Making a decision to do wrong.
- **I**niquity (*a' won*): Wickedness and wrongdoing.
- **N**ot knowing (*opheilo*): To be ignorant of what is right.
- **G**odlessness (*asibeia*): To deliberately refuse to do God's will.

✐ CONTEMPLATION

They answered him, 'We are Abraham's descendants and have never been slaves of anyone. How can you say that we shall be set free?'

Jesus replied, 'I tell you the truth, everyone who sins is a slave to sin.'

JOHN 8:33–34

Sometimes our slavery to sin is very obvious: The anorexia of the ballerina, the pornography of the businessman, the gossip of the church busybody, the alcohol of the man wandering the streets... Always it seems to lurk in the dark corners of our secret thoughts – an everpresent slavemaster that refuses to let our souls be free.

Sin disqualifies us from heaven, disrupts our relationship with God and destroys our life. I mean, think about it: Hasn't sin completely trashed everything? It wrecks our relationships; it pollutes our thoughts; it destroys our world...

❧ QUOTATION

You have not yet considered the heavyweight sin is.

ST ANSELM, ARCHBISHOP OF CANTERBURY (1093–1109)

The Apostle Paul fought against the insidiousness of sin. Honest and open about his struggles, he described the tension between indwelling sin and the desire to obey God in his spirit:

> *For we know that the Law is spiritual, but I am of flesh, sold into bondage to sin. For what I am doing, I do not understand; for I am not practising what I would like to do, but I am doing the very thing I hate... For I know that nothing good dwells in me, that is, in my flesh; for the willing is present in me, but the doing of the good is not. For the good that I want, I do not do, but I practise the very evil that I do not want... Wretched man that I am! Who will set me free from the body of this death? Thanks be to God through Jesus Christ.*   ROMANS 7:14–15, 18–19, 24–25 (NASB)

I don't have to describe to you the emotion behind those words, do I? You know the feeling. Something in our body is programmed to sin... and yet something in our spirit deeply desires to obey. Indwelling sin is like a sliver in our finger; it is certainly present and it is a real pain, but it is not who we are! This is the struggle of all authentic believers and it's actually an encouraging sign that your spirit has been made new by God's Spirit. But it's still frustrating and it still entangles us.

How are we set free? Thank God that it's been done through Jesus Christ!

? QUESTION

In what ways are you currently experiencing the power of sin? What sins from your past continue to bind you with guilt and shame?

Freed by forgiveness

> *Search me, O God, and know my heart; test me and know my anxious thoughts. See if there is any offensive way in me, and lead me in the way everlasting.*

PSALM 139:23–24

Freedom is never free. Freedom for our soul was purchased by Jesus Christ that dark day he hung on the cross. The price has been paid. His blood has been shed instead of ours. His resurrection confirms the victory. He has come to set the captives free...

The Prophet Daniel showed the way. From all outward appearances he was a good man – yet he seemed to be experiencing that gnawing grind of sin stirring in himself and in his people. Then through the Prophet Jeremiah he saw the coming judgment for his sin and the sins of the Israelites – a 'desolation' of their beloved Jerusalem that would last seventy years.

Daniel 9 reveals the essential steps that break the strength of the STRINGs. It starts in the heart in a *posture* of humility (Daniel 9:3) and an awareness of God's holiness that causes *praise* (9:4). Daniel never forgets that God is God and that he is not. So when it's time to *pray* Daniel approaches his almighty Creator from a healthy *perspective* that opens the door of forgiveness's freedom.

1. Admit your sin

We have sinned and done wrong. We have been wicked and have rebelled; we have turned away from your commands and laws...   DANIEL 9:5

2. Admit your shame

Lord, you are righteous, but this day we are covered with shame... O Lord, we and our kings and our princes and our fathers are covered with shame because we have sinned against you... We have not obeyed the Lord our God or kept the laws he gave us through his servants the prophets...   DANIEL 9:7–10

3. Admit your stubbornness

You have fulfilled the words spoken against us and against our rulers by bringing upon us great disaster... yet we have not sought the favour of the Lord our God by turning from our sins and giving attention to your truth... yet we have not obeyed him.   DANIEL 9:12–14

4. Admit your smallness

Now, O Lord our God, who brought your people out of Egypt with a mighty hand and who made for yourself a name that endures to this day, we have sinned, we have done wrong.   DANIEL 9:15

After Daniel gets his perspective right, he's in a *position* to make his requests of God:

- 'Don't be angry' (verse 16).
- 'Hear my prayer' (verse 17).
- 'Look with favour' (verse 17).
- 'See my distress' (verse 18).
- 'Show your mercy' (verse 18).
- 'Forgive my sin' (verse 19).

Those who approach God as Daniel did need not fear that forgiveness will be withheld. The Almighty forgives immediately and completely, cleansing us from sin's guilt and shame.

> *If we confess our sins, he is faithful and just and will forgive us our sins and purify us from all unrighteousness.*   1 JOHN 1:9

But what about freedom?

In his book *The Grace Awakening*, Chuck Swindoll reminds us of a powerful lesson from history: On 18 December 1865 slavery was legally abolished by the Thirteenth Amendment of the Constitution of the United States – *yet the vast majority of slaves in the South continued to live just as they had before.* A war had been fought, a president assassinated and the Constitution amended – but their blood-bought freedom was not being experienced.

Tragic? Yes. But the tragedy continues in the human soul today. Christ has died. Good Friday was our Eternal Emancipation Proclamation – the day that sinners were officially set free... *yet the vast majority of Christians are still living as though they were slaves to sin.* Swindoll puts it this way:

> *President Grace legally freed us from our lifelong master Sin and his wife Shame. Theoretically we were freed when we believed in Christ, but practically speaking, our plantation owners do everything in their power to keep us ignorant, afraid, and thinking like a slave.*[46]

I say, 'Enough!'

The fullness of forgiveness

Can I ask you to say a quick prayer right now? We are standing on the threshold of four powerful forgiveness principles – ones that can liberate your soul and absolutely transform your life. Just stop for a moment and ask God that he would speak to you directly through his Word and his Spirit.

Did you pray? Come on, I'm serious! If you don't ask God to illuminate the power in this, there's no way you're going to be able to grasp it with just your brain. The Spirit has got to make it real in your soul...

Legally forgiven

> *In him we have redemption through his blood, the forgiveness of sins, in*
> *accordance with the riches of God's grace.*   EPHESIANS 1:7

Jesus said he came to *fulfil* the Law of God, not to abolish it (Matthew 5:17). God created the laws of justice, so the payment for forgiveness must be made or our sin cannot be legally paid for. Who has paid the price? Jesus Christ, with his own blood, because of grace. When we get to the so-called 'Pearly Gates' we will have the *legal right* to enter.

✒ DEFINITION

redemption (rĭ-dĕmp'sh[e]n) *n.* 1. The total recovery of something pawned or mortgaged. 2. The complete payment of an obligation or debt.

Personally forgiven

But what about now? I simply cannot offer a more beautiful picture of the *personal* forgiveness of God than the story of the Prodigal Son. In this heart-wrenching parable we see a young man who took his father's inheritance, walked away from his home, and immersed himself in every pleasure that money could buy. This dude pulled out all the stops. But the STRINGs began to tighten their grip. As the money ran out he found himself with nothing except empty shame and an empty stomach. His thoughts began to turn towards home and he began to rehearse his plea: 'Father, I have sinned against heaven and against you. I am no longer worthy to be called your son; make me like one of your hired men.'

Hoping for nothing more than to be allowed back on the property as a workman, he headed for home. *But* (there's that word again!)...

> *But while he was still a long way off, his father saw him and was filled with*
> *compassion for him; he ran to his son, threw his arms around him and kissed*
> *him.*   LUKE 15:20

The son returned not to a scolding but to a full-on celebration... And so it is with you. *God runs to you!* He's so excited to be back together with you that he just throws his arms around you and kisses you... Why? Because he really loves you and because he *can*. In Christ you are redeemed completely, so God can forgive you on a *personal* level absolutely.

This was a big part of my problem. When it came to forgiveness, my theology was right, but my biography was all screwed up. I could tell *you* what to believe, but *I* wasn't living it. Deep inside I was still trying to earn God's unconditional love, I was still trying to make myself worthy of his grace. It was burning me out, of course. In my own strength I was trying to do something that has already been done.

⑆ QUOTATION

I'd love you unconditionally, but you just don't deserve it.   AUTHOR UNKNOWN

? QUESTION

Why might the Prodigal Son have chosen not to return to his father? Do you see any of those tendencies in yourself?

Continually forgiven

The next time I was in the counsellor's office, the thoughts about grace and forgiveness were still flying through my head. Just when I thought I was getting it figured out, he dropped another new concept on me: *God's grace covers my sin in Christ the very moment the sin is committed.* It is gone, forgotten, as though it never happened. I'll still have to deal with the consequences, but my sin is *continually* forgiven!

Continual forgiveness is awesome because our struggles with sin are continually awful. It would be nice if temptation went away when you become a Christian, but it doesn't. In fact, sometimes it gets much worse. Open the Bible to almost any book and you'll find men and women entangled with their sinful behaviour... and you'll also find a God who continually forgives. (You'll also see that God continually uses these people for mighty works and eternal purposes!) Consider Peter who denies (Matthew 26) or Moses who doubts (Exodus 3) or David who commits adultery and murder (2 Samuel 11)... These are the people God used to build his church, deliver his people, and lead a mighty nation.

How is that possible? Because of continual forgiveness.

Let's take a look back at Daniel 9. This next section is so awesome that you just have to read it yourself:

While I was speaking and praying, confessing my sin and the sin of my people Israel and making my request to the Lord my God for his holy hill – while I was still in prayer, Gabriel, the man I had seen in the earlier vision, came to me in swift flight about the time of the evening sacrifice. He instructed me and said to me, 'Daniel, I have now come to give you insight and understanding. As soon as you began to pray, an answer was given, which I have come to tell you, for you are highly esteemed.'
                                                                    DANIEL 9:20–23

Now that's about the clearest picture of God's continual forgiveness that I have ever seen. The instant Daniel began to pray, God's answer was given. As soon as Daniel started getting his posture right, God started running to him and hugging him and kissing him and telling him it's all right. In fact, God was there all along. Even though Daniel and his people had turned their backs on him, he had not deserted them or left them. (If you think about it, where could they go where God wasn't?! It's pretty ridiculous to think that they could ditch an omnipresent being!) They only needed to turn around in their hearts to find him still there, arms still open, forgiveness continually flowing.

✍ CONTEMPLATION

Where can I go from your Spirit? Where can I flee from your presence? If I go up to the heavens, you are there; if I make my bed in the depths, you are there. If I rise on the wings of the dawn, if I settle on the far side of the sea, even there your hand will guide me, your right hand will hold me fast.   PSALM 139:7–10

Doesn't that say something about how badly God wants a relationship with you? What an incredible God we serve! *He wants the relationship even more than we do, and his continual forgiveness allows us to be one in Christ with him always.* Because our redemption is total, our forgiveness is continual: That's his promise.

That realization can radically change the way that we pray about forgiveness. Rather than continually *asking* for forgiveness, we can continually *thank* him for forgiveness. We can focus on the fact that we *are* forgiven in Christ. Our confession of sin becomes agreeing with God about sin, and our praise erupts because he has already granted us forgiveness for that sin. Some of us are still begging and asking for freedom that we already have!

Transformationally forgiven

> *For we know that our old self was crucified with him so that the body of sin might be done away with*, that we should no longer be slaves to sin – *because anyone who has died has been freed from sin.*
> ROMANS 6:6–7

Back in the counsellor's office, things were starting to come together. It was almost embarrassing. I had grown up in a great Christian family, gone to a Christian college, and had a Masters of Divinity degree from a respected seminary... and I still hadn't gotten it. I was much closer now, but freedom from sin was still one significant realization away:

He hasn't just forgiven my *sin*; he has forgiven *me*, the person. He can do that because through the cross I have been *transformed* into a new creature.

The book of Romans teaches that all are 'in Adam' when we are born. This means that before the Holy Spirit came in and made you new, your *old self* (some call this the 'old man') was enslaved to *indwelling sin* (the voice inside you that tells you to do sinful things). But the moment you put your trust in Christ, you were 'in Christ'. Your *old self* has been crucified and a new creation has taken its place. This new self is not enslaved to indwelling sin like the old one was.

✐ CONTEMPLATION

Don't you know that all of us who were baptized into Christ Jesus were baptized into his death? We were therefore buried with him through baptism into death in order that, just as Christ was raised from the dead through the glory of the Father, we too may live a new life... We know that our old self was crucified with him so that the body of sin might be done away with, that we should no longer be slaves to sin – because anyone who has died has been freed from sin... In the same way, count yourselves dead to sin but alive to God in Christ Jesus.   ROMANS 6:3–4, 6–7, 11

Some might ask, 'How could I have been crucified with Christ when I wasn't even born yet?' My wife Libby explains it this way. The moment we trust Christ, we are one with him. Our sins are erased and his life indwells us. Because his life is eternal (going back into eternity and forward into everlastingness) and because we are now united with him, he can take us to the cross. It is incredible, isn't it? We were baptized (identified) in his death; the person we once were died that day.

That's enough scriptural meat to keep you chewing for a lifetime! With each morsel you swallow and digest, a new surge of energy flows through the soul:

Live a new life... old self crucified... no longer slaves to sin... freed from sin... alive to God in Christ...

When I was in seminary I worked at a restaurant. I had never waited on tables before and the manager was always on my case. He was critical and demanding for the whole two years I was there. I quit right after I graduated. What a relief!

A few weeks later Libby and I went back, but this time to eat. When I walked in the front door the manager was there as usual, staring at me. I stood tall, smiled at him and walked to my seat. I felt his eyes on me but it didn't matter any more – I was free from him and I knew it. I suppose he could have come over and demanded, 'Pete, get your apron back on and take care of the table in the corner! Now!' And I suppose I could have chosen to obey him and fall back into the bondage I had been liberated from. But the joy was that now I didn't have to! I could choose to say 'no' to him because I was different – I was a graduate instead of a waiter and he had no power over me any more.

Do you see the parallel here? the manager is indwelling sin, but because I am a new person in Christ, I don't have to obey sin any more! I'm forgiven; I'm free; I'm transformed.

The same goes for you. Your old history ended at the cross; your new history begins with the resurrection. Slavery to sin has ended. You can now choose to walk in freedom. It is now 'normal' to walk in holiness as you allow Jesus to live through you. We will certainly have our moments of temporary insanity when we forget who we are and sin again, but it doesn't have to be that way any more.

That's the freedom of complete forgiveness: Legal, personal, continual and transformational forgiveness.

The forgiveness of other people's sin

Now, let's head in another direction. What about the forgiveness of the sins committed against us?

> *Therefore, as God's chosen people, holy and dearly loved, clothe yourselves with compassion, kindness, humility, gentleness and patience. Bear with each other and forgive whatever grievances you may have against one another. Forgive as the Lord forgave you. And over all these virtues put on love, which binds them all together in perfect unity.* COLOSSIANS 3:12–14

Unless we are willing to allow God to work through us in order to forgive the sins of others toward us, we will again be enslaved and tied by the STRINGs of sin.

Unforgiveness leads to bitterness, anger, resentment, hatred, stress, conflict ulcers (and that's just for starters). Who wants to live like that?! Satan wins on all accounts if you allow yourself to become a judgmental victim. Be free! Cut the strings of sins committed against you by asking God to work his healing of forgiveness through you toward those who have wronged you.

In the book *Rest Assured*, Bill Ewing said:

> *Forgiveness is the divine transaction, paid in full by the blood of Jesus, which frees both the offender and the offended from the bondage of sin. The act of forgiveness follows in the footsteps of Christ to the very shadow of the Cross.*

Are you willing to follow in these footsteps? If so, another facet of freedom from sin will be yours.

✍ CONTEMPLATION

Do not repay anyone evil for evil. Be careful to do what is right in the eyes of everybody. If it is possible, as far as it depends on you, live at peace with everyone. Do not take revenge, my friends, but leave room for God's wrath, for it is written: 'It is mine to avenge; I will repay,' says the Lord. On the contrary: 'If your enemy is hungry, feed him; if he is thirsty, give him something to drink.'   ROMANS 12:17–20

Seeking forgiveness from others

> *Therefore, if you are offering your gift at the altar and there remember that your brother has something against you, leave your gift there in front of the altar. First go and be reconciled to your brother; then come and offer your gift.*
>
> MATTHEW 5:23–24

What are the four toughest words to say in the English language? No, they aren't 'supercalifragilisticexpialidocious', 'Constantinople' or 'Timbuktu', nor the longest official word in the English dictionary: 'antidisestablishmentarianism'. The toughest words to say are unquestionably *Will you forgive me?*

? QUESTION

In your opinion, why is it so hard to ask for forgiveness? What is the risk? What is the reward of seeking forgiveness?

In asking for forgiveness, you can follow the same pattern that Daniel used:

1. Admit your sin in clear terms: 'I did _____.'
2. Then admit your shame, stubbornness and smallness as necessary.
3. Then choke out those four words: *Will you forgive me?*

They may or may not actually forgive. Many will choose to hang onto the feelings of anger and vengeance... and even if they do forgive, you may have many natural consequences to contend with... but that doesn't matter. You'll still feel free, because while it may take two people to reconcile, it only takes one to forgive.

M.A.P.S.

✆ *Meditate*
Ask God to guide your thoughts as you consider these words from the Creed:

> *I believe in... the forgiveness of sins...*

✤ *Apply*
You will need some time and you'll need some quiet for this one. Find a place where you can be alone with the Lord. Ask him to begin searching your heart. As the Holy Spirit leads you:

- Posture yourself humbly.
- Praise God passionately.
- Position yourself accordingly.

And then:

- Admit your sin.
- Admit your shame.
- Admit your stubbornness.
- Admit your smallness.

Praise God for the forgiveness granted at the cross, then proclaim God's promise: *God has forgiven me in Christ!*

❧ *Plot the passages*

- Key word: *Forgiven*.
- Key passage: Daniel 9:1–23.
- Supporting passages: Proverbs 5:22; Psalm 139:23–24; Ephesians 1:7; Colossians 3:12–14; Matthew 5:23–24; Romans 8:1–2.

❧ *Speak*

Speak to self

Often, the hardest person to forgive is yourself. For some reason we continue to hold onto the sins that even God lets go of.

Tell yourself, boldly and out loud:

- I have been legally forgiven.
- I have been personally forgiven.
- I am being continually forgiven.
- God hasn't just forgiven my *sin*; he has forgiven *me*. Through the cross I have been *transformed* into a new creature.

And if you just don't seem to get it (like I didn't get it), I really suggest spending some time with a trusted Christian mentor or counsellor like I did. The fullness of forgiveness has transformed my life.

Speak to others

I sometimes wonder if we should talk about forgiveness and freedom *before* we preach about sin and guilt. Sin is so serious that it's tough to be truly honest about our sin until we understand God's solution for it.

When speaking with others, remember: It's the Holy Spirit's job to convict of sin (John 16:8). It's our job to simply allow the Spirit to proclaim the good news of the gospel through us (Romans 10:9–10).

And then, who is out there who needs to hear you speak those four words: *'Will you forgive me?'*

Speak to God

> Gracious and merciful God,
> Thank you for your forgiveness. Thank you for your forgiveness. Thank you for your forgiveness.
> Amen.

*   *   *

No one likes to hear, 'You don't believe…' – particularly if you're an educated pastor who is supposed to know it all (a delusion I do not subscribe to, by the way). Wasn't I supposed to be the one giving advice? But my counsellor had struck a chord attached to a strongly felt need… and as I continued to read the story of the girl from Travers City, Yancey's words resonated with where I was.

Shortly after freeing herself from her parents, her life spirals into a nightmare of slavery to sin. Alcohol, drugs, the horror of prostitution… In a desperate moment her mind drifts back to her home. She leaves a message on the answering machine at her parents' home, telling them she's decided to travel back towards home on a bus, stopping briefly at the bus station to see if anyone would be there for her. Not to worry, she said. If no one is there she'll just keep riding to Canada.

As the bus rolls toward home, she rehearses her speech of contrition, just in case someone shows up… but nothing prepares her for the scene she sees as the bus pulls into the station:

> *There in the concrete-walls-and-plastic-chairs bus terminal in Traverse City, Michigan, stands a group of forty brothers and sisters and great-aunts and uncles and cousins and a grandmother and great-grandmother to boot. They're all wearing goofy party hats and blowing noise-makers, and taped across the entire wall of the terminal is a computer-generated banner that reads, 'Welcome home!'*
>
> *Out of the crowd of well-wishers breaks her dad. She stares through the tears quivering in her eyes like hot mercury and begins the memorized speech, 'Dad, I'm sorry. I know…'*
>
> *He interrupts her. 'Hush, child; we've got no time for that. No time for apologies. You'll be late for the party. A banquet is waiting for you at home.'*[47]

It's been years since I first read that story. But even now as I write about it, tears flow. It is, of course, a modern reliving of the Prodigal Son story – but now I understand it.

I am the prodigal; I am that girl… and so are you.

Do I believe in 'grace'? Am I being honest when I say, 'I believe in… the forgiveness of sins'?

Truthfully, I am still working through the scandal of grace… and find myself convinced that this side of glory I won't fully grasp it. But I'm tasting it now, feasting on grace more and more as I live with this God of continual second chances.

The Lord is compassionate and gracious, slow to anger, abounding in love. He does not treat us as our sins deserve or repay us according to our iniquities. For as high as the heavens are above the earth, so great is his love for those who fear him; as far as the east is from the west, so far has he removed our transgressions from us. PSALM 103:8, 10–12

Therefore, there is now no condemnation for those who are in Christ Jesus, because through Christ Jesus the law of the Spirit of life set me free from the law of sin and death. ROMANS 8:1–2

*I believe in God the Father Almighty, maker of heaven and earth; and in Jesus Christ his only Son our Lord; who was conceived by the Holy Ghost, born of the Virgin Mary, suffered under Pontius Pilate, was crucified, dead and buried. He descended into hell; the third day he rose again from the dead. He ascended into heaven, and sits on the right hand of God the Father Almighty. From thence he shall come to judge the quick and the dead. I believe in the Holy Ghost, the holy catholic church, the communion of saints, the forgiveness of sins, **the resurrection of the body,** and the life everlasting. Amen.*

CHAPTER 15

Starting Over

It is possible to provide security against other ills, but as far as death is concerned, we men live in a city without walls.

EPICURUS

I'm not afraid of death; I just don't want to be there when it happens.

WOODY ALLEN

I walked away, wiping the dirt from my hands – my mind a blur of thoughts, my heart awash in emotion. Retracing my family's roots had brought us to this place: the gravesite of my paternal grandparents in the Lake District of England. My Dad hadn't been back for years and the years had had their way. In the shadow of the weathered little church the graveyard had fallen into disrepair. The stone etched with the name 'Stanley Briscoe' had fallen over and my father's face reflected a pensive disappointment. The weeds had won the battle for the dirt in front of the tipped slab of stone. We huffed and heaved as we righted the slab and pulled a few weeds from the sacred ground...

Reality check-up

The graves of those who have gone before us conjure up such a strange mixture of feeling and thought. The feelings can be intense; the thoughts vital. They wash over us from every side; like tsunamis crashing down on the soul. One wave comes from the sea of faith and hope; another wave swells up from the ocean of loss. And finally, the third wave hits: The blatant reality that one day it will be us. *My body will die. My life will be over.*

Or will it?

As the Apostles' Creed heads down the home stretch, it addresses a topic of high importance: The human body. This topic is of immense concern in our culture (and not just at graveyards either). Consider women's 'body language'. I don't mean what you probably think I mean. I mean that women's conversation almost invariably ends up focused on their body: Clothes, make-up, hair... and the dreaded 'F' word: *fat*. Women, it seems, are always talking about their bodies. But it's not just a female thing; men like to talk about women's bodies too! (And who says we don't have anything in common!)

? Question

Why is there no good answer to that question that strikes fear in the heart of every husband: 'Do I look fat in this dress?'

Look at the diet ads on television, the plastic surgeons' ads in the yellow pages, the magazine rack at the grocery store... I mean, should we really be concerned about which emaciated Hollywood star has gained three ounces over the holidays? Maybe not; but we are.

But enough about what *we* say about our bodies, and who cares what the books and tabloids say about the body... What does *God* say about the body?

I want you to imagine something with me right now: Imagine that you're walking into a doctor's office – but not just any doctor; you're in the office of the Great Physician. God has given you a thorough examination. The results are in. Now comes the moment of truth. God is going to give you a *diagnosis*, a *prognosis*, and a *prescription*.

Listen carefully, because some of the news is going to be good, some of it very sobering, and some of it really exciting. And while some of it might be somewhat disconcerting, hang in there. In the end you'll be able to rejoice when you can say from the heart: *I believe... in the resurrection of the body.*

Your diagnosis

Your body is incredible

> *I praise you because I am fearfully and wonderfully made; your works are wonderful, I know that full well.*   PSALM 139:14

Dr Lang, a friend who is now the Head of Cardiology at John's Hopkins in Baltimore, told me some things about how incredible our body really is: There are 74 trillion cells in the human body. The white blood cells in the lymph tissue can form up to 100,000 different antibodies. They fight against foreign tissue and can make these antibodies at a rate of 2,000 per second. A single white blood cell can kill as many as a hundred bacteria (tough little guys). Over the course of a lifetime the heart will pump an average of 52,560,000 gallons of blood. (That's enough to fill a New York skyscraper...)

Modern technology has uncovered a phenomenal biological world inside the human body. Its complexity far exceeds anything that anyone ever imagined... and in many ways, we haven't even begun to explore it.

Your body is indispensable

May your whole spirit, soul and body be kept blameless at the coming of our Lord Jesus Christ.   1 THESSALONIANS 5:23

The Bible says that human beings are made up of a spirit, soul and body. Counsellor Bill Gillham calls the human body an 'earth suit'. Just as a spacesuit keeps an astronaut alive, the body is indispensable for our earthly existence. Like it or not, you just can't live in this world without it.

Your body is susceptible

Do not join those who drink too much wine or gorge themselves on meat.   PROVERBS 23:20

God designed the human body to be used in a certain way. If it's used differently than he intended, there will be natural consequences. Too much alcohol, too much food, sex outside of the context of a monogamous marriage… if you don't follow the guidelines he has given us in Scripture, you can bring upon yourselves obesity, heart disease, alcoholism, sexually transmitted diseases…

Because we live in a world bombarded by the effects of the fall and sin, many of these things may come upon us through no fault of our own, because the body is susceptible.

? QUESTION

Consider a few people whom you know well. Are their health issues a consequence of their own choices or the result of living in a fallen world? Do you think one type of illness is 'fair' and the other one is not? Why or why not?

Your body is trainable

Everyone who competes in the games goes into strict training. They do it to get a crown that will not last; but we do it to get a crown that will last forever. Therefore I do not run like someone running aimlessly; I do not fight like a boxer beating the air. No, I strike a blow to my body and make it my slave…   1 CORINTHIANS 9:25–27

Life is like a marathon. It's a good long race that lasts a long time (Lord willing). But you don't decide on Saturday to run a marathon on Sunday. Marathons take preparation, vision and training. The Apostle Paul says that we're supposed to do the same thing in life. We are supposed to discipline and train our bodies, for the race ahead of us is long.

It's actually very exciting news because the Scriptures also say that training and disciplining our bodies is *worship*:

> *Therefore, I urge you, brothers, in view of God's mercy, to offer your bodies as living sacrifices, holy and pleasing to God – this is your spiritual act of worship.*
> ROMANS 12:1

Training and disciplining the body is also *worthwhile*:

> *Do not offer the parts of your body to sin, as instruments of wickedness, but rather offer yourselves to God, as those who have been brought from death to life; and offer the parts of your body to him as instruments of righteousness.*
> ROMANS 6:13

What a great perspective to have about your body: It is a living sacrifice, an instrument of righteousness in the hands of God!

Your prognosis

Okay, you're sitting in the office of the Great Physician. He's finished with his charts and explanations. Now you're going to hear what you came for: *What's going to happen to me?!* With gentle but serious eyes, God asks you to sit down.

'Do you want the good news or the bad news?' he asks.

Let's get the bad news out of the way, shall we?

Your body is going to deteriorate

> *Therefore we do not lose heart. Though outwardly we are wasting away, yet inwardly we are being renewed day by day.*   2 CORINTHIANS 4:16

We might not be aware of this fact until we hit the mid-twenties or even early thirties, but by then it becomes pretty clear that it's a downhill slide toward the grave. When I was playing basketball in college I set a life goal for myself: to be able to dunk a basketball on my fiftieth birthday. The week of my thirtieth birthday, however, I got an excruciating pain in my lower back... three bad discs in the lower portion of my spine. It's tough to work out now – though eating still comes easily. Combine all this with sitting at a desk ten hours a day, and my once strong legs now resemble white threads hanging harmlessly from my belt. The ultimate humiliation was when my thirteen-year-old son beat me at a game of one-on-one in our driveway and blocked one of my shots! (And at six feet five, I stand five inches taller than he does!) At the beginning of my forty-fifth year I decided to get serious about dunking that basketball again. With a fresh New Year's resolution I set out on a short run on 1 January. 'Pop!' By the middle of January I'm on the operating table having my torn meniscus repaired – 2 Corinthians 4:16 indeed!

✒ QUOTATION

He is no fool who gives what he cannot keep to gain what he cannot lose.

JIM ELLIOT

But don't worry, it gets worse...

Your body will die

Why, you do not even know what will happen tomorrow. What is your life? You are a mist that appears for a little while and then vanishes.   JAMES 4:14

A pastor named Steve Brown was on a plane to the West Coast – a plane filled with people who had just got off cruise ships in Miami. Everybody was still in the party mood, trying to make the most of the remaining seconds of their little break from reality. But then reality caught up with them. One of the women in the front of the plane began having a hard time. Then all at once she slumped forward... dead. Right there in the middle of the airborne party. They landed in Dallas, took off the body and resumed their journey towards Los Angeles.

Steve told the flight attendant, 'Ma'am, I'm a pastor. If anyone would like to talk to me about what's happened, I'm in seat 12A.'

The flight attendant responded, 'No problem sir. We are going to give everyone free drinks for the rest of the flight.'

And she was right. Within an hour everyone was back in the party festive mood.

Isn't that the way most of us try to deal with death? It's like we're floating along on this big old cruise-ship called *Life*. Every once in a while somebody around us drops dead and falls out of the party. It catches our attention for a moment, but rather than dealing with it, we grab onto anything we can to numb our thoughts and feelings so that the party can continue. We might grab onto alcohol, or work, or friends, or denial, or exercise... but if we stop for a moment and are honest, we must face the fact that all of us will die physically.

Full stop.

That's a cold, clammy reality. Even the great philosophers of centuries and centuries ago had a hard time with death. Aristotle said that death is the 'most terrible' of all things. Epicurus said that death is 'the most terrifying' of all things. Sophocles said, 'Of all great wonders, none is greater than man. Only for death can he find no cure.'

Your body will decompose

All go to the same place; all come from dust, and to dust all return.

ECCLESIASTES 3:20

Yuck. No need to talk about this one much. Whether your body is cremated, put in a casket or donated to medical science... the result will be the same: 'Dust to dust.'

Okay, that's the bad news. And it's plenty bad. But that's only half of the prognosis. There is definitely a flip-side of the coin and it's really awesome *if* you know Jesus Christ personally.

Your spirit will dwell

We live by faith, not by sight. We are confident, I say, and would prefer to be away from the body and at home with the Lord.   2 CORINTHIANS 5:8

This passage reveals the heart of a godly and yet struggling man. Paul says that he would prefer to be away from the body... he would rather be *dead*. If his body dies, he believes that he will be at home with the Lord. His body may be decomposing six feet under, but the spirit and soul will be alive and aware somewhere else.

Not everybody believes this. There are several other very popular theories out there (but none of them can be backed up with the Bible):

- *Soul sleep.* This is the 'eternal nap' theory. The soul still exists, but in death it goes into an unconscious snooze forever.
- *Nihilism.* After death, the soul and spirit just kind of evaporate and cease to exist altogether.

- *Reincarnation.* This is the 'repeat' theory. When any living thing dies, its soul goes into other living things – actually becoming something else over and over again in a never-ending cycle of life and death.

Your body will be determined

> *But someone may ask, 'How are the dead raised? With what kind of body will they come?' How foolish! What you sow does not come to life unless it dies. When you sow, you do not plant the body that will be, but just a seed, perhaps of wheat or of something else. But God gives it a body as he has determined, and to each kind of seed he gives its own body.*   1 CORINTHIANS 15:35–38

Have you ever seen a chrysanthemum seed? (It's easier to see it than it is to pronounce it!) They look like little brownish shrivelled-up things. *But*, if you take that seed and you bury it in the dirt, what happens? You get this amazing flower – totally unlike the seed that was planted.

Do you see what Paul is getting at here? If our body (usually little brownish shrivelled-up things) dies, how will God raise us and what will we look like when that happens? We are foolish to even ask the question, because the difference between what dies and what is resurrected is as great as the difference between the chrysanthemum seed and its flower. I think it's fair to let our imaginations run with this for a little while, because I believe that our new bodies will be *beyond* anything that we can imagine.

Your body will be different

> *The sun has one kind of splendour, the moon another and the stars another; and star differs from star in splendour. So will it be with the resurrection of the dead. The body that is sown is perishable, it is raised imperishable; it is sown in dishonour, it is raised in glory; it is sown in weakness, it is raised in power; it is sown a natural body, it is raised a spiritual body... in a flash, in the twinkling of an eye, at the last trumpet. For the trumpet will sound, the dead will be raised imperishable, and we will be changed.*   1 CORINTHIANS 15:41–44, 52

Imagine something right now: You are still in the doctor's office and the Great Physician has sat down in front of you. The diagnosis of death and decay has left you stunned; your soul is reeling with that reality. But now he's leaning towards you; he's taking you by the hand and he's lifting your chin and looking you in the eyes – he has something to say:

'My child, the death, the pain, the decay... it is all temporary – an immeas-urably small moment in light of the eternity that awaits you. What lies beyond is incomparable. The asthma, the cancer, the bruises and scabs and scars... these will not last. Dream of an existence where nothing perishes, where the physical is shed and you are raised in a body spiritual. Trust me, look to the future and see with the eyes of faith a heavenly, timeless, and painless existence – an exist-ence of an entirely different kind, a body of an entirely different kind. Be patient, my child; have faith. For with a flash of light you will be changed.'

The Great Physician has finished talking for the moment. God pushes back and gives you a moment to let this soak in. But he's not done, either. In light of your diagnosis and prognosis, he has some things for you to do.

✣ QUOTATION

Death is no more than passing from one room into another. But there's a difference for me, you know. Because in that other room I shall be able to see.

HELEN KELLER

Your prescription

Care for your body

A number of years ago the legendary professor Howard Hendricks was speaking at Dallas Theological Seminary, an all-male school at the time. He stood up and said something to this effect: 'Gentlemen, I need to talk to you. I've decided that I'm not going to waste my time on many of you any more.' (A major attention-getter from a highly respected educator!) 'Here's why,' he continued. 'Some of you are so hopelessly out of shape that I'm not going to invest my time in you. I would rather invest my time on someone who is going to live for a long time. So get in shape or get out of school!'

Harsh? Absolutely. But the point he was making was deathly serious: You only get one body. There are no returns and there's no warranty. When it's done, it's done; so take care of that 'earth suit'. Give it exercise; fuel it with good food. Give it enough sleep and rest; optimize its efficiency with vitamins and nutri-tional supplements. Dr Hendricks spoke with authority on the issue because he had been similarly challenged as a young 'out of shape' man. He made lifelong lifestyle adjustments that, to date, have enabled him to serve at the seminary for over fifty years!

❧ QUOTATION

Arise, O Sluggard! In the grave there will be sleeping enough.   BENJAMIN FRANKLIN

And what about your weaknesses? Remember that the body is susceptible. Alcohol? Tobacco? Junk food? Figure out your weak spot and turn it over to Christ. Allow him to be your strength; trust in him moment by moment to deliver you, because your body is an instrument of worship and righteousness. Keep it tuned up so that it can do its job as effectively and as long as possible.

But remember: *You are destined to failure when you try to change your flesh in the strength of your flesh. Any lasting success is the result of trusting the Lord to do these things through you, rather than trying to do it on your own.*

✍ CONTEMPLATION

If anyone would come after me, he must deny himself and take up his cross and follow me. For whoever wants to save his life will lose it, but whoever loses his life for me and for the gospel will save it. What good is it for a man to gain the whole world, yet forfeit his soul?   MARK 8:34–36

Live in the shadow of death

Even though I walk through the valley of the shadow of death, I fear no evil, for You are with me...   PSALM 23:4 (NASB)

If you believe the prognosis given to you by the Great Physician, it will not only change your perspective on physical death and the fact that it is unavoidable, it will change your life *now*. There is a very tangible sense of peace that comes with aligning your beliefs with what is true about the death and resurrection of your body. Stress and worry evaporate in the presence of this type of true belief.

What's the *worst* that can happen to you? You will die. What's the *best* that can happen to you? You will die!

There is freedom in this truth. There's no sense in denying it or avoiding it: Your body will die. *So why not live fearlessly? Why not live with focus? Why not live with fervour?*

If you only have one earthly life to live, why not take calculated risks? Why not push the envelope of your comfort zone and allow Christ to live through you and lead you into worthwhile and demanding new endeavours?

Benjamin Franklin lived in the shadow of death. He lived without fear and he lived boldly for the things that he believed in. He was a great writer, but few words of his (or anyone else's, for that matter) are as powerful as the words that he wrote for his tombstone. Knowing that these would be his last words left for the world to read long after he was gone, he wrote:

> The body of Benjamin Franklin, printer, like the cover of an old book, its contents torn out and stripped of its lettering and gilding, lies here. Yet the work itself shall not be lost. But it will, as he believed, appear once more in a new and more beautiful edition, corrected and amended by the Author.

? QUESTION

What do you want written on your tombstone?

Share the hope

This is truly good news. It's real and it's honest. Belief in the resurrection of the body embraces both the harsh realities of physical death and the glorious future that gives perspective and purpose to our present. This is a great hope – a hope that will naturally flow into conversations and into our life message when we truly can say: *I believe... in the resurrection of the body!*

M.A.P.S.

Meditate

Ask God to guide your thoughts as you consider these words from the Creed:

> *I believe... in the resurrection of my body.*

Apply

Review the diagnosis and the prognosis the Great Physician has given you regarding your physical body. Consider the three-point prescription God gives you in light of the resurrection of your body.

Pray through these points with the Lord. What attitudes or actions do you think God wants to change in your life? Are you willing to allow him to make those changes?

Plot the passages

- Key word: *Body*.

- Key passage: 1 Corinthians 15:35–58.
- Supporting passages: 2 Corinthians 4:16; James 4:14; Psalm 23:4; 2 Corinthians 5:8–9.

✵ *Speak*

Speak to self
I believe:

- My body is incredible.
- My body is indispensable.
- My body is susceptible.
- My body is trainable.
- It's going to deteriorate.
- It's going to die.
- It's going to decompose.
- My spirit and soul will live on.
- I will be given a new, different body of God's perfect design.

Because of this, as God empowers me, I will care for my body, I will live fearlessly in the shadow of death, and I will share this hope with others around me.

Speak to others
How might the current events in our world and in your community give you the opportunity to share about the hope of the resurrection of the body?

Think through three or four ways that you can turn a conversation about our bodies toward conversation about the resurrection of our bodies.

Is God specifically placing people on your heart who need to hear about the resurrection of their body? How can you make this message most relevant to them in light of their felt needs?

Speak to God

Great Physician,

Thank you for my physical body. I confess that there are plenty of things that I would like to change about it, but by faith I accept it as your perfect gift to me, my earth suit, for as many or as few years as you give me on this planet.

I ask that you would give me a true of awareness of my mortality. Give me a true belief in the fact that my physical body will die. Give me a vision for what life will be like with a resurrected body that will not perish and has none of the pain and limitations of this earthly one.

And finally, in light of my belief in these truths, I pray that you would ignite my temporal life on this earth to burn for things that are eternal and will never end. Let my physical body be an instrument of worship, a living sacrifice that makes beautiful music for you. Play me well, that the souls of many might lift their voice in praise to you.

Amen.

*   *   *

I wish I had known my grandfather. The day we stood beside the grave, my Dad filled in some of the gaps with tales of the man: Keeping the family grocery store open through the Great War and the Depression. A man of his word... a man of the Word. A lay preacher who spoke what he knew each weekend in a corrugated metal building they called 'The Tin Church'...

Nothing fancy here. Just a simple faith that knew the value of community and honesty, the value of the truth, the value of investing life in something worth dying for... I thought a lot about Stanley Briscoe, about the dirt and dust beneath my feet. Would he be as concerned as us about the condition of the grave? I think not. He sounded like the kind of man who knew that the grave was not the full stop on his life... it was merely a comma.

The grave: That's reality – both the good news and the bad news. In between birth and the coffin there are an unknown number of days that God gives us to live for his purposes in this physical body we have been given. Some day it will be changed into a perfect body, but for now it is wearing out... Yet it continually waits to be used for eternal purposes.

Soon enough the dust of my body, of your body, will mix with the soil beneath a tilting headstone. Will the cemetery be kept up? Will weeds grow there too? Does it matter? Perhaps it is best to let the gravestone lie, because:

When the perishable has been clothed with the imperishable, and the mortal with immortality, then the saying that is written will come true: 'Death has been swallowed up in victory. Where, O death, is your victory? Where, O death, is your sting?' The sting of death is sin, and the power of sin is the law. But thanks be to God! He gives us the victory through our Lord Jesus Christ. Therefore, my dear brothers, stand firm. Let nothing move you. Always give yourselves fully to the work of the Lord, because you know that your labour in the Lord is not in vain.

1 CORINTHIANS 15:54–58

I believe in God the Father Almighty, maker of heaven and earth; and in Jesus Christ his only Son our Lord; who was conceived by the Holy Ghost, born of the Virgin Mary, suffered under Pontius Pilate, was crucified, dead and buried. He descended into hell; the third day he rose again from the dead. He ascended into heaven, and sits on the right hand of God the Father Almighty. From thence he shall come to judge the quick and the dead. I believe in the Holy Ghost, the holy catholic church, the communion of saints, the forgiveness of sins, the resurrection of the body, **and the life everlasting.** *Amen.*

CHAPTER 16

The Sustained Life

It's not that life is too short; it's that eternity is so long.   AUTHOR UNKNOWN

He has made everything beautiful in its time. He has also set eternity in the hearts of men; yet they cannot fathom what God has done from beginning to end.
ECCLESIASTES 3:11

'Mythstake'

What a great word, if I may say so myself – which I can; because I invented it. I keep checking in Webster's dictionary and they haven't put that word in there yet, but twenty years from now, when 'mythstake' is in all of the dictionaries of the world, you can say to your sons and daughters, 'I remember, back in the day, when Pete Briscoe first used this now famous word...'

A *mythstake* is a combination of a *mistake* and a *myth*. Unlike a mistake, however, a mythstake is not an accident. It's an error that is a consequence of believing a myth (a commonly held notion that has no basis in truth). Mythstakes show up everywhere you care to look for them.

A business mythstake

In 1958, 80 per cent of all watches were made in Switzerland. Japan made 0 per cent. In 1968, only 20 per cent of all watches were Swiss made and over 70 per cent were made in Japan. Wow, what happened? Blame it on the quartz watch – and a major mythstake by the Swiss.

You see, up until 1958, the Swiss believed that *a watch must have a mainspring in order to work*. But that year, two inventors approached the Swiss with a working concept model of a miniature mechanism that kept time by measuring the vibrations in quartz crystals. The Swiss said this was impossible; *a watch must have a mainspring*. So the inventors took the idea to Japan and the rest is history. What's ironic about this? The two inventors were Swiss... and then neither of them thought to patent this idea. Japan got it all and the Swiss made a major mythstake.

A sexual mythstake

Hundreds of millions of people in the Western world believe that *protected sex is safe sex*. The statistics prove that this is a myth. 'Protection' can reduce some risks, but it's just a fallacy to say that it makes sex 'safe'. As a result, hundreds of thousands of people are making mythstakes that lead to unwanted pregnancies and the contraction of numerous sexually transmitted diseases. The AIDS epidemic clearly shows that some mythstakes can be very, very deadly. And sadly, they are discovering that there is nothing that can protect the heart from the emotional implications of inappropriate sexual unions.

It doesn't matter how strongly you believe that protected sex is safe sex. If what you believe is not true, the consequences of believing the myth will follow you the rest of your life. We need the facts, not the fantasy.

I remember the day my Dad taught me the 'facts of life'. Since he's a preacher who made a living by talking, I was bracing myself for a full sermon – or at least a brief conversation – but when we sat down at the table, we looked at each other in awkward silence. I blinked; he blinked. More silence. Blink. Blink. Finally his mouth opened and he consolidated his entire message on the birds and the bees into three words: 'Here, read this.' That was it. No diagrams, no special words, no hand motions. Just a book. (It didn't even have pictures in it. Rats.) But I read that book and I thank God that it saved me from many of the mythstakes that others have believed and lived to regret.

? QUESTION

What do you think is one of the biggest mythstakes that has ever been made? In your opinion, what were some of the factors that led up to this error? Could it have been avoided?

All mythstakes can have serious earthly consequences, but some mythstakes impact not only this life, but the life to come as well. When the Apostles' Creed proclaims, *'I believe in... the life everlasting'*, it is talking about belief about what happens beyond the grave – what happens in eternity... as in *forever*.

That's both exciting and scary, because people believe things about eternal life that are myths. If they buy into those myths, they will make mistakes that last a long, long, long time. If we want to avoid these mythstakes, we need to know more than the facts of life; we need to know the facts about *eternal* life.

Eternal consequences

To be honest, I really don't like preaching 'hellfire and brimstone'. It always reminds me of red, puffy-faced, bald men with neckties that are way too tight. They yell at me from the television. I wear jeans and T-shirts to work at my church and I would just as soon avoid topics that sound judgmental and condemning.

The problem is that the Bible teaches 'hellfire and brimstone'. If belief matters – which it truly does – then we have to be committed to being seekers of true belief... even when the truth is uncomfortable, unpopular, and controversial. And while we can certainly avoid the yelling and the red faces and the neckties that are too tight, we must share the commitment to be a warning to those headed in the wrong direction.

Jesus did that. He warned those around him – as in this unnerving story he told to the Pharisees and the disciples:

> There was a rich man who was dressed in purple and fine linen and lived in luxury every day. At his gate was laid a beggar named Lazarus, covered with sores and longing to eat what fell from the rich man's table. Even the dogs came and licked his sores.
>
> The time came when the beggar died and the angels carried him to Abraham's side. The rich man also died and was buried. In hell, where he was in torment, he looked up and saw Abraham far away, with Lazarus by his side. So he called to him, 'Father Abraham, have pity on me and send Lazarus to dip the tip of his finger in water and cool my tongue, because I am in agony in this fire.'
>
> But Abraham replied, 'Son, remember that in your lifetime you received your good things, while Lazarus received bad things, but now he is comforted here and you are in agony. And besides all this, between us and you a great chasm has been fixed, so that those who want to go from here to you cannot, nor can anyone cross over from there to us.'   LUKE 16:19–26

There are many lessons to be learned from this passage, but the blaring message is this: *There is a heaven, and there is a hell, and after death it is impossible to move from one to the other. An eternal barrier is fixed between these two places and the decisions we make on earth will determine where we spend eternity.*

Throughout the Bible we find various snapshots of heaven to give us a little glimpse of what *kind* of place it will be:

- A place of joy (Luke 15:7, 10).
- A place of reward (Matthew 5:11–12).
- A place of peace (Luke 16:25).

- A place of righteousness (2 Peter 3:13).

But quite frankly, eternal life in heaven is *indescribable*. When we step out of the time/space dimension of this screwed-up and fallen world, when we begin to navigate through the timelessness of eternity with perfect and glorified bodies... nothing on earth will compare to that. It's everything that is good and beautiful and pure and blessed, going on forever and ever and ever. The Bible also speaks of a new heaven and new earth (2 Peter 3:13) that will be ours to enjoy and explore. Revelation 21 – 22 gives a vivid word-picture of this place. It's an inspiring read, but like much of Revelation, it's hard to tell what is literal and what is symbolic. When we get down to it, there is no direct description – no earthly comparison to heaven. It simply cannot be described in human terms.

The Bible actually is most explicit about what heaven will *not* be like. No more pain (Revelation 21:4), no more tears (Revelation 7:17), no more death (Luke 20:36)... and no more Satan.

✐ CONTEMPLATION

There will be no more night. They will not need the light of a lamp or the light of the sun, for the Lord God will give them light. And they will reign for ever and ever.   REVELATION 22:5

While heaven is indescribable, the alternative, on the other hand, is *intolerable*.

- Hell is torment (Revelation 14:11).
- Hell is darkness (Matthew 8:12).
- Hell is a bottomless pit (Revelation 20:1–2).
- Hell is continual and eternal (Revelation 14:11).

Hell is the opposite of heaven. Heaven is all good; hell is all evil. When you're deciding between heaven and hell, it's not like you're deciding between Dallas and Chicago. The decision is more like the decision between Maui and a Rwandan refugee camp... multiplied times a million and experienced all the way through eternity... that's the decision you're making.

If we truly believe this, then I guess we have to give the red-faced, yelling preachers a little credit. Maybe they're just trying to scare the hell out of people, which is, by comparison, better than sitting idly by as people unknowingly rush to arrive there. Maybe some people will be smart enough to grasp the message even if they never want to be like the messenger.

☙ CONTEMPLATION

God so loved the world that he gave his only begotten Son that whoever should believe in him would not *perish* but have *eternal life.*   JOHN 3:16 (ITALICS MINE)

Eternal mythstakes

With so much riding on the decision, it's eternally critical that what we believe about heaven and hell is true and accurate. When it comes time to decide how to get off the road to hell and head toward heaven, however, many people base their beliefs on myths and not on the Word of God.

The 'good guy' mythstake

This is by far the most popular mythstake of our time. It basically says that *if you're a good enough person, you'll get to heaven.* The words of Jesus, however, destroy this notion.

> *As Jesus started on his way, a man ran up to him and fell on his knees before him. 'Good teacher,' he asked, 'what must I do to inherit eternal life?'*
>
> *'Why do you call me good?' Jesus answered. 'No one is good – except God alone.'*   MARK 10:17–18

By human standards, the man that Jesus was talking to was a 'good' man. He had kept all the law since he was young – and yet Jesus stopped mid-track and said, 'No one is good.' Jesus obliterated the assumption of being a 'good guy' before the conversation even got started.

Here's the problem with the 'good guy' mythstake: We compare ourselves to other humans. It's not too tough to find somebody who is more of a scumbag than we are. So in our minds we think, 'Compared to that other guy, I'm a pretty good guy.'

But Jesus says that if you want to compare yourself to someone, compare yourself to God. He is the ultimate standard of what is good. Hmmm, that's a little tough, isn't it? Compared to God, we are anything but good. 'Good guys' are just an illusion created by human-to-human comparison.

> *... for all have sinned and fall short of the glory of God.*   ROMANS 3:23

The 'good try' mythstake

Okay, so maybe we aren't good. But maybe God rewards a good effort. The 'good try' mythstake says, *'If you sincerely try to do your best, God will let you in.'* So let's keep our noses clean and skip the cracks in the cement! Let's pray and read our Bibles and go to church. Certainly this will at least improve our chances, right?

The Christian religion gives people an endless number of opportunities to give life a 'good try'. Religion tells you *what* you're supposed to do and what you're not supposed to do; and tells you exactly *how* you're supposed to do or not do all those things that you're trying to do or not do. The problem is that Scripture says good deeds are irrelevant when it comes to getting into heaven.

✒ CONTEMPLATION

For it is by grace you have been saved, through faith – and this not from yourselves, it is the gift of God – not by works, so that no one can boast.

EPHESIANS 2:8–9

The consequences of this mythstake are going to come as a shock for a lot of people – particularly those who have been trying to impress God through their religious efforts.

Not everyone who says to me, 'Lord, Lord,' will enter the kingdom of heaven, but only he who does the will of my Father who is in heaven. Many will say to me on that day, 'Lord, Lord, did we not prophesy in your name, and in your name drive out demons and perform many miracles?' Then I will tell them plainly, 'I never knew you. Away from me, you evildoers!'   MATTHEW 7:21–23

Ouch. That means you can call Jesus 'Lord', and even be a prophet, exorcist, or do miracles in Jesus name... and he will still turn you away.

The bottom line is this: God is perfect; if you are going to work your way into heaven, you will have to do it perfectly. God doesn't grade on the curve. It's pass or fail. You can try if you want, *but the problem isn't your sincerity or your effort, it's your failure.*

✒ CONTEMPLATION

But if you show favouritism, you sin and are convicted by the law as lawbreakers. For whoever keeps the whole law and yet stumbles at just one point is guilty of breaking all of it.   JAMES 2:9–10

? QUESTION

If you asked ten of your co-workers how to get to heaven, how many of them do you think believe the 'good guy' or 'good try' mythstakes? Why do you think this is such a popular error?

The 'cockeyed' mythstake

A classmate in high school once told me, 'I'd rather party in hell with my friends than go to heaven without them!' If he had known what the Bible teaches us about hell, I suspect his attitude would have been different. You have to be cock-eyed to verbalize this myth (let alone believe it), but many people do. It can be summarized by a poem on a birthday card:

> *Why worry?*
> *Either you are well or you are sick.*
> *If you are well you have nothing to worry about.*
> *If you are sick you only have two things to worry about:*
> *either you will live or you will die.*
> *If you live you have nothing to worry about.*
> *If you die you only have two things to worry about:*
> *either you will go to heaven or you'll go to hell.*
> *If you go to heaven you have nothing to worry about.*
> *If you go to hell, you'll be so busy shaking hands with friends*
> *that you won't have time to worry!*
> *Happy Birthday!*

The myth is that *hell is going to be an eternal continuation of the party here on earth.* It's simply not true.

What do souls do in hell?

- They experience agony (Luke 16:24).
- They weep (Luke 13:28).
- They wail (Matthew 13:42).
- They grit and grind their teeth in frustration (Luke 13:28).

Sorry; this will be no party.

If someone says they would rather be in hell with their friends than in heaven alone, ask them *why* they think their friends are going to hell, and *why* they think they are going to be together? (They won't have an answer, by the way.

People believe this myth blindly for no real reason.) The haunting descriptions we have of hell in Scripture indicate that they may exist in suspended isolation and darkness... forever (Matthew 8:12; Revelation 20:1–2).

The 'pass-him-by' mythstake

This person believes the myth that *it's okay to meet Jesus in a casual way and then go on with life as usual.* I said the prayer; I met Jesus Christ, now I have eternal life. So I'm going to have my fun now and go to be with Jesus later. Eighties rock star Eddie Van Halen took that approach to life. In his hit song *Best of Both Worlds* he confesses the fleeting desire to have heaven on earth... a place where he can chase his earthly passions without compromising eternity.

The problem is that Scripture doesn't say that's the way it works at all. Just because you said a prayer doesn't mean that you know Jesus. Anyone can say the words, but a salvation prayer is not a magical password into heaven. Only the person who personally *knows* Jesus will enter. Those who know Christ are marked by an inspirational change of life-focus that alters their purpose and vision for life.

Eternal life starts the day that you believe in Jesus Christ and receive him into your life. Your life becomes his life, and his life becomes yours (Galatians 2:20). If you truly believe that you have had this encounter with Christ, your life can never be the same again.

First of all, your *attitude* changes.

> *For the love of money is a root of all kinds of evil. Some people, eager for money, have wandered from the faith and pierced themselves with many griefs. But you, man of God, flee from all this, and pursue righteousness, godliness, faith, love, endurance and gentleness. Fight the good fight of the faith. Take hold of the eternal life to which you were called when you made your good confession in the presence of many witnesses.*   1 TIMOTHY 6:10–12

The person with a genuine relationship with Jesus Christ knows that they're going to have a 'good fight' on their hands. They 'take hold of eternal life' with purpose, knowing that the things of the world will continually try to draw them away and distract them from the battle at hand – and they take that seriously, not flippantly.

Second, your *behaviour* changes.

A great example of this is recorded in John 4, where Jesus is talking with a Samaritan woman at a well:

Jesus answered, 'Everyone who drinks this water will be thirsty again, but whoever drinks the water I give him will never thirst. Indeed, the water I give him will become in him a spring of water welling up to eternal life.'   JOHN 4:13–14

The words 'welled up' indicate a spontaneous welling and overflow from within. The person who is filled with Jesus' water will have a natural outpouring of Christ through their life. Jesus changes us from the inside and out.

The person who is comfortable passing by Jesus and then going on with life as normal would be wise to stop and question whether or not they know him at all. It is far better to search your heart now, rather than live with the consequences of the 'pass him by' mythstake.

The 'standby' mythstake

This myth is pretty basic. It says *'Yeah, I believe that, but I'll deal with it later.'* It sounds like the words of another man Jesus described:

Then he said, 'This is what I'll do. I will tear down my barns and build bigger ones, and there I will store all my grain and my goods. And I'll say to myself, "You have plenty of good things laid up for many years. Take life easy; eat, drink and be merry."' But God said to him, 'You fool! This very night your life will be demanded from you. Then who will get what you have prepared for yourself?'   LUKE 12:18–20

I don't have to explain how foolish that is, do I? Like most mythstakes, this one dissolves with the least bit of thought. *That night* the man lost his life...

The 'need not apply' mythstake

Of all the people out there making eternal mythstakes, these are the ones that I have the most compassion for. These people actually believe the 'good guy' and 'good try' myths – but they are honest enough to know that they don't have a chance to make the grade. They believe that only the good will make it... and they know that they are not good. Their honesty deflates their hope, for they know they are guilty, a lost cause, a hopeless case, a reject. *Why even try? There is no point. It's useless. No need to apply.*

And they are right. Partially.

The gospel is truly good news to people who know that they are bad. The supernatural and transforming message of truth is like a crystal-clear splash of ice-water to those dying of thirst in the deserts of sin and shame. The people who are making this mythstake are often stunned when they hear the rest of the story – what God has done for them through the person of Jesus Christ:

> *What benefit did you reap at that time from the things you are now ashamed of?*
> *Those things result in death! But now that you have been set free from sin and*
> *have become slaves to God, the benefit you reap leads to holiness, and the result*
> *is eternal life. For the wages of sin is death,* but *the gift of God is eternal life in*
> *Christ Jesus our Lord.*   ROMANS 6:21–23

Yeah, the wages of sin is death, *but...* (I love that word 'but'! It means that something is coming that wipes out the bad news...) *but* the free gift of God is eternal life in Christ. Wow. That's the best news possible to a humble, honest soul.

This was a huge *but* for the Apostle Paul (the guy God used to write this passage of the Bible) because Paul was anything but a 'good guy'. Before he met Christ, he carried huge amounts of religious pride and arrogance with him. He was actually an accomplice to the murder of the Apostle Stephen... *but...*

The word 'but' shows up in Jesus' confrontation with the rich 'good guy' mentioned above too. Remember Jesus told the guy that he wasn't good at all; only God is good, and then Jesus pointed out that he hadn't even sold his possessions to give to the poor. The man walked away in defeat, understanding that he was a selfish man.

> *The disciples were amazed at his words. But Jesus said again, 'Children, how*
> *hard it is to enter the kingdom of God! It is easier for a camel to go through the*
> *eye of a needle than for a rich man to enter the kingdom of God.'*
>
> *The disciples were even more amazed, and said to each other, 'Who then*
> *can be saved?'*
>
> *Jesus looked at them and said, 'With man this is impossible,* but *not with*
> *God; all things are possible with God.'*   MARK 19:24–27

Impossible to enter into heaven? Yes, *but* not with God. *All* things are possible with him – even an everlasting life in heaven for those who are far, far from perfect.

✐ CONTEMPLATION

You who are trying to be justified by law have been alienated from Christ; you have fallen away from grace. But by faith we eagerly await through the Spirit the righteousness for which we hope.   GALATIANS 5:4–5

Jesus died on the cross for your sins so that they can be removed, so you can confidently enter an everlasting life in heaven based on what God has done for you, rather than what you have tried and failed to do for him.

Consider one of the two thieves who were crucified beside Jesus. He was neither a 'good guy', nor did he have the opportunity to change his ways and give it a 'good try'. *But*, when the man asked for pardon, Jesus said, 'Today, you will be with me in Paradise.'

The two of them hung together in the midday heat. In a matter of hours, Jesus Christ, the sinless Son of God, breathed his last and completed his earthly work. A short time later the thief, a man fully worthy of an eternal hell, also died. But across the threshold of death, Jesus was waiting for him, ready to invite him into everlasting life.

... Just as he will be waiting for you if you have humbly and honestly received this free gift.

Make no mythstake about it.

? QUESTION

What are you most excited about that heaven has? What are you most excited about that heaven does **not** *have?*

M.A.P.S.

❧ Meditate
Ask God to guide your thoughts as you consider these words from the Creed:

I believe... in the life everlasting.

❧ Apply
Go back to the list and pinpoint the myths that influence your thinking. (Be honest! To differing degrees we are all affected by at least a couple of them.)

- The 'good guy' mythstake.
- The 'good try' mythstake.
- The 'cockeyed' mythstake.
- The 'pass-him-by' mythstake.
- The 'standby' mythstake.
- The 'need not apply' mythstake.

Go back and review the passages from the Bible that correct these mythstakes. Ask God to set you free with the truth!

❧ *Plot the passages*

- Key word: *Heaven*.
- Key passage: Luke 16:19–26.
- Supporting passages: Revelation 21:1 – 22:5; Matthew 5:11–12; 2 Peter 3:13; Mark 10:24–27.

❧ *Speak*

Speak to self

I believe:

- That without Christ in my life, there would be nothing good about me.
- That without Christ in my life, I could do no good thing and I would have zero chance of earning my way to heaven.
- That hell is a real place – empty, dark and burning.
- That Jesus is far too valuable to pass by.
- That the decision to choose him is urgent.
- That the reward for choosing him is indescribable!

And I believe that he is willing and able to save us all... if only we apply.

Speak to others

Everlasting life is a very easy topic to enter into with friends or even strangers. Again, just ask questions!

I once asked a young woman at a shopping centre the following questions:

'Do you believe in heaven?'

'Yes,' she replied.

'Is heaven a perfect place?'

'Yes, absolutely!' she said.

'Do you think you will go there?'

'I think I have a pretty good shot,' she answered. (She had bought into the 'good try' mythstake.)

'Have you lived a perfect life?'

'Well, of course not – who has? But I'm better than most people I know.'

'Well,' I continued, 'if heaven is a perfect place and you have not lived a perfect life, what makes you think you can go there without wrecking it?'

Now there is a conversation starter! What other conversation starters do you think would open the door to conversation about everlasting life?

Speak to God

Eternal God,

Burn into my soul the reality of heaven and hell. Search my heart and reveal the myths that have infiltrated my beliefs about everlasting life and replace them with truth from your living Word.

Empower me and motivate me with your love. Give me a sincere heart for those who are bound for a Godless eternity. Equip me and make me willing to allow you to use me to destroy myths and share the truth about your love with any and all people whom you place in my path.

I thank you, Father, for all you have done for me: for the cross, for your Word, for the power of your Spirit and the encouragement of the church around me. Use us as mouthpieces of your grace for your glory.

Amen.

* * *

I believe... in the life everlasting.

Those are powerful words – words that affect where we will spend eternity; words that affect our attitudes and behaviour moment by moment.

When these and all other beliefs from the Apostles' Creed become an integrated part of our thinking, life becomes truly transformed... and our lives become instruments of transformation in the world.

Some time ago my mother shared with me a letter – a letter that characterizes this type of focused devotion and commitment. The letter had been found in the office of a young pastor in Zimbabwe in Africa:

I am part of the Fellowship of the unashamed. I have the Holy Spirit power. The dye has been cast and I've stepped over the line. The decision has been made. I am a disciple of his. I won't look back, let up, slow down, back away, or be still. My past is redeemed. My present makes sense. My future is secure. I'm finished and done with low living, sight walking, smooth knees, colourless dreams, tamed visions, worldly talking, cheap giving and dwarfed goals. I no longer need pre-eminence, prosperity, position, promotions, plaudits, or popularity. I don't have to be right, first, tops, recognized, praised, regarded or rewarded, I now live by faith. Lean in his presence, walk by patience, I'm uplifted by prayer and labour with power. My face is set, my gauge is fast. My goal is heaven and my road is narrow. My way is rough, my companions are few, my guide is reliable and my mission is clear. I cannot be bought, compromised, detoured, lured away, turned back, eluded, or delayed. I will not flinch in the face of sacrifice, hesitate in the presence of the enemy, pander at the pool of popularity, or meander in the maze of mediocrity. I won't give up, shut up, let up until I have stayed up, stored up, prayed up, paid up and preached up for the cause of Christ. I am a disciple of Jesus. I must go till he comes. Give till I drop. Preach until all know, and work until he stops me. And when he comes for his own, he will have no problem recognizing me. My banner will be clear.

The letter was found by the saints of the church he led. They were cleaning out his office in the days after his body had been found battered and mutilated. He was a man who died as a living sacrifice of worship on this earth, propelled into everlasting life by the same grace that he preached and showed to those around him.

May the God of peace, who through the blood of the eternal covenant brought back from the dead our Lord Jesus, that great Shepherd of the sheep, equip you with everything good for doing his will, and may he work in us what is pleasing to him, through Jesus Christ, to whom be glory for ever and ever. Amen... Grace be with you all.   HEBREWS 13:20–21, 25

*I believe in God the Father Almighty, maker of heaven and earth; and in Jesus Christ his only Son our Lord; who was conceived by the Holy Ghost, born of the Virgin Mary, suffered under Pontius Pilate, was crucified, dead and buried. He descended into hell; the third day he rose again from the dead. He ascended into heaven, and sits on the right hand of God the Father Almighty. From thence he shall come to judge the quick and the dead. I believe in the Holy Ghost, the holy catholic church, the communion of saints, the forgiveness of sins, the resurrection of the body, and the life everlasting. **Amen.***

CHAPTER 17
Saying 'Amen!'

Live your beliefs and you can turn the world around.   HENRY DAVID THOREAU

There are three words that have the same usage in the Christian church where ever you go in the world... The first one is 'amen'. The second one is 'alleluia'. The third one is 'Coca-Cola'.   STUART BRISCOE[48]

The children of Israel are coming back home; they're coming back to Jerusalem after years in foreign exile. A mixture of joy and sobriety is there to meet them. Yes, they are back in the Promised Land but Jerusalem has been devastated. The holy Temple has been demolished, looted, ravaged... nothing but a pile of rubble and broken dreams.

For decades they have been stripped of their heritage, drifting without aim before the winds of oppression. But now, upon their return, as they begin to rebuild, they find their anchor: The Word of God.

So on the first day of the seventh month, Ezra the priest brought the Law before the assembly, which was made up of men and women and all who were able to understand. He read it aloud from daybreak till noon as he faced the square before the Water Gate in the presence of the men, women and others who could understand. And all the people listened attentively to the Book of the Law.
NEHEMIAH 8:2–3

All is not lost. Hope emerges from the ashes. They have something to believe again...

And so do we.

Like the Israelites, we live in a world that has been decimated, destroyed and ravaged by lies and deception – masses of humanity wandering without aim or direction, trying to find their home. But we have found God's Word too. We have explored that Word and we have something to believe. We have true belief.

✖ QUOTATION

The contemporary world still needs this testimony to the victory of the Father Almighty, Maker of heaven and earth, the victory of Jesus the crucified risen Lord, the victory of the Spirit, the giver of life. May the Creed of the saints and the martyrs become again today the public and courageous testimony to the victory of the Father, Son, and Holy Spirit.   THEODORE W. JENNINGS, JR[49]

When we set out on this journey for truth, we had four goals:

1. To be able to outline the major theological aspects of your faith.
2. To be able to turn to a series of key Bible passages which support your beliefs.
3. To be able to communicate the depth and details of your faith with those who don't believe as you do.
4. To be able to explore the wonders of the Christian faith at new levels.

If you have made it through all my crazy stories, wrestled with the questions, pondered the quotes and (most importantly) followed the M.A.P.S. through God's Word, you should be able to do the four things pretty well, far better than if we hadn't learned to use the Creed as a tool.

I like tools... when I have the *right* tool. Years ago I tried to scrape old tiles off the kitchen floor in an apartment Libby and I were renting at the time. The stuff was glued down with an ancient black tar-like substance. I wasn't doing very well. With a chisel and a hammer I had only removed about six square feet by noon. When Libby came home and looked at the mess (both the floor and her husband), she said, 'Why not use a heat gun?' I dashed to the hardware store, and 120 volts later, I was in business... the hot tiles almost popped off the floor.

With the Apostles' Creed now in your tool-belt, you'll find that it's the right tool for many, many jobs as you apply the Word of God to many, many different tasks.

You are *able* to use that tool now... but are you *willing* to use it?

That depends on what you mean when you say 'Amen.'

Saying 'Amen'

I used to think that the word 'Amen' was a sort of Hebrew full stop – a punctuation mark at the end of a prayer that told you it was okay to open your eyes and look up again.

In some churches 'Amen' bounces around during the sermon like a rubber ball ricocheting off the walls. In other churches, though, you wonder if anybody is even conscious. Is the congregation nodding or nodding off? Hard to tell sometimes. Some Sunday mornings we look like a bunch of nodding-dogs in rush-hour traffic. On those days an 'Amen' sounds pretty empty.

What does 'Amen' mean? It means 'so be it!' It means *Yes! What was just said, I agree with. What I was just taught, I buy. What was just prayed, include me in that prayer. That's my prayer too!* 'Amen' is the standing ovation after the concert, the crowd cheering after the game-winning goal. 'Amen' is the soft kiss of parents when they tuck their children in at the end of the day. Throughout the Bible we find this word used in four different ways:

When we say 'Amen' we are saying 'I appreciate God's Word'

After the Israelites came back to a pulverized Jerusalem, they continued eagerly and extensively listening to the reading of the Word of God:

> *Ezra opened the book. All the people could see him because he was standing above them; and as he opened it, the people all stood up. Ezra praised the Lord, the great God; and all the people lifted their hands and responded, 'Amen! Amen!' Then they bowed down and worshipped the Lord with their faces to the ground.*
>
> NEHEMIAH 8:5–6

Wow. They got it. What an ideal response to God's Word – 'So be it!' Why not respond with 'Amen! Amen! I appreciate the Word!'

❧ QUOTATION

> *The creeds are not merely laundry lists of statements about the Christian faith. In fact, they are really much more like prayers. When we say them, we are not merely announcing what we think or describing the state in which we find ourselves; we are also asking God for help and guidance in living into the faith that the creeds attempt to articulate.* DAVID S. CUNNINGHAM[50]

When we say 'Amen' we are saying 'I agree with God's decisions'

In 1 Kings 1, King David chose Solomon to succeed him on the throne. Solomon was Bathsheba's son, but David and Bathsheba didn't exactly start their relationship off on the right foot. David had had an affair with Bathsheba, the wife of one of his soldiers, and when she got pregnant David had her husband killed!

So, David was worried about what people would think if a son conceived in an adulterous, murderous affair took the throne. He was at peace with God, however. David knew first hand about the forgiveness of sins; he knew God is in the business of turning a mess into something marvellous... and he believed that Solomon was the man for the job. So he called the leaders of Israel together to tell them what he had chosen. How did they respond?

> *Benaiah son of Jehoiada answered the king, 'Amen! May the Lord, the God of my Lord the king, so declare it. As the Lord was with my Lord the king, so may he be with Solomon to make his throne even greater than the throne of my Lord King David!'*
> 1 KINGS 1:36–37

When the leaders said 'Amen!' they said that they agreed with the choice God had made. That's what we mean too.

✿ QUOTATION

We dare not say or sing this word glibly... To utter 'amen' is to place ourselves within the very sanctuary of God, confronting his holiness and righteousness, his justice and truth, and declaring our willingness to stand fast for what we believe.
D. BRUCE LOCKERBIE[51]

When we say 'Amen', we are saying 'I understand God's boundaries'

In Deuteronomy 27 God drew some serious lines for the Israelites:

> *Then Moses and the priests, who are Levites, said to all Israel, 'Be silent, O Israel, and listen! You have now become the people of the Lord your God. Obey the Lord your God and follow his commands and decrees that I give you today'...*
> *The Levites shall recite to all the people of Israel in a loud voice: 'Cursed is the man who carves an image or casts an idol – a thing detestable to the Lord, the work of the craftsman's hands – and sets it up in secret.'*
> *Then all the people shall say, 'Amen!'*
> *'Cursed is the man who dishonours his father or his mother.'*
> *Then all the people shall say, 'Amen!'* DEUTERONOMY 27:9–10, 14–16

This goes on for about another ten verses as God clearly defined boundaries of behaviour for his chosen people. We have boundaries all around us that God has drawn too. Many of these boundaries have been illuminated during this study of the Creed. If we want to live within those boundaries we say 'Amen!'

? QUESTION

What 'boundaries' are people pushing in your community? What do you think they are hoping to gain by what they do?

We say 'Amen' when we want to punctuate God's praise

The original Christian praise-book is found in the Old Testament Psalms. It's really an anthology of 150 Hebrew worship lyrics. Psalm 41 says:

> *Praise be to the Lord, the God of Israel, from everlasting to everlasting. Amen and Amen!*
>
> PSALM 41:13

'Amen' is the applause at the end of the song; it's the exclamation mark at the end of the poem. Punctuating God's praise with 'Amen' is still a part of Christian worship – particularly in some of those good old-fashioned hymns. You may not get excited about the style of music, but you can't beat the words!

> *O for a thousand tongues to sing*
> *my great Redeemer's praise,*
> *the glories of my God and King,*
> *the triumphs of his grace!*
> *Amen!*
>
> *And when I think that God his Son not sparing,*
> *sent him to die, I scarce can take it in.*
> *But on the cross my burden gladly bearing,*
> *he bled and died to take away my sin.*
> *When Christ shall come with shouts of acclamation,*
> *and take me home, then joy shall fill my heart.*
> *Then I shall bow in humble adoration and then proclaim,*
> *'My God, how great Thou art!'*
> *Amen!*

Oh, that's good stuff. Whether you prefer electric guitars or pipe organs, when you feel truth resonating deep down inside you, cap it off with a grand proclamation of 'Amen!'

'Amen.' It's the way to say to God, *'I really mean those words. I'm not just saying these words because everyone else is singing them; they really mean something to me. So be it! Amen.'*

If you have made it all the way through this study, I want to offer up a very hearty 'Amen!' You did it! Phrase by phrase, verse by verse, you've been accumulating truth from God's Word. With a clear sense of accomplishment, I want to encourage you to stand back and look at what God has done: The hundreds of small pieces of truth now form a massive mosaic of belief, *true belief...* belief that matters.

My prayer for all of us, as we part ways for now, is the same prayer that Paul prayed for his friends in the church of Ephesus:

> *For this reason I kneel before the Father, from whom his whole family in heaven and on earth derives its name. I pray that out of his glorious riches he may strengthen you with power through his Spirit in your inner being, so that Christ may dwell in your hearts through faith. And I pray that you, being rooted and established in love, may have power, together with all the saints, to grasp how wide and long and high and deep is the love of Christ, and to know this love that surpasses knowledge – that you may be filled to the measure of all the fulness of God.*
>
> *Now to him who is able to do immeasurably more than all we ask or imagine, according to his power that is at work within us, to him be glory in the church and in Christ Jesus throughout all generations, for ever and ever! Amen.*
> EPHESIANS 3:14–20

May God continue to grant us the privilege and honour of being stewards of the truth. And when our days come to and end – when our hearts beat their last and the last molecules of air are expended from our lips – may our parting whisper be 'Amen.'

M.A.P.S.

❧ *Meditate*

One last time, ask God to guide your thoughts as you consider the words of the Apostles' Creed:

> *I believe in God the Father Almighty, maker of heaven and earth; and in Jesus Christ his only Son our Lord; who was conceived by the Holy Ghost, born of the Virgin Mary, suffered under Pontius Pilate, was crucified, dead and buried. He descended into hell; the third day he rose again from the dead. He ascended into heaven, and sits on the right hand of God the Father Almighty. From thence he shall come to judge the quick and the dead. I believe in the Holy Ghost, the holy catholic church, the communion of saints, the forgiveness of sins, the resurrection of the body, and the life everlasting. Amen.*

Apply

I've intentionally kept this chapter short to allow you some time to reminisce a bit. Skim back through the entire book. Ponder all the passages you have absorbed. Take a look at the way you plotted the passages through your Bible and formed a web of doctrinal truth that you can use for the rest of your life.

- What phrase from the Creed has meant the most to you?
- Which Bible passages have made an impact on your heart?
- If you were to ask God to make just three changes in your life because of the truths you have learned, what would they be?

Plot the passages

- Key word: *Amen*.
- Key passage: Nehemiah 8:2–6.
- Supporting passages: 1 Kings 1:36–37; Deuteronomy 27:9–16; Psalm 41:13.

Speak

Speak to self

I believe in saying 'Amen.'

- I say 'Amen' because I agree with God's decisions.
- I say 'Amen' because I respect God's boundaries.
- I say 'Amen' because I appreciate God's Word.
- I say 'Amen' to punctuate my life of worship and praise!

Think this next one all the way through before you say it. Rethink all that you have come to realize as you have used the Creed to comb through the foundational theologies of the Christian faith. Are you willing to allow God to make this your biography as well as your theology? If so...

- I say 'Amen' to the Apostles' Creed.

Speak to others

The Creed is a tool that you can use for many jobs. It is useful because it allows us to access God's Word easily when communicating with others. Take out the 'Plot the Truth' sheet that lists all the 'Key passages' and 'Supporting passages' from the Apostles' Creed. That's an important tool in your hand.

But I have a question for you:

Are you willing to be an important tool in the hand of God? Throughout this study I have emphasized an indispensable, essential principle of the Christian faith: *Allowing Christ to live through you.* He has created you and re-created you for a purpose, and he has given you gifts and abilities that can be used as part of God's team to glorify Christ by sharing the truth about him to the multitudes and the individuals that need to hear.

Are you willing to say 'Amen' to that?

Speak to God

My God,

You have given me the truth of your Word. You have filled me with the Spirit of your Son, Jesus. My life is yours because he gave his life for mine. I now place my whole self in your hands. Use me in any way to bring glory to your Son in this world.

I believe; help my unbelief.

Amen and Amen.

*   *   *

Belief matters.

It is quite impossible to over-emphasize that fact.

Belief matters.

Belief determines our perceptions of reality.

Belief shapes every thought, decision and action.

Belief defines the parameters of what is possible.

Belief emerges from the soul – from that inner core of our being that defines who we are and what we do, even altering the contours of eternity.

Belief matters and what we believe matters.

The Apostles' Creed is a remarkable tool for discovering belief, solidifying belief and articulating belief.

It takes thirty seconds to recite the Creed.

It takes a lifetime to ponder it.

It will take an eternity to experience it.

May the journey continue.

Amen?

Belief Matters: Plotting the Truth

Tear or cut this page out and insert it in your Bible for permanent reference.

I believe...
- Key word: *Belief*.
- Key passage: Romans 4:17–21.
- Supporting passages: Mark 9:23–24; John 6:28–29; Acts 16:31; Romans 4:2–3.

... in God the Father...
- Key word: *Father*.
- Key passage: Exodus 33:12–17.
- Supporting passages: Hosea 6:3; Psalm 103:8–14; Zephaniah 3:17; 2 Chronicles 30:9; 1 John 4:7–10.

... Almighty...
- Key word: *Almighty*.
- Key passage: Luke 1:37.
- Supporting passages: Isaiah 55:8–9; 44:8–10; Hebrews 7:25; 2 Corinthians 9:8; Ephesians 3:20–21; Jude 24–25.

... maker of heaven and earth...
- Key word: *Creator*.
- Key passage: Genesis 1:1–31.
- Supporting passages: Hebrews 11:3; Psalm 139:13–14; 2 Corinthians 5:17–20; Ephesians 2:10.

... and in Jesus Christ his only Son our Lord...
- Key word: *Son*.
- Key passage: John 1:1–14.
- Supporting passages: John 11:35; 10:30–33; Acts 10:36; Philippians 2:9–11; John 13:1–5.

... who was conceived by the Holy Ghost, born of the Virgin Mary...
- Key word: *Conception*.
- Key passage: Luke 1:28–38.
- Supporting passages: Genesis 3:14–15; Isaiah 7:14; Matthew 1:18–23; Revelation 12:1–5; Hebrews 2:14–15.

... suffered under Pontius Pilate, was crucified, dead and buried...
- Key word: *Crucified*.
- Key passage: 1 John 4:9–10.
- Supporting passages: 1 Peter 2:22–24; Isaiah 53:4–5; Colossians 2:13–14; Galatians 2:20–21; Hebrews 4:14–16.

... He descended into hell; the third day he rose again from the dead...
- Key word: *Risen*.

- Key passage: John 19:31 – 20:18.
- Supporting passages: 1 Corinthians 15:3–8, 14–19; 1 Peter 1:3–9; 3:18–19.

… He ascended into heaven, and sits on the right hand of God the Father Almighty…
- Key word: *Seated*.
- Key passage: Hebrews 12:2–3.
- Supporting passages: Hebrews 10:19–20; Ephesians 2:4–7; Colossians 3:1–4; Matthew 11:28–30.

… From thence he shall come to judge the quick and the dead…
- Key word: *Return*.
- Key passage: John 14:1–4.
- Supporting passages: Matthew 24:43–44; John 14:1–4; 3:18–36; 1 Thessalonians 5:24.

… I believe in the Holy Ghost…
- Key word: *Spirit*.
- Key passage: John 16:5–15.
- Supporting passages: Ezekiel 36:26–27; John 14:15–27; Ephesians 4:30.

… the holy catholic church, the communion of saints…
- Key word: *Saints*.
- Key passage: 1 Peter 2:9.
- Supporting passages: Ephesians 4:4–11; Matthew 24:14; 28:16–20; Revelation 7:9–12.

… the forgiveness of sins…
- Key word: *Forgiven*.
- Key passage: Daniel 9:1–23.
- Supporting passages: Proverbs 5:22; Psalm 139:23–24; Ephesians 1:7; Colossians 3:12–14; Matthew 5:23–24; Romans 8:1–2.

… the resurrection of the body…
- Key word: *Body*.
- Key passage: 1 Corinthians 15:35–58.
- Supporting passages: 2 Corinthians 4:16; James 4:14; Psalm 23:4; 2 Corinthians 5:8–9.

… and the life everlasting…
- Key word: *Heaven*.
- Key passage: Luke 16:19–26.
- Supporting passages: Revelation 21:1 – 22:5; Matthew 5:11–12; 2 Peter 3:13; Mark 10:24–27.

… Amen.
- Key word: *Amen*.
- Key passage: Nehemiah 8:2–6.
- Supporting passages: 1 Kings 1:36–37; Deuteronomy 27:9–16; Psalm 41:13.

FROM *BELIEF MATTERS* BY PETE BRISCOE, PUBLISHED BY MONARCH BOOKS

Belief Matters: Plotting the Truth

I believe...
- Key word: *Belief.*
- Key passage: Romans 4:17–21.
- Supporting passages: Mark 9:23–24; John 6:28–29; Acts 16:31; Romans 4:2–3.

... in God the Father...
- Key word: *Father.*
- Key passage: Exodus 33:12–17.
- Supporting passages: Hosea 6:3; Psalm 103:8–14; Zephaniah 3:17; 2 Chronicles 30:9; 1 John 4:7–10.

... Almighty...
- Key word: *Almighty.*
- Key passage: Luke 1:37.
- Supporting passages: Isaiah 55:8–9; 44:8–10; Hebrews 7:25; 2 Corinthians 9:8; Ephesians 3:20–21; Jude 24–25.

... maker of heaven and earth...
- Key word: *Creator.*
- Key passage: Genesis 1:1–31.
- Supporting passages: Hebrews 11:3; Psalm 139:13–14; 2 Corinthians 5:17–20; Ephesians 2:10.

... and in Jesus Christ his only Son our Lord...
- Key word: *Son.*
- Key passage: John 1:1–14.
- Supporting passages: John 11:35; 10:30–33; Acts 10:36; Philippians 2:9–11; John 13:1–5.

... who was conceived by the Holy Ghost, born of the Virgin Mary...
- Key word: *Conception.*
- Key passage: Luke 1:28–38.
- Supporting passages: Genesis 3:14–15; Isaiah 7:14; Matthew 1:18–23; Revelation 12:1–5; Hebrews 2:14–15.

... suffered under Pontius Pilate, was crucified, dead and buried...
- Key word: *Crucified.*
- Key passage: 1 John 4:9–10.
- Supporting passages: 1 Peter 2:22–24; Isaiah 53:4–5; Colossians 2:13–14; Galatians 2:20–21; Hebrews 4:14–16.

... He descended into hell; the third day he rose again from the dead...
- Key word: *Risen.*
- Key passage: John 19:31 – 20:18.
- Supporting passages: 1 Corinthians 15:3–8, 14–19; 1 Peter 1:3–9; 3:18–19.

... He ascended into heaven, and sits on the right hand of God the Father Almighty...
- Key word: *Seated*.
- Key passage: Hebrews 12:2–3.
- Supporting passages: Hebrews 10:19–20; Ephesians 2:4–7; Colossians 3:1–4; Matthew 11:28–30.

... From thence he shall come to judge the quick and the dead...
- Key word: *Return*.
- Key passage: John 14:1–4.
- Supporting passages: Matthew 24:43–44; John 14:1–4; 3:18–36; 1 Thessalonians 5:24.

... I believe in the Holy Ghost...
- Key word: *Spirit*.
- Key passage: John 16:5–15.
- Supporting passages: Ezekiel 36:26–27; John 14:15–27; Ephesians 4:30.

... the holy catholic church, the communion of saints...
- Key word: *Saints*.
- Key passage: 1 Peter 2:9.
- Supporting passages: Ephesians 4:4–11; Matthew 24:14; 28:16–20; Revelation 7:9–12.

... the forgiveness of sins...
- Key word: *Forgiven*.
- Key passage: Daniel 9:1–23.
- Supporting passages: Proverbs 5:22; Psalm 139:23–24; Ephesians 1:7; Colossians 3:12–14; Matthew 5:23–24; Romans 8:1–2.

... the resurrection of the body...
- Key word: *Body*.
- Key passage: 1 Corinthians 15:35–58.
- Supporting passages: 2 Corinthians 4:16; James 4:14; Psalm 23:4; 2 Corinthians 5:8–9.

... and the life everlasting...
- Key word: *Heaven*.
- Key passage: Luke 16:19–26.
- Supporting passages: Revelation 21:1 – 22:5; Matthew 5:11–12; 2 Peter 3:13; Mark 10:24–27.

... Amen.
- Key word: *Amen*.
- Key passage: Nehemiah 8:2–6.
- Supporting passages: 1 Kings 1:36–37; Deuteronomy 27:9–16; Psalm 41:13.

Notes

1. John Foxe, *Foxe's Christian Martyrs of the World*, Barbour Publishing, 1990.
2. Ron James, *Creed and Christ*, Nashville: The Upper Room, 1986, p. 15.
3. Bill Ewing, *Rest Assured*, Rapid City, SD: Real Life Press, 2003.
4. Wolfhart Pannenberg, *The Apostles' Creed in the Light of Today's Questions*, Philadelphia: Westminster Press, 1972.
5. D. Bruce Lockerbie, *The Apostles' Creed: Do You Really Believe It?*, Wheaton, Illinois: Victor Books, 1977, p. 19.
6. Stephen Covey, 7 *Habits of Highly Successful People,* London, Simon & Schuster, 1999.
7. Tim Hansel, *Holy Sweat*, Word Publishing, 1987, p. 26.
8. A.W. Tozer, *The Knowledge of the Holy*, Harper, 1961, p. 1.
9. Todd Hillard, *Lead Me to the Rock: Exploring the Heart of God in Uncertain Times*, Rapid City, SD: Real Life Press, 2005, p. 54.
10. David S. Cunningham, *Reading is Believing*, Grand Rapids: Brazos Press, 2002, p. 34.
11. As quoted in Pete Briscoe (ed.), *Christianity: A Follower's Guide*, B&H 200, p. 25.
12. Chip Ingram, *God as He Longs for You to See Him*, Grand Rapids: Baker Books, p. 46.
13. A.W. Tozer, *The Knowledge of the Holy*, Harper, 1961, p. 10.
14. From Stuart Briscoe, *The Apostles' Creed: Beliefs that Matter*, Wheaton, Illinois: Harold Shaw, 1994, p. 12.
15. Ron James, *Creed and Christ*, Nashville: The Upper Room, 1986, p. 25.
16. Stuart Briscoe, *The Apostles' Creed: Beliefs that Matter*, Wheaton, Illinois: Harold Shaw, 1994, p. 43.
17. John R. May, *Nurturing Faith through Fiction: Reflections of the Apostles' Creed in Literature and Film*, Lanham, MD: Rowman & Littlefield, 2001, p. 43.
18. Theodore W. Jennings, *Loyalty to God*, Nashville: Abingdon Press, 1992, p. 54.
19. Ron James, *Creed and Christ*, Nashville: The Upper Room, 1986, p. 25.
20. Ron James, *Creed and Christ*, Nashville: The Upper Room, 1986, p. 31.
21. Don Miller, *Blue Like Jazz*, Nashville: Thomas Nelson, 2003, p. 237.
22. In Stuart Briscoe, *The Apostles' Creed: Beliefs that Matter*, Wheaton, Illinois: Harold Shaw, 1994, p. 51.
23. Douglas J. Soccio, *Archetypes of Wisdom*, New York: Wadsworth, 1998, p. 46.
24. In Tim Hansel, *Holy Sweat*, Word Publishing, 1987, p. 26.
25. C.S. Lewis, *Mere Christianity*, London: Fount, 1997, p. 41.
26. J. I. Packer, *Knowing God*, London: Hodder & Stoughton, p. 54.
27. Theodore W. Jennings, *Loyalty to God*, Nashville: Abingdon Press, 1992, pp. 99–100.

28. Phillip Yancey, *Disappointment with God*, Zondervan, 1997, p. 100.
29. Brennan Manning, *The Ragamuffin Gospel*, Authentic Lifestyle, 2001, p. 103.
30. Wayne Grudem, *Systematic Theology*, Inter-Varsity Press, p. 568.
31. Wayne Grudem, *Systematic Theology*, Inter-Varsity Press, p. 575.
32. Bruce D. Lockerbie, *The Apostles' Creed: Do You Really Believe It?*, Wheaton, Illinois: Victor Books, 1977, p. 52.
33. Theodore W. Jennings, *Loyalty to God*, Nashville: Abingdon Press, 1992, p. 105.
34. D. Bruce Lockerbie, *The Apostles' Creed: Do You Really Believe It?*, Wheaton, Illinois: Victor Books, 1977, p. 51.
35. Theodore W. Jennings, *Loyalty to God*, Nashville: Abingdon Press, 1992, pp. 99–100.
36. I. Howard Marshall, *1 Peter*, Downers Grove, Illinois: Inter-Varsity Press, 1991, p. 122.
37. Watchman Nee, *Sit, Walk, Stand*, Wheaton, Illinois: Tyndale, 1985, pp. 15–16.
38. Ron James, *Creed and Christ*, Nashville: The Upper Room, 1986, p. 74.
39. Stuart Briscoe, *The Apostles' Creed: Beliefs That Matter*, Wheaton, Illinois: Harold Shaw, 1994, p. 140.
40. Theodore W. Jennings, *Loyalty to God*, Nashville: Abingdon Press, 1992, p. 164.
41. In Tim Hansel, *Holy Sweat*, Word Publishing, 1987, p. 27.
42. Theodore W. Jennings, *Loyalty to God*, Nashville: Abingdon Press, 1992, p. 68.
43. http://www.joshuaproject.net/index.php
44. Stuart Briscoe, *The Apostles' Creed: Beliefs that Matter*, Wheaton, Illinois: Harold Shaw, 1994, p. 81.
45. Phillip Yancey, *What's So Amazing About Grace*, Zondervan, 1997, p. 70.
46. Chuck Swindoll, *The Grace Awakening,* Word Publishing, 2006.
47. Phillip Yancey, *What's So Amazing About Grace*, Zondervan, 1997, p. 51.
48. Stuart Briscoe, *The Apostles' Creed: Beliefs That Matter*, Wheaton, Illinois: Harold Shaw, 1994, p. 235.
49. Theodore W. Jennings, *Loyalty to God*, Nashville: Abingdon Press, 1992, p. 224.
50. David S. Cunningham, *Reading is Believing*, Grand Rapids: Brazos Press, 2002, p. 235.
51. D. Bruce Lockerbie, *The Apostles' Creed: Do You Really Believe It?*, Wheaton, Illinois: Victor Books, 1977, p. 140.